IMAGES
of America

SCRANTON'S HILL SECTION

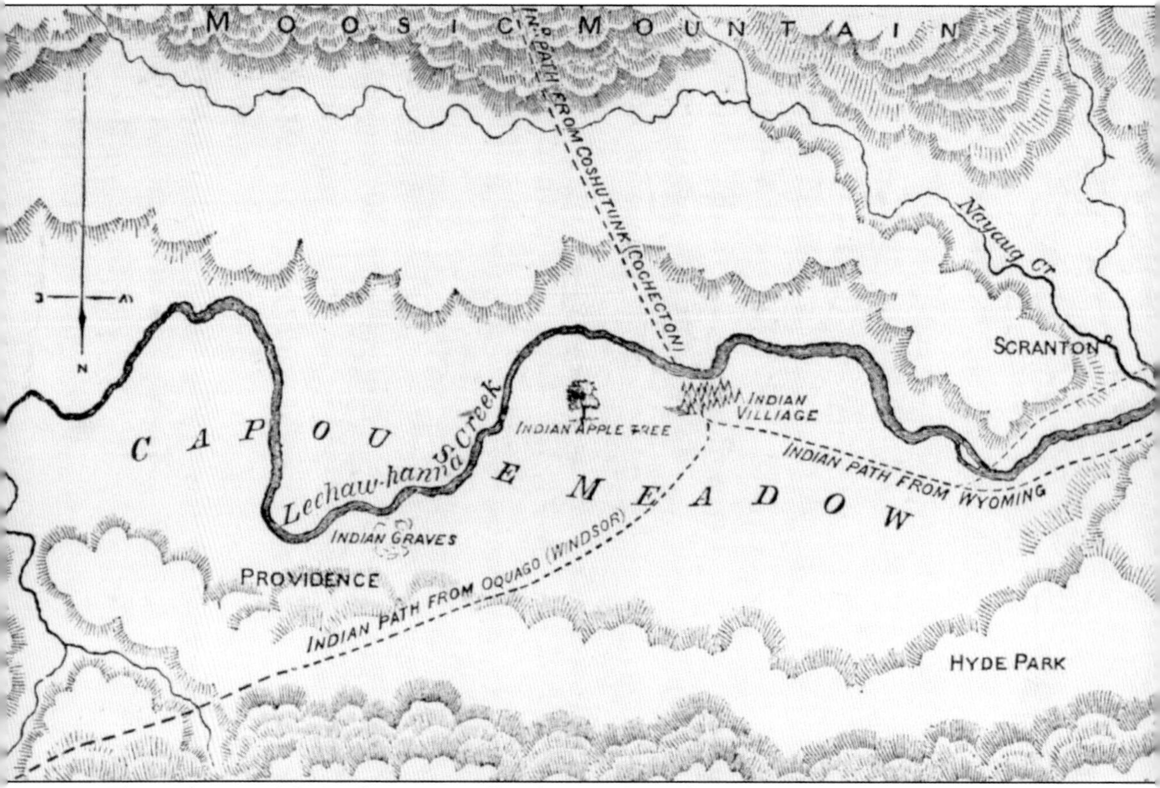

This early map of the Lackawanna Valley dates to the mid-1800s. Eventually, the city of Scranton would annex Providence and Hyde Park and extend across most of the area shown here. Scranton's Hill Section would eventually develop on the lands between Nay Aug Creek (Roaring Brook) and the Indian Trail from Cochecton on the upper right of this map. (Courtesy of the Lackawanna History Society.)

ON THE COVER: Looking east, this panoramic image shows Scranton's Hill Section around the turn of the century. (Courtesy of the Lackawanna History Society.)

IMAGES
of America

SCRANTON'S HILL SECTION

Jack Shean

ARCADIA
PUBLISHING

ISBN 978-1-4671-2335-8

Published by Arcadia Publishing
Charleston, South Carolina

Printed in the United States of America

Library of Congress Control Number: 2014953322

For all general information, please contact Arcadia Publishing:
Telephone 843-853-2070
Fax 843-853-0044
E-mail sales@arcadiapublishing.com
For customer service and orders:
Toll-Free 1-888-313-2665

Visit us on the Internet at www.arcadiapublishing.com

This book is dedicated in memory of my mentor and Lackawanna Historical Society president Alan Sweeney.

Contents

ACKNOWLEDGMENTS

I would first and foremost like to acknowledge my parents, Christine and Timothy Shean, for their unyielding support and guidance. I could not have done any of this without them. I am forever in their debt.

I would also like to acknowledge the Lackawanna Historical Society, including Mary Ann Moran Savakinus (executive director), Sarah Piccini (assistant director), Olivia Bernardi (office manager), and the trustees, for their assistance. There would not be many stories to tell if not for the Lackawanna Historical Society. I cannot thank Mary Ann, Sarah, and last but not least, Olivia enough for their help in every aspect of this project.

I would furthermore like to acknowledge Jack Hiddlestone for his many memories and postcards about the Hill Section and Luna Park, as well as the McHugh Special Collections of the University Archives at the University of Scranton's Weinberg Memorial Library for its immense collection of images and historical materials. I would also like to acknowledge Gertrude Hawk Chocolates and David Hawk for their help and interest, Jack and Pat Chipak for their images and information, the Albright Memorial Library's Lackawanna Valley Digital Archives for its collections, and the office of Sen. Robert P. Casey Jr., Judge Robert D. Mariani, Mayor David Wenzel, Councilman Bill Gaughan, Nancy J. Weinberger, and Adele Pollack for their knowledge and assistance.

Additionally, I would like to acknowledge the following individuals and groups for their help and support: Holy Cross High School, Covenant Presbyterian Church, Elm Park Methodist Church, Temple Israel, the Hill Neighborhood Association, Frank Homer PhD, Elizabeth Shomaker, Charles "Sandy" Connell, Dorothy Smith, Granville Smith Jr., Jane Oppenheim, Pattie Ollendyke, Joe Sadowski, Scott Thomas, Lois Kiertoch, George Lowry, Jim Guthrie, Fr. Brian J.T. Clarke, Michael Costello, Emily Savino Perry, Judy Sweeney, Mary Catherine Smith, and the staff of Arcadia Publishing.

Finally, I would like to acknowledge all those individuals who have contributed to the history of Scranton's Hill Section. This book is a testament to their lives and legacies.

Unless otherwise noted, all images are courtesy of the Lackawanna Historical Society.

INTRODUCTION

Scranton's Hill Section has a long and intriguing history. A myriad of geological forces led to the formation of the series of hills in the eastern portion of the Lackawanna Valley, between the marshy plateau on the eastern banks of the Lackawanna River and the rocky channel of the Roaring Brook. Dense deciduous forest took root on these hills, fed by groundwater springs that formed several small swamps and streams. The first people to settle in the Lackawanna Valley were Iroquois Indians of the Delaware, Monsey, and Capouse tribes, who created the name *Lackawanna*, meaning "place where streams meet," for the valley where the Lackawanna River and Roaring Brook converge. Europeans did not settle in the region until the mid-18th century, when settlers from the colonies of Connecticut and Pennsylvania began arriving. The British Crown had previously granted the lands around the Lackawanna and Wyoming Valleys to both Connecticut and Pennsylvania, which claimed it as Westmoreland and Pennsylvania, respectively, setting the stage for numerous conflicts in the 1760s and early 1770s. During the American Revolution, the Iroquois allied themselves with the British and effectively destroyed the largest European settlement in the region in an event known as the Wyoming Massacre at what is today Forty Fort in the Wyoming Valley. Despite this tragedy, American general John Sullivan led a campaign now known as Sullivan's March and defeated the Iroquois and British, firmly establishing American control over the region.

Following the American Revolution, the settlements in the region began experiencing tremendous growth, with the brothers Ebenezer and Benjamin Slocum founding the community of Slocum's Hollow. During this period, the land disputes between Connecticut Yankees and Pennsylvanians were finally settled when the Connecticut settlers relinquished their claims to Westmoreland in return for property guarantees from the Commonwealth of Pennsylvania. Economic activity in the region also began to blossom with the establishment of several mills along the Roaring Brook in Slocum's Hollow and iron ore and anthracite coal mines throughout the valley. However, it was not until 1840 when William Henry, Selden T. Scranton, George W. Scranton, and Sanford Grant of Belvidere, New Jersey, acquired 503 acres of land and founded an iron furnace operation in Slocum's Hollow that the area's economy began to boom.

The iron operation initially took the name of Scranton and Grant, and despite an abundance of resources at its disposal, it struggled to produce a profitable product. It was not until the late 1840s when the company began producing rails for the Erie Railroad that a profit was finally turned. From this point on, the iron furnaces and the community around them grew without inhibition. Slocum's Hollow was transformed into a new community named after and led by the Scranton family. George W. Scranton used his connections as a Pennsylvania senator and, later, US congressman to help Scranton annex the surrounding communities of Providence, Hyde Park, and Minooka and lobby for a new railroad connecting Scranton to the New York City area. This new railroad would eventually become the Delaware, Lackawanna & Western Railroad (DL&W), which would finally extend from Hoboken, New Jersey, to Buffalo, New York. The railway greatly accelerated Scranton's growth by allowing thousands of immigrants to pour into the valley and thousands of tons of anthracite and iron to pour out. The tremendous growth of Scranton was further fueled by an elite class of capitalists who also made their way into the valley. Sanford Grant sold his share of the iron furnace operation to Joseph Hand Scranton and Joseph C. Platt, an in-law to the Scranton family. These men were instrumental in attracting numerous individuals to relocate and invest in Scranton. As a result, a new upper class developed in Scranton, one that needed a place to call home.

The Scrantons' iron operation, which now called itself the Lackawanna Iron and Coal Company, owned most of the land on the east and south sides of Scranton. It used the lands around the Roaring Brook for its industrial operations and for the DL&W's main line. The organization used the lands on Scranton's South Side for company housing and subdivided the marshy plateau along the Lackawanna River for use as the new city's commercial center. This left only the hills of east Scranton for elite residential development. At this time, these hills were barely settled. Only a small German immigrant community called Petersburg existed on the hills' far side. Near the end of the Civil War, architect and city planner Joel Amsden extended his grid design for the city eastward. In this design, the roads running north to south would be called avenues, with the first six named after the first six American presidents in the order that they served and the remaining avenues named after other prominent Northern political leaders. The roads going east to west were named after various species of trees, and the alleys that would bisect each block from north to south would be called courts and named after prominent local figures. With a street plan in place, the Lackawanna Iron and Coal Company began the decades-long process of subdividing the land, with one of the first parcels going to a company executive.

Joseph Hand Scranton build a palatial estate in the lower Hill Section, near the Iron Furnaces and the DL&W main line, in the late 1860s. His Anglo-Saxon business partners and peers soon followed, building numerous mansions for their families throughout the lower hill. Scranton's elites were very fond of the new neighborhood because it afforded a cleaner environment high above the city's industrial developments. These individuals built palatial mansions designed by various architects from Scranton and across the country in a myriad of architectural styles, ranging from English Tudor, Queen Anne, Georgian Colonial, and Victorian to Neoclassical, Venetian Gothic, Richardsonian Romanesque, and Craftsman. The homes were designed to impress, as their lofty positions put them on display for the entire city. In the latter part of the 19th century, returning Civil War veterans and new immigrants who succeeded in amassing impressive fortunes from coal mining, coal supportive industries, and commercial services added to Scranton's ever-growing population and moved to the neighborhood in significant numbers. These prominent figures also built magnificent residences and began to develop an interrelated and extensive aristocracy centered in what Scrantonians began calling "the Hill Section."

By the dawn of the 20th century, Scranton's economy had heavily diversified, which helped to not only minimize the impact of the relocation of the newly renamed Lackawanna Iron and Steel Company to Lackawanna, New York, in 1902 but also create a large middle class. These middle-class residents gradually moved into the Hill Section, establishing residences on the terraced blocks surrounding its many mansions. As the influx of wealthy and middle-class residents into the Hill Section steadily increased, the older community of Petersburg, as well as the Italian immigrant communities of Little England and Bunker Hill on the Hill Section's far side, were absorbed. By the 1920s, a prolific number of eclectic homes was being built throughout the Hill Section. Among these was a large number of duplex and triplex homes occupied by the service workers of Scranton, who helped to make the Hill Section into a diverse, heavily populated, mixed-income neighborhood. During Scranton's golden age, the Hill Section was home to the most influential people in the area. Millionaire tycoons and leading politicians all called the Hill Section their home.

To serve the Hill Section's growing population, civic leaders began to organize religious and community institutions throughout the neighborhood. Eventually, nine Protestant churches, three Catholic parishes, and five Jewish temples would be established in the Hill Section. Religious organizations were also closely related to many community organizations that developed in the Hill Section, including youth and community centers as wells as social clubs. Merchants also began developing prosperous commercial enterprises in the Hill Section, with Mulberry Street, Prescott Avenue, and Petersburg Corners becoming thriving commercial centers. Light industry sprang up on the Hill Section's periphery, and professional and business offices began expanding from downtown onto the lower hill. The Scranton Transit Company, which had established the first electric streetcar line in the United States in 1888, also operated three lines in the Hill Section.

During this time, the Hill Section became the center of medical care and education for the Scranton area. Three hospitals were established by various groups in the Hill Section, and the Scranton School District opened five primary schools. Several private schools were also founded in the Hill Section by local elites, Catholics, and Jews. By the late 1930s, St. Thomas College had taken over the former Scranton estate. Under the guidance of the Jesuit order, the school became the University of Scranton and dramatically expanded into a highly ranked college with a campus encompassing a vast tract of the lower Hill Section. Nay Aug and other public parks were also developed throughout the area, and an eclectic amusement park called Luna Park was built by the interurban Lackawanna & Wyoming Valley Railroad, also called the Laurel Line.

Scranton began to change dramatically in the 1930s. With the Great Depression, Scranton's economy entered a period of decline that inflicted great harm on the entire region and country. Nonetheless, the Hill Section managed to survive and, in some ways, thrive. Many of the elites who had built the Hill Section did begin to relocate, taking their fortunes with them, but they were replaced with a new class of Irish Catholic and Jewish families whose progression into the Hill Section mirrored their progression in society. African Americans also began moving to the Hill Section, where they established the first substantial African American community in northeastern Pennsylvania. The flood caused by Hurricane Diane in 1955 destroyed Little England, causing many of the Hill Section's Italian residents to migrate to the nearby borough of Dunmore. These residents were replaced by an even larger number of Jewish residents, which the floods had displaced from the flats on the South Side. The Hill Section generated many fine memories in the postwar years. During these years, it was full of children and a unique assortment of people who managed to live in harmony. However, Scranton's economy continued to worsen in the following decades, leading the Hill Section to experience urban blight, as many businesses, including the Scranton Transit Company, closed. The new millennium has brought new hope for the Hill Section, which is now more diverse than ever with a significant number of new Hispanic and Asian immigrants. The efforts of its many devoted residents, local medical and educational institutions, and the Hill Neighborhood Association and Lackawanna Historical Society have managed to initiate a minor renaissance for this community.

Scranton's Hill Section is a unique and incredible place with stories that are impossible to amalgamate into one book. The goal of the subsequent text is to depict the history of Scranton's Hill Section in a manner that will preserve its past and promote its future. There is no other place like it. The previously described events culminated in the creation of a unique environment, where people of all ethnic groups and classes lived together for over a century in a manner that is in stark contrast to most other American communities. The progression of individuals into the Hill Section mirrored their progression in society. Moving up to the Hill Section was very much akin to the attainment of the American Dream—a dream that the lives of so many of the Hill Section's residents have and continue to embody.

Unfortunately, there are many aspects of the history of Scranton's Hill Section for which there are no surviving images to depict them. Nonetheless, a sampling of these aspects deserves to be in included in this volume. The life story of African American businesswoman Louise Tanner Brown is one fine example. Brown was born in Beaver, Pennsylvania, in the early 1900s and later moved to Scranton upon her marriage to George W. Brown, the owner and operator of a local draying business. The couple settled in the 500 block of Prescott Avenue, but George died, leaving his entire business to his young widow in 1923. Louise Brown faced a difficult situation:

either she had to sell her family's business or go it alone as an African American woman in the 1920s. Louise Brown chose the latter; she led G.W. Brown Trucking Company to expand and prosper even during the Great Depression, transcending some of the 20th century's most intimidating barriers. In the late 1940s, Louise Brown sold G.W. Brown Trucking to one of her young employees, Granville Smith Sr., who continued to operate the business and lived the Hill Section for many years.

There are also many historic Hill Section residences of which there are no surviving images, such as the Samter family residences in the 700 block of Webster Avenue. Samuel Samter, who owned a large men's clothing store in Scranton's downtown, built a large home for himself at 701 Webster Avenue. He later built two homes, both with inward-facing doors, adjacent to his for his daughters. The first home was built for Minnie Samter Levi and her husband, A.J. Levi, who took over Samuel's store upon his retirement, and the second was built for Jean Samter Heinz, whose husband, Bernard Heinz, operated Heinz's, a women's clothing store. Similarly, the Connell family, who made their fortune from the coal, banking, button, textile, and milling industries, developed an entire enclave of eclectic mansions along Vine Street, between Webster and Clay Avenues. Sadly, few of these homes still stand today.

Small mom-and-pop shops like Johnny's Market at the corner of Quincy Avenue and Pine Street and Dorfman's Drug Store and Soda Fountain at the corner of Madison Avenue and Pine Street are great examples of the numerous corner stores that filled the Hill Section. But images of these successful and iconic enterprises have been lost over time. The Nay Aug Park Zoo, once Scranton's largest public park, has also left behind very little in terms of photographic memories. At one time, the zoo had numerous exotic animals on display and a petting zoo with a Winnie the Pooh theme. The elephant exhibit was particularly well known, with elephants named Queenie, Tillie, Princess Penny, and Toni. These elephants shared an enclosure with a donkey companion that helped complete a classic scene of political satire. These stories all contributed to the history of Scranton's Hill Section, a history that I have done my best to depict in the following seven chapters.

One

HOMES

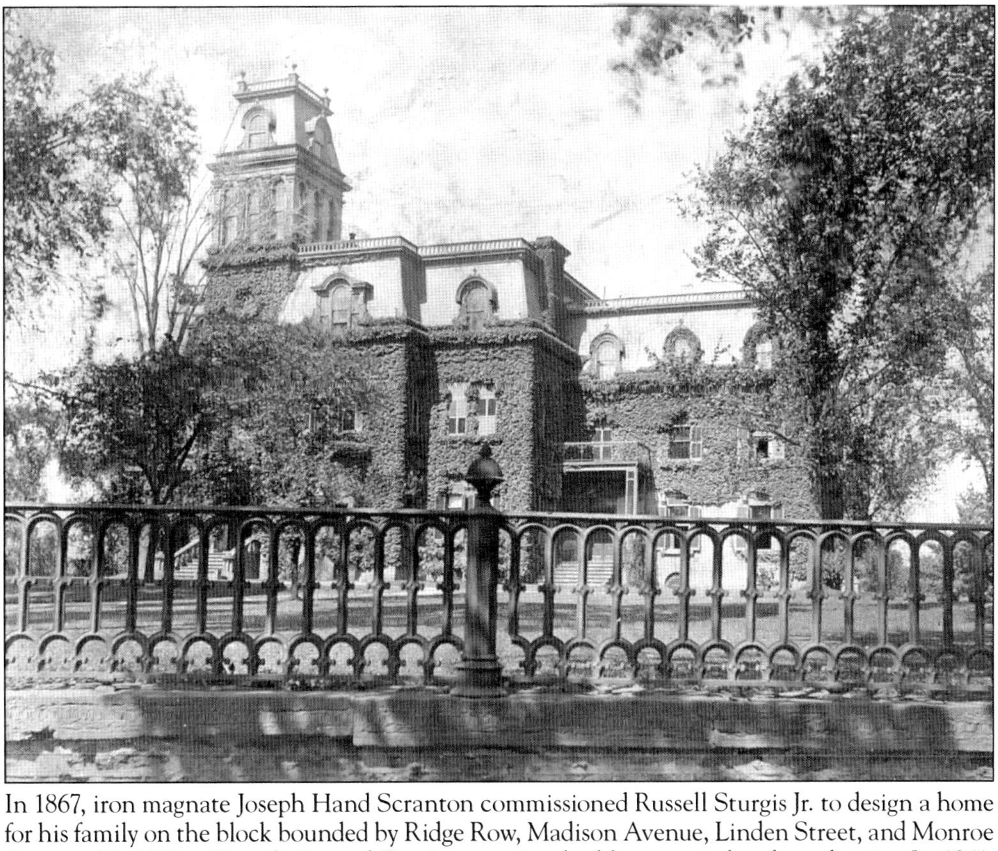

In 1867, iron magnate Joseph Hand Scranton commissioned Russell Sturgis Jr. to design a home for his family on the block bounded by Ridge Row, Madison Avenue, Linden Street, and Monroe Avenue. By 1871, a French Second Empire mansion had been completed on the site. In 1941, Worthington Scranton, Joseph Hand Scranton's grandson, donated the family home and its grounds to the Diocese of Scranton's St. Thomas College.

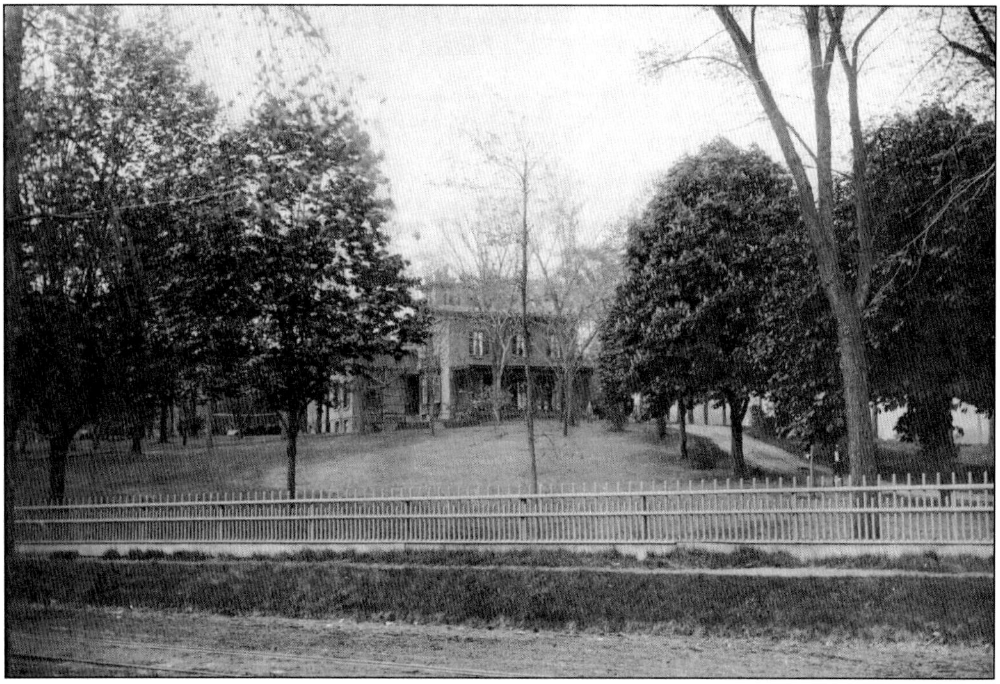

The Archbald estate was constructed at the corner of Monroe Avenue and Ridge Row in the years following the Civil War for businessman and civil engineer James Archbald. The estate was eventually the residence of Archbald's daughter Mary Archbald and son-in-law George H. Catlin, a prominent lawyer and banker. The estate was demolished in 1925, and the University of Scranton's Loyola Science Center now occupies its former location.

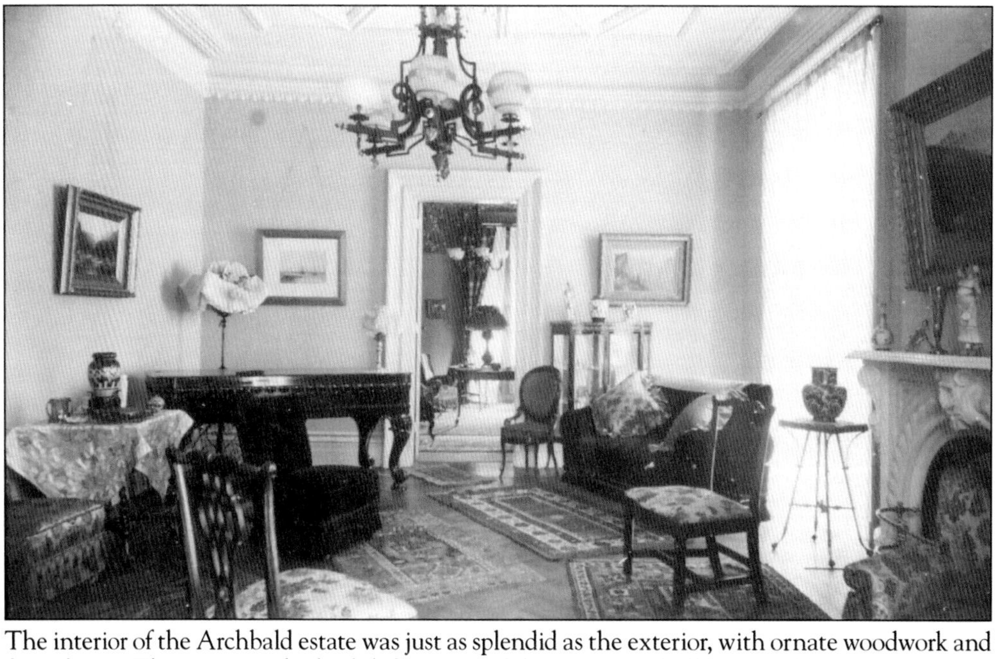

The interior of the Archbald estate was just as splendid as the exterior, with ornate woodwork and furnishings. The piano in the back left corner of the reception hall, pictured here, is on display at the Lackawanna Historical Society.

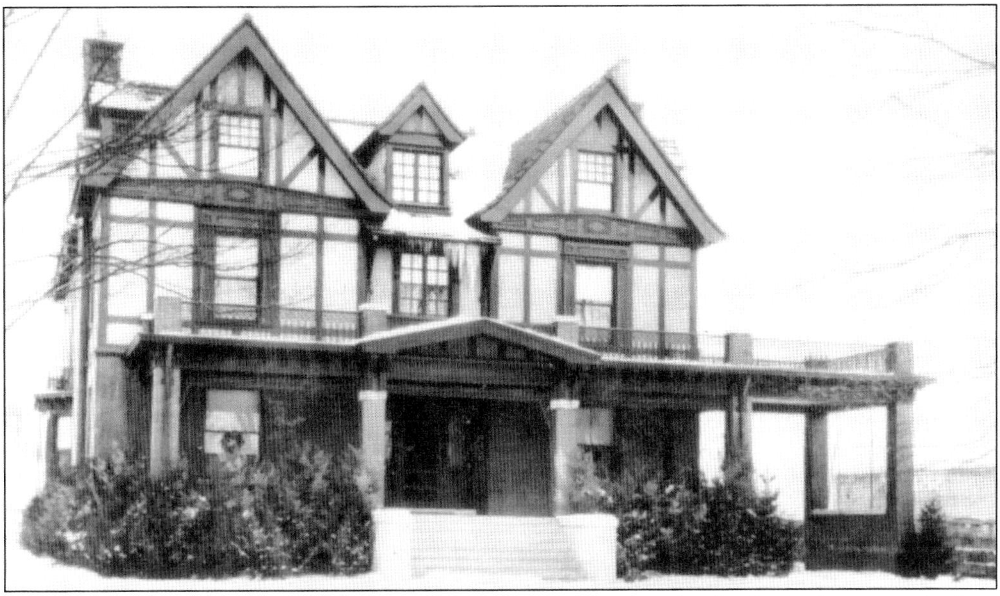

Designed by architect Edward Langley in the Tudor Craftsman style, the Catlin house was built at 232 Monroe Avenue for lawyer and banker George H. Catlin and his second wife, Helen Walsh, in 1912. George and Helen Catlin never had any children, and following their deaths in 1935 and 1942, respectively, the home was willed to George's beloved Lackawanna Historical Society for use as the organization's headquarters.

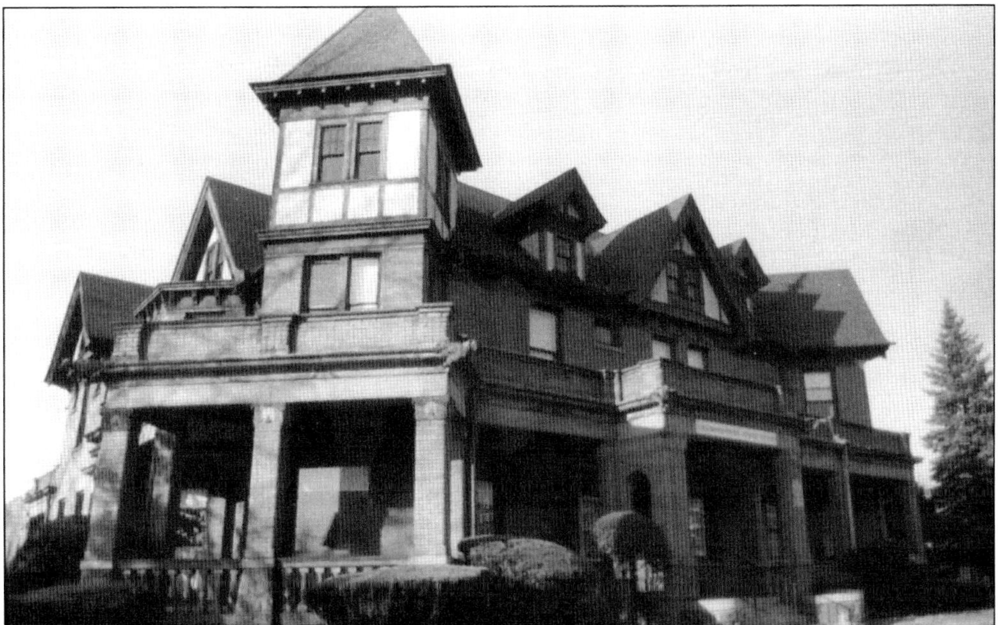

The Crawford mansion at 313 Monroe Avenue was built by James L. Crawford, president of the Peoples Coal Company. Following the deaths of James L. Crawford and his wife, Huldah Wilcox, the home was acquired by the Lackawanna County government for use as a juvenile detention center, nicknamed "Mrs. Duggan's." The home was later demolished, and the University of Scranton's McDade Center now stands on its former site.

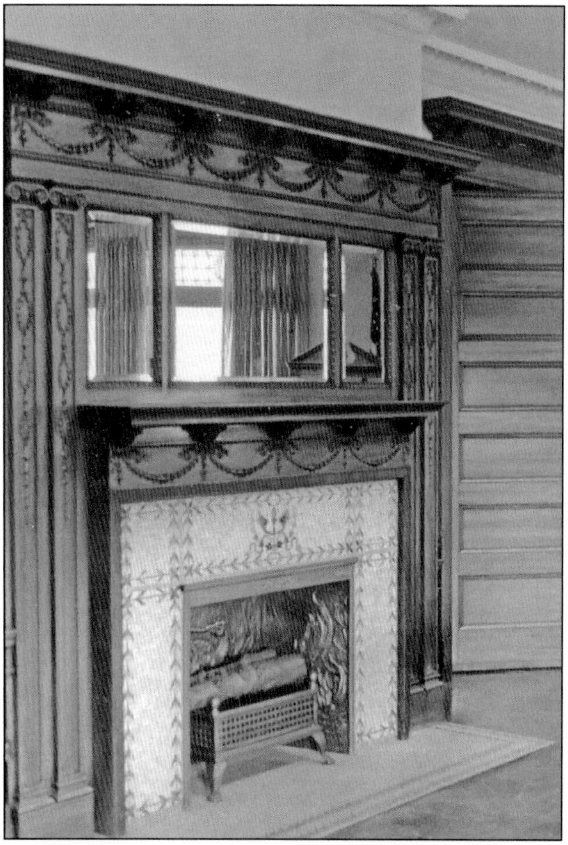

Shown here is the fireplace of the Crawford mansion. Although this fireplace is particularly opulent, similar fireplaces graced the living spaces of many Hill Section mansions.

This is a stained-glass window from the Crawford mansion. Ornate stained-glass windows were prominent features of many residences of the Gilded Age and common in the Hill Section. The Crawford mansion was no exception, with English playwright William Shakespeare depicted in the one seen here.

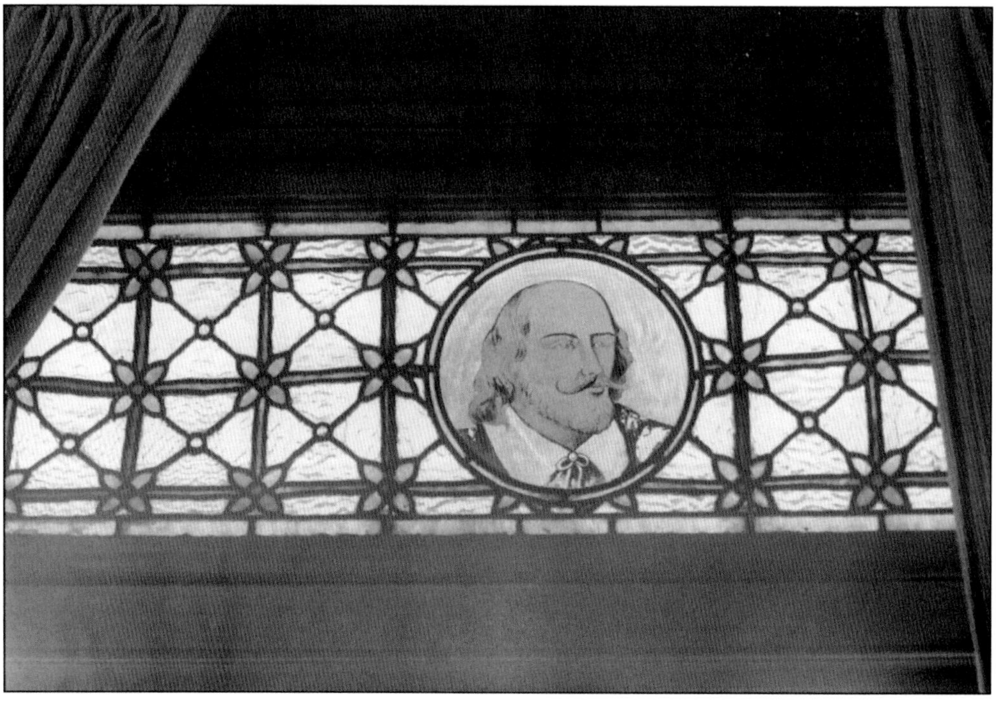

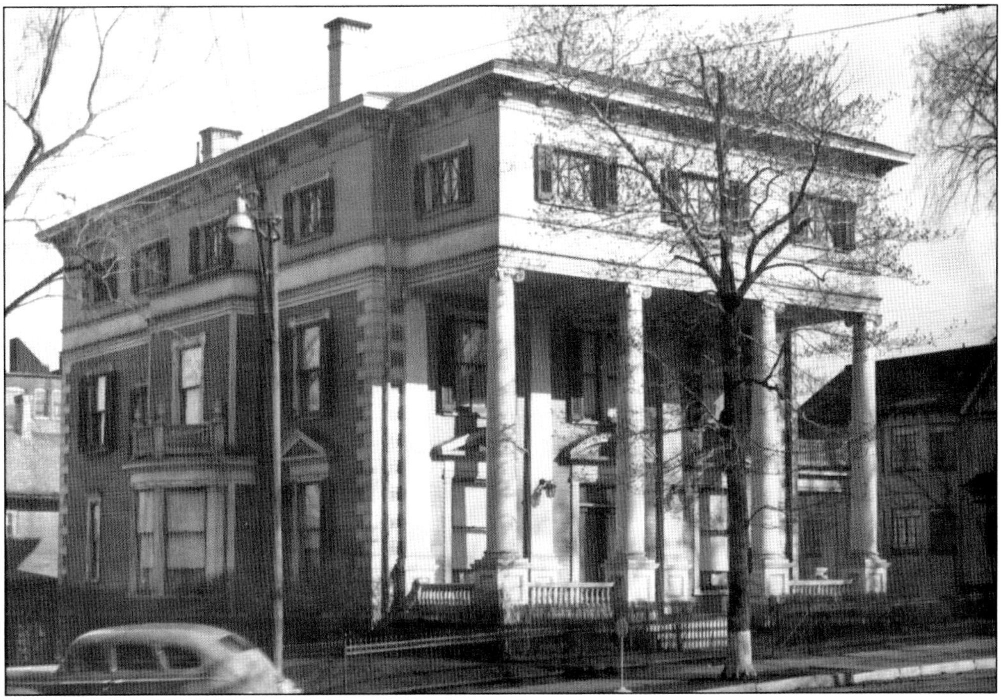

The grand home of banker Austin Blair located at 401 Jefferson Avenue is among the most recognizable in Scranton. Originally constructed in the Victorian style, the home was extensively remodeled in the early 1900s, when it took on its present Neoclassical form. In the early 2000s, the home underwent a historically sensitive renovation and was turned into an elegant event space and bed-and-breakfast known as the Colonnade.

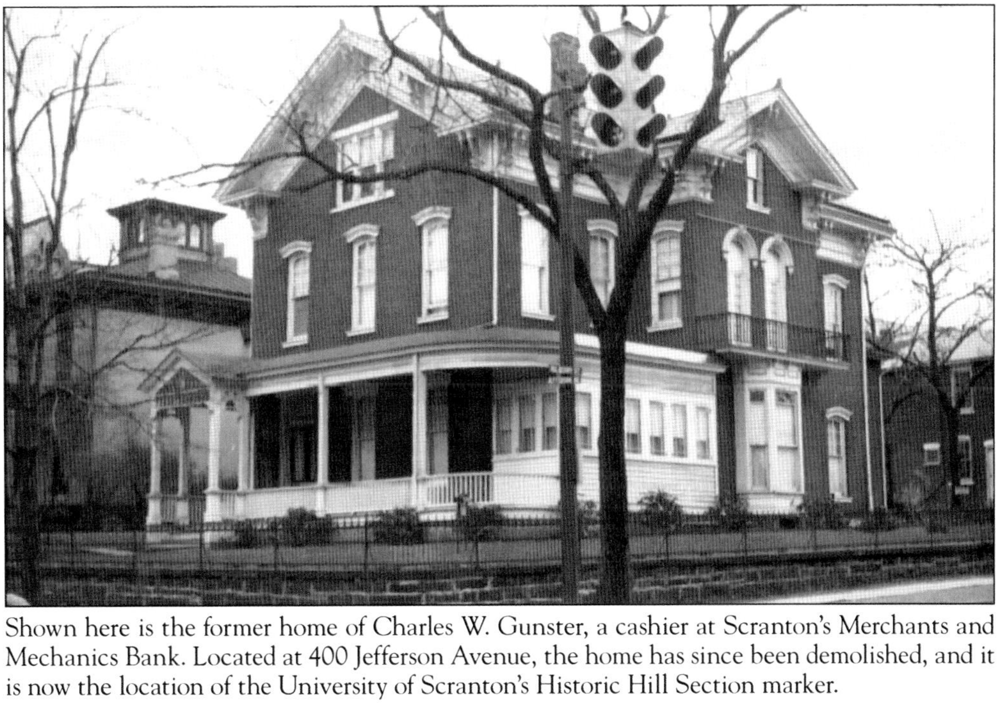

Shown here is the former home of Charles W. Gunster, a cashier at Scranton's Merchants and Mechanics Bank. Located at 400 Jefferson Avenue, the home has since been demolished, and it is now the location of the University of Scranton's Historic Hill Section marker.

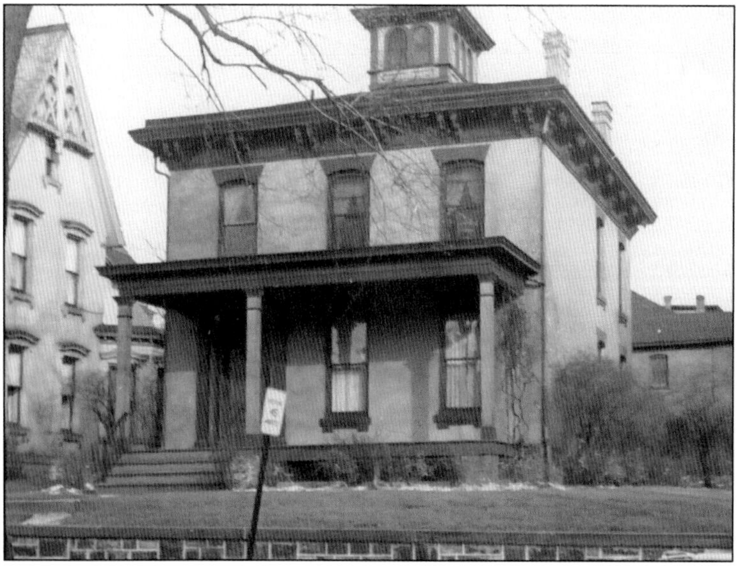

This home at 402 Jefferson Avenue was originally the residence of Jacob Bryant of the construction firm Kierstad & Bryant. Samuel Hines, a prominent real estate agent, later occupied the home before the nearby Immanuel Baptist Church purchased it for use as a rectory. The home has since been converted to offices and still stands today.

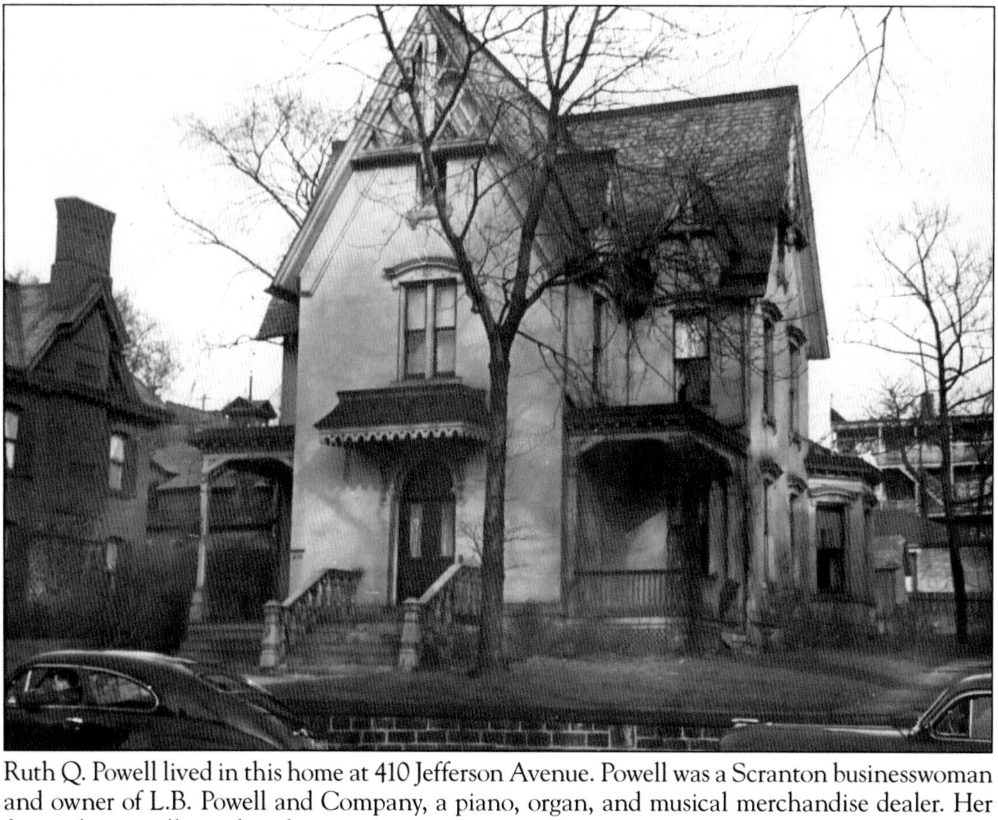

Ruth Q. Powell lived in this home at 410 Jefferson Avenue. Powell was a Scranton businesswoman and owner of L.B. Powell and Company, a piano, organ, and musical merchandise dealer. Her former home still stands today.

James Archbald Jr. and his wife, Augusta Brooks, lived in this home at 422 Jefferson Avenue. James Archbald Jr. was the son of affluent engineer James Archbald and brother-in-law of prominent lawyer and banker George Catlin. Augusta Brooks was the daughter of local stockbroker Reese Brooks. The Archbald home has since been demolished and replaced by modern structures.

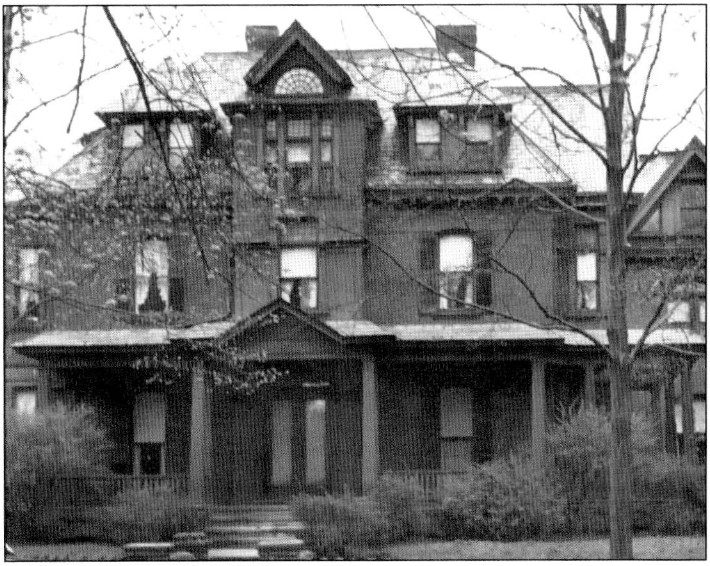

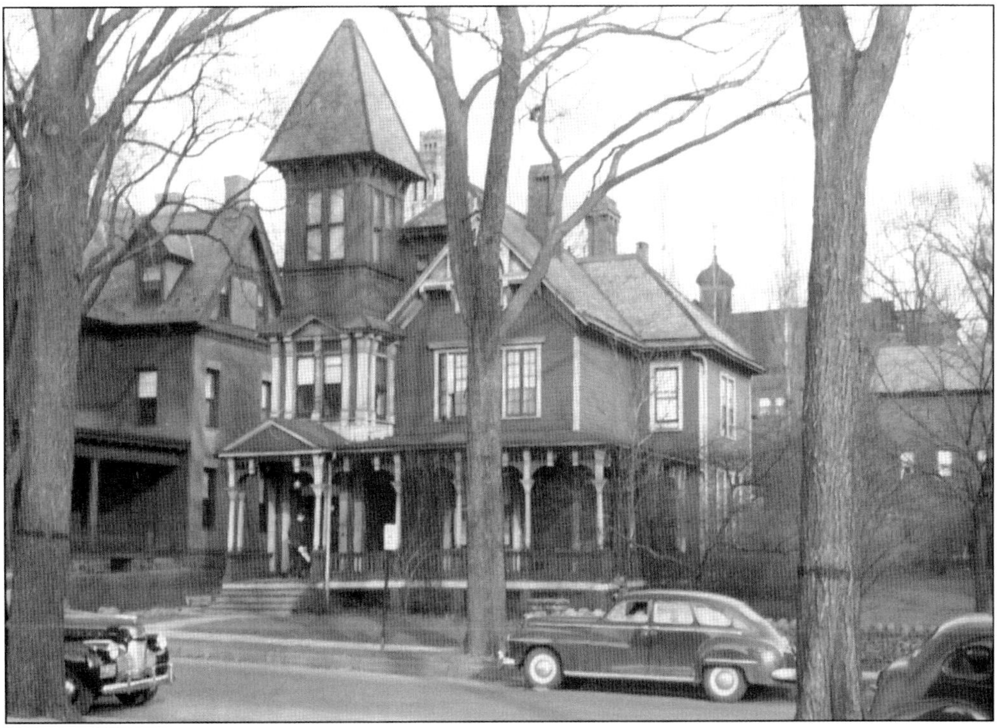

The president of the Stipp Construction Company, Mathias Stipp, resided in this home at 436 Jefferson Avenue. Stipp and his brothers were prolific real estate developers and used their construction business to build many Hill Section structures. Although heavily remodeled, the Stipp home still stands today.

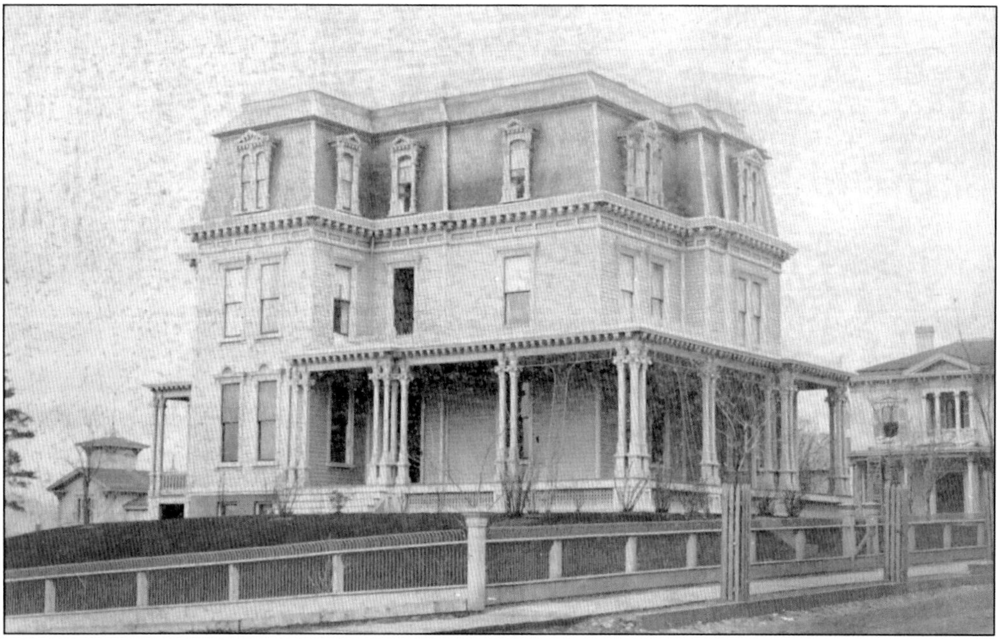

The French Second Empire mansion seen here was located at 447 Jefferson Avenue and served as the residence of Henry Belin Jr., an explosive powder magnate and the founder of the Scranton Lace Curtain Company. The Belin mansion has long since been demolished; St. Matthew's Lutheran Church now owns its former site.

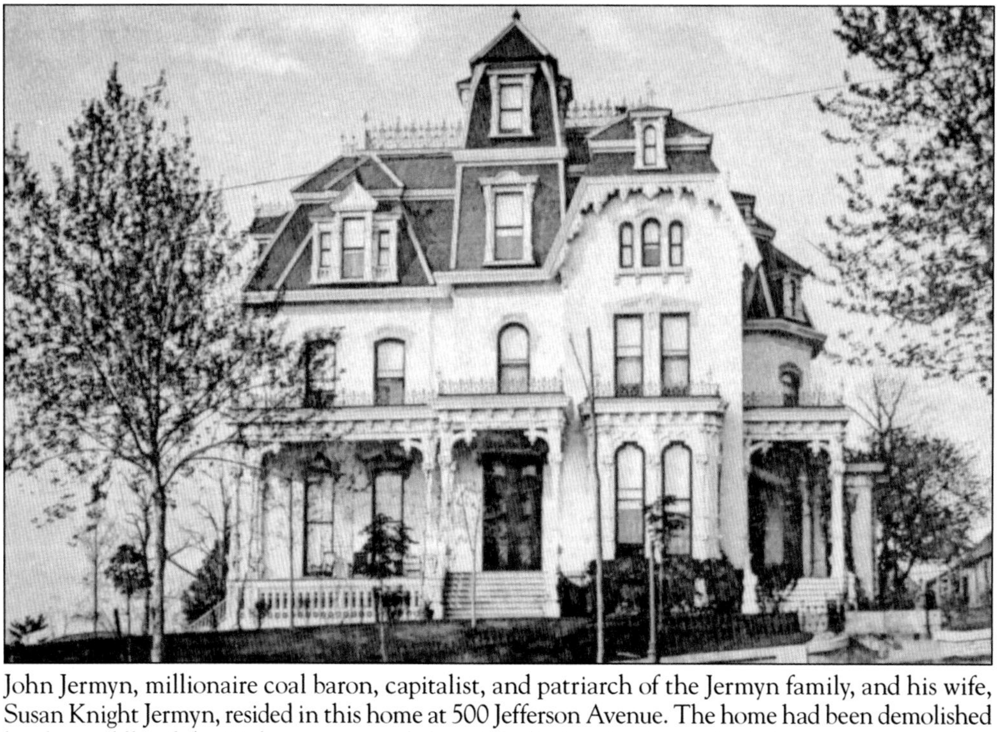

John Jermyn, millionaire coal baron, capitalist, and patriarch of the Jermyn family, and his wife, Susan Knight Jermyn, resided in this home at 500 Jefferson Avenue. The home had been demolished by the middle of the 20th century, and the Catholic Youth Center (CYC) was constructed on its former site in the 1940s.

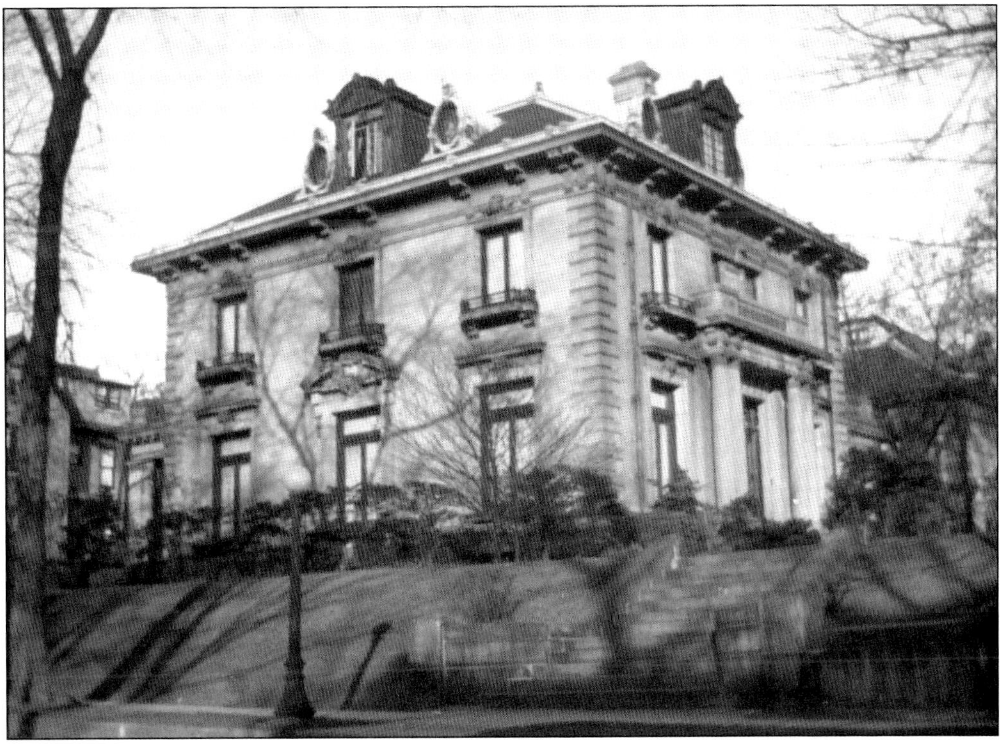

Charles Sumner "C.S." Woolworth resided in this palatial Beaux-Arts mansion at 520 Jefferson Avenue. Woolworth was cofounder of the F.W. Woolworth Company, which operated an empire of five-and-dime stores. After Woolworth's death, his home was acquired by Mercy Hospital's Nursing School, which used it until the 1970s. In the early 2000s, the home was purchased by a private owner and extensively renovated.

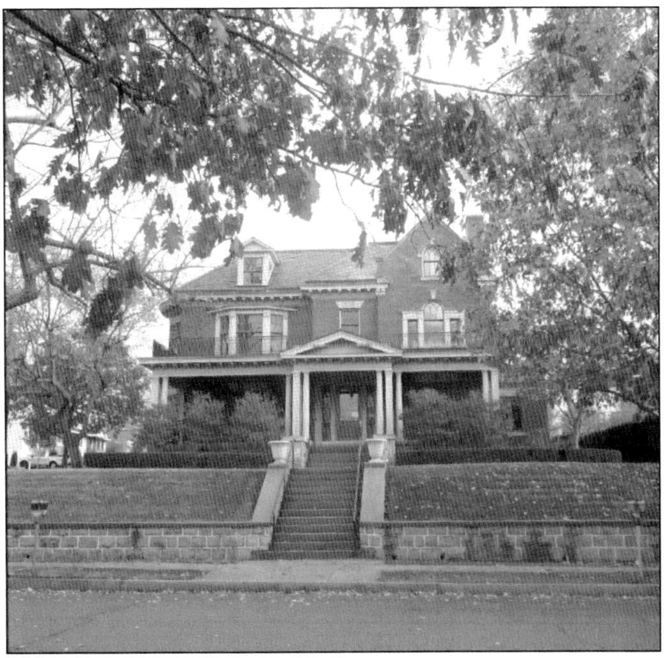

This Victorian Colonial Revival residence at 544 Jefferson Avenue was originally the home of John T. Potter, a wholesale grocer and trustee at Elm Park Methodist Church. Later, the home was occupied by Potter's daughter Elizabeth and son-in-law Ralph E. Weeks, a prominent hardware merchant. In the early 2000s, the home was renovated, and it is now the headquarters of a local software business. (Author's collection.)

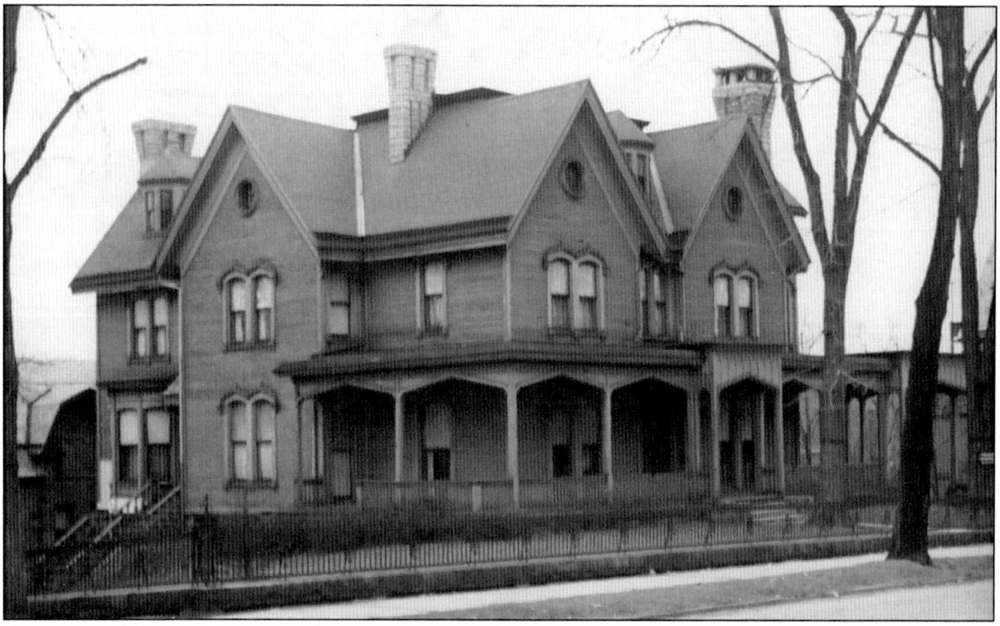

William Tallman "W.T." Smith resided in this home at 615 Jefferson Avenue. Smith made his fortune directing the Mount Pleasant Coal Company, and after his death, his widow endowed the W.T. Smith Manual Training School in his honor. The W.T. Smith home no longer stands, and its former site is now the location of the Jewish Community Center (JCC).

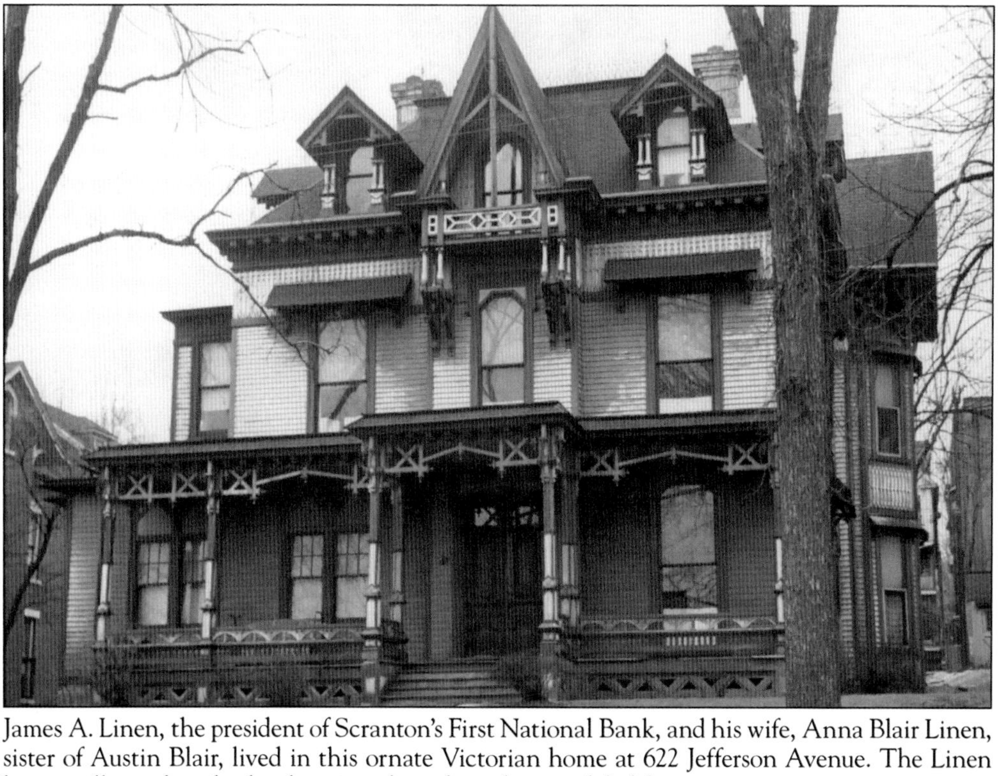

James A. Linen, the president of Scranton's First National Bank, and his wife, Anna Blair Linen, sister of Austin Blair, lived in this ornate Victorian home at 622 Jefferson Avenue. The Linen house still stands today but has since been heavily remodeled for use as apartments.

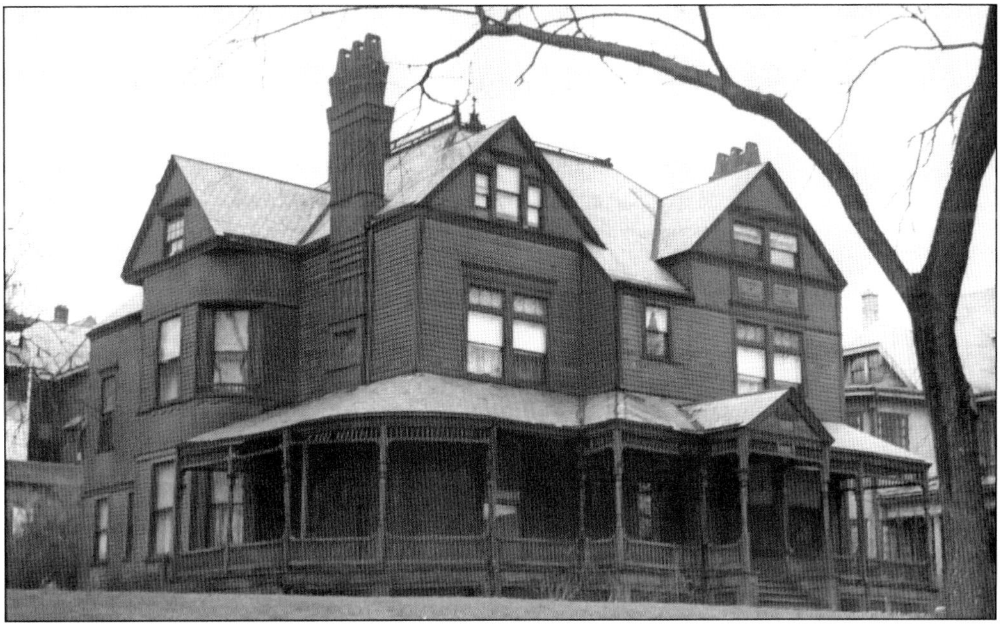

Railway and salt magnate Edward Laton Fuller built this home at 632 Jefferson Avenue. Edward Fuller's son, Mortimer B. Fuller, president of the International Salt Company and subsequent family patriarch of the prominent Fuller family, later resided here. The home still stands today as a private residence.

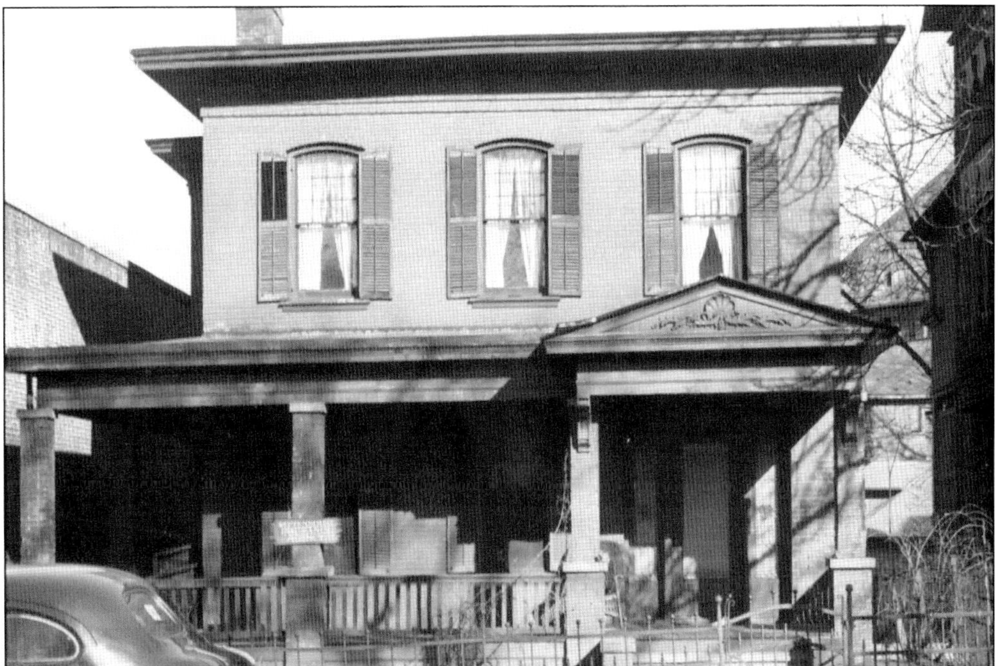

This home at 339 Madison Avenue was the residence of insurance agent John W. Rittenhouse. In the 1940s, when this image was taken, the home was converted for use as offices, and the small sign visible on the front porch denotes the Rittenhouse Insurance Agency. The home has since been demolished.

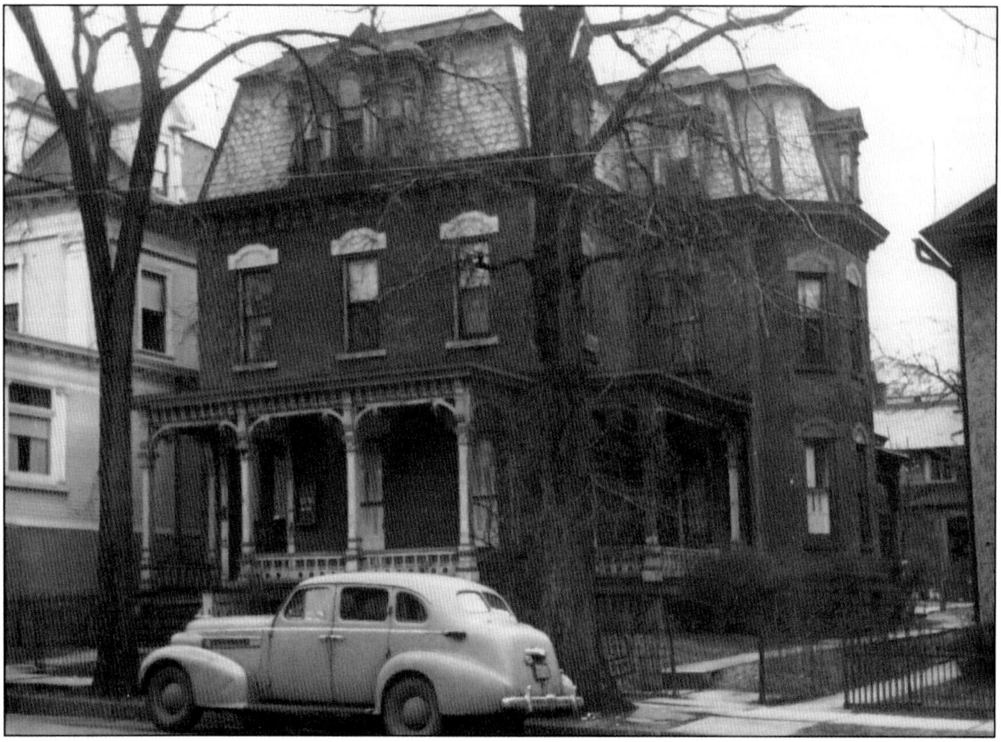

This home at 338 Madison Avenue was the residence of T.J. Foster, the president of the International Text Book Company and International Correspondence School. It has since been demolished and is now the location of the University of Scranton's Mulberry Plaza dormitories.

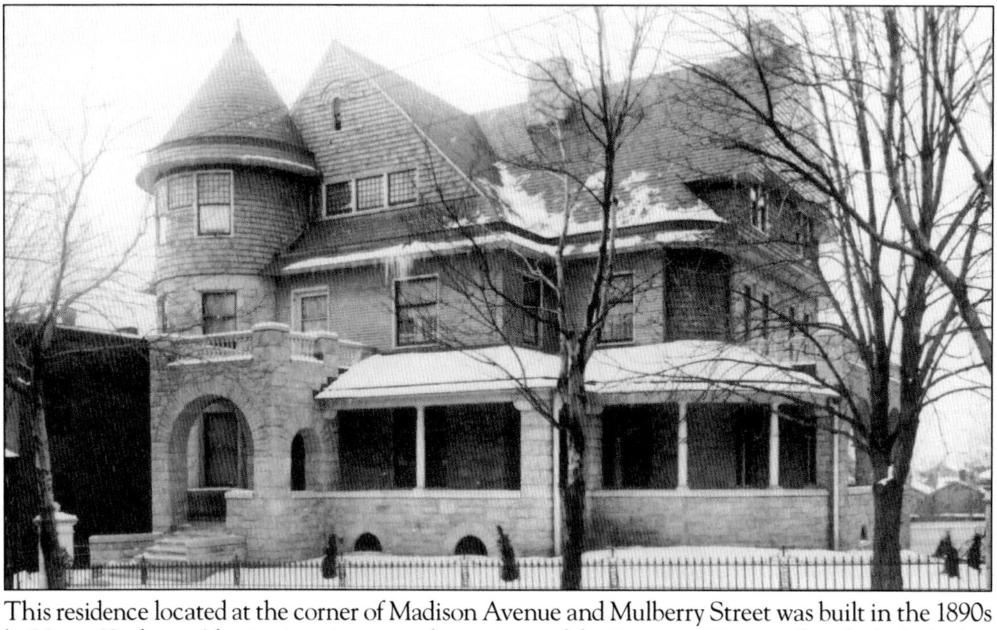

This residence located at the corner of Madison Avenue and Mulberry Street was built in the 1890s by Victor Koch, an Alsatian immigrant and proprietor of the Scranton House, a hotel. Koch died in the 1930s, and his family sold the home to Samuel and John Chipak in 1948. The Chipaks converted the home into the Chipak Funeral Home, which continues to occupy the structure today.

The front living room of the Koch residence is an excellent example of Gilded Age woodwork and interior artistry. The room's fireplace mantel and woodwork are made from bird's-eye maple, and the ceiling is decorated with a painting of angels. At one time, the Koch family used this space as a music room and had a baby grand piano in the front window area. (Courtesy of the Chipak Funeral Home.)

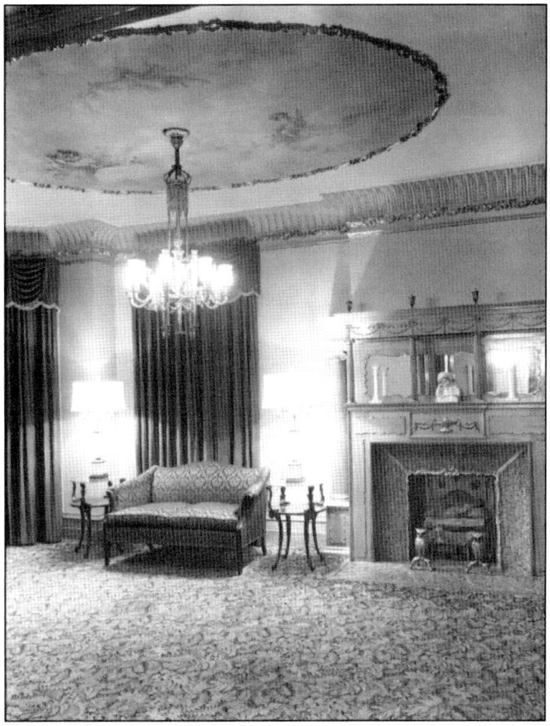

The main staircase of the Koch residence is made entirely from cherry wood and illuminated by large stained-glass windows. The staircase begins in the home's basement and terminates at its third floor, with several spacious landings in between. After the Koch residence became the Chipak Funeral Home, John Chipak used the landing seen here as his personal office. (Courtesy of the Chipak Funeral Home.)

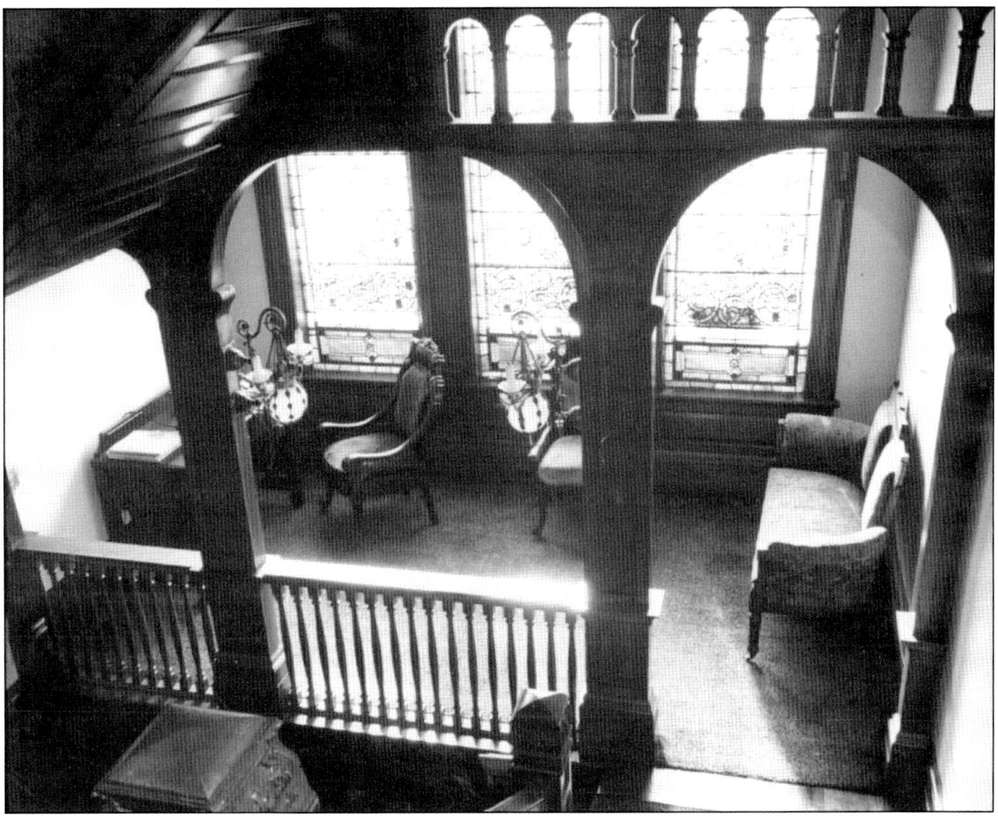

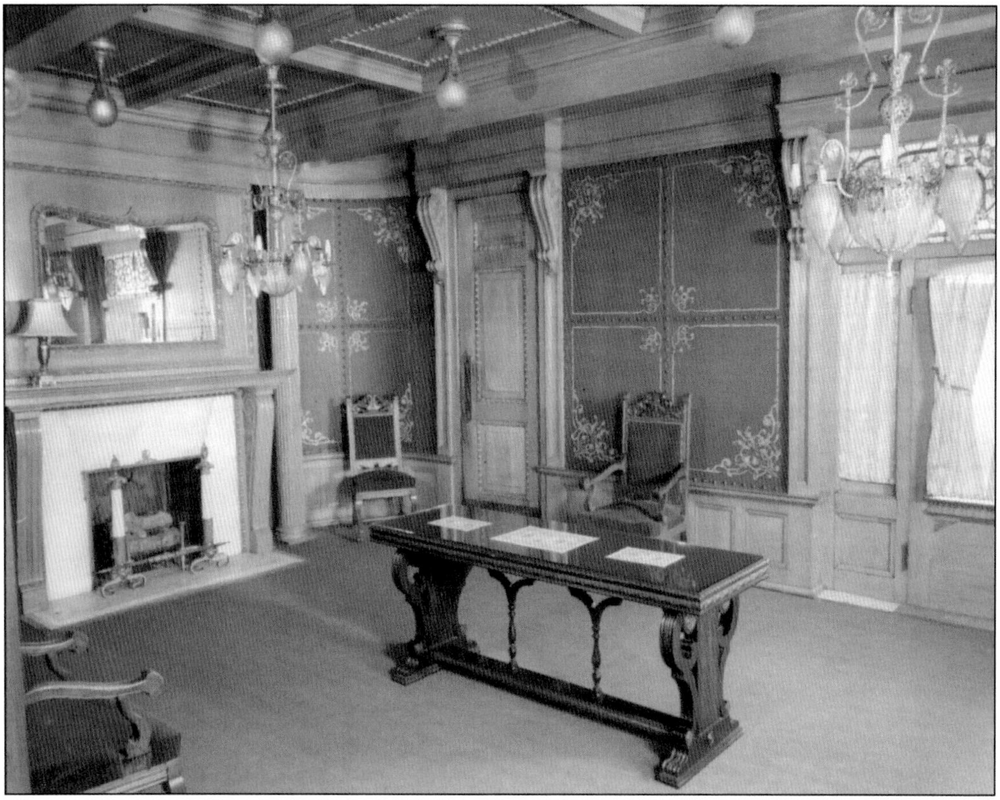

The dining room of the Koch residence is a decorative masterpiece. The room's walls are adorned with studded leather panels, its extensive woodwork is made from solid oak, and its fireplace is made of highly polished onyx. Today, the room looks much like it did when the Koch family used it. (Courtesy of the Chipak Funeral Home.)

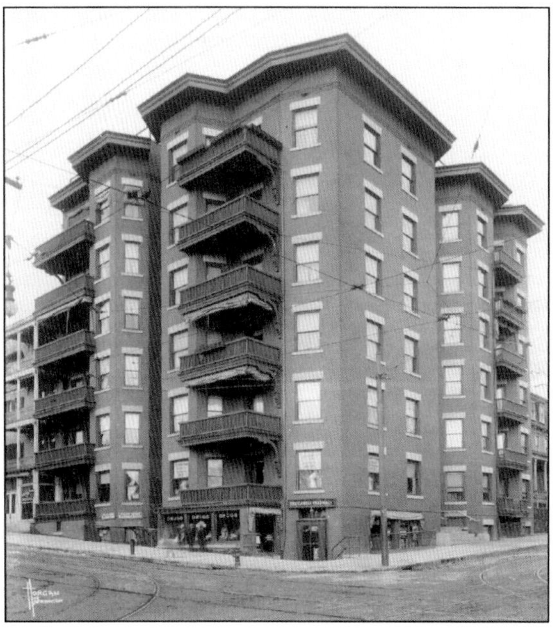

Shown here are the Carter Apartments. This multistory residential complex was located on the northeastern corner of Madison Avenue and Mulberry Street. The Carter Apartments were very similar to many other named apartment buildings of varying architectural styles that once filled the Hill Section. The building was torn down in the early 2000s, and the University of Scranton's Madison Square dormitories now occupy the site.

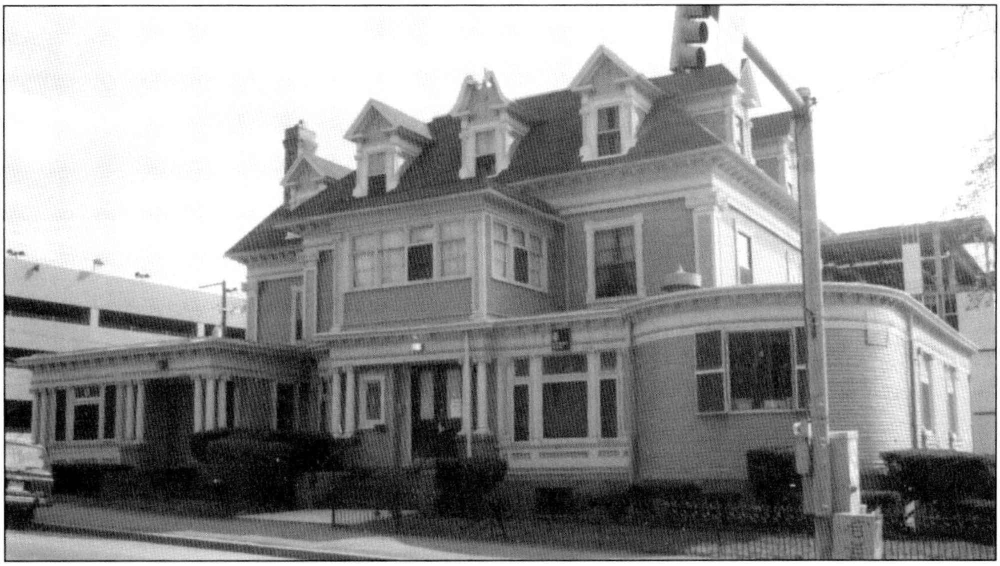

This Colonial Revival home at 800 Mulberry Street was originally built for Dr. L.A. Gates in 1901. In the 1930s, it became a music conservatory; in the 1950s, it became Snowdon's Funeral Home; and in the 1960s, it became the Jefferson Townhouse, a catering and party venue. In 1982, the home became dormitories for the University of Scranton, and in the early 2000s, the structure was demolished and replaced by the University's Mulberry Plaza dormitories.

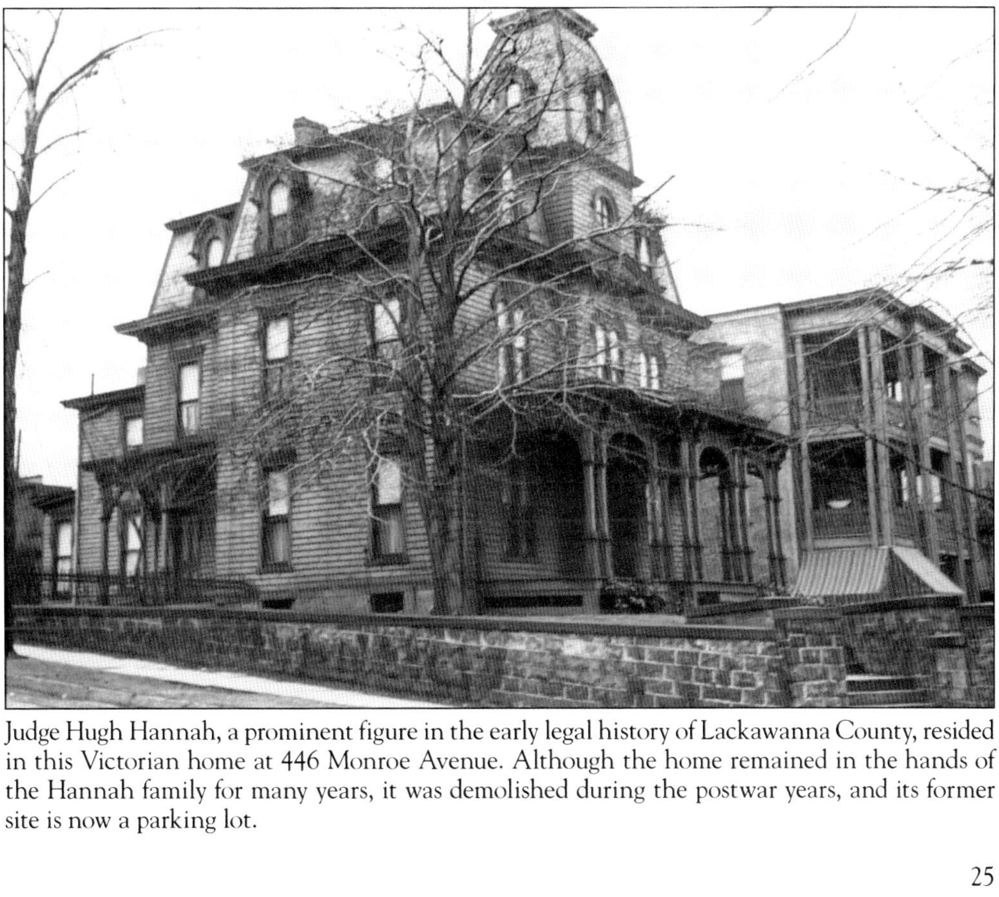

Judge Hugh Hannah, a prominent figure in the early legal history of Lackawanna County, resided in this Victorian home at 446 Monroe Avenue. Although the home remained in the hands of the Hannah family for many years, it was demolished during the postwar years, and its former site is now a parking lot.

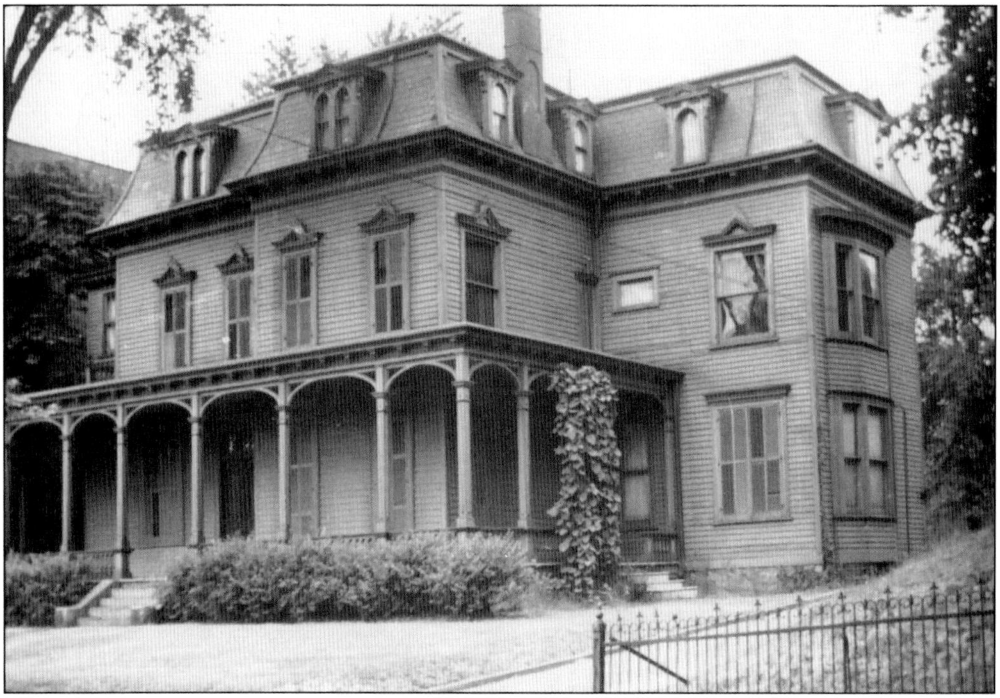

Shown here is the residence of Charles H. Welles, a lawyer and onetime partner in the well-known law firm Welles & Torrey. This Victorian residence has long since been demolished, and its former site is now the location of the St. Nicholas Orthodox Church.

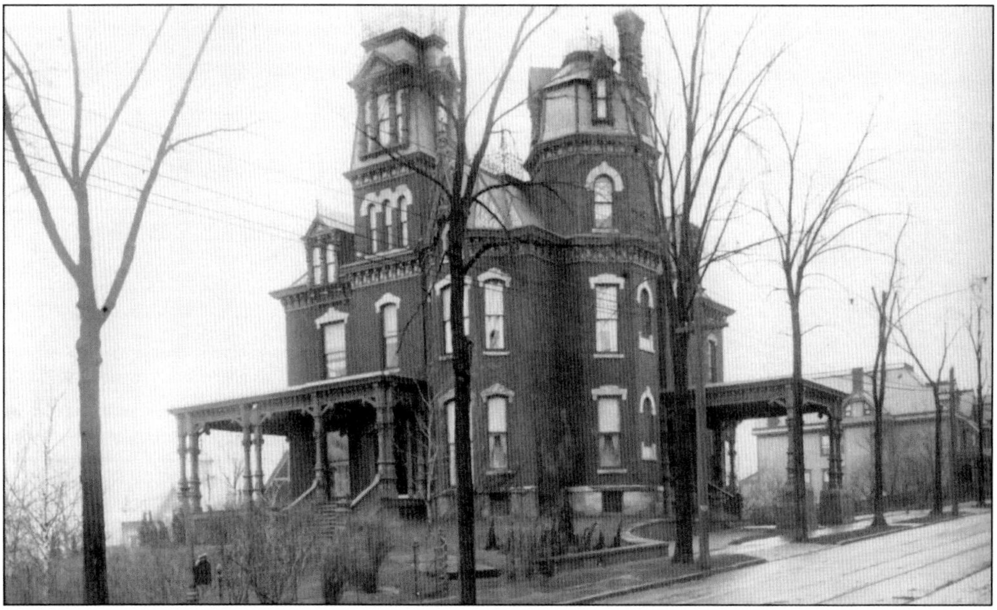

Joseph A. Scranton, a US congressman and Joseph H. Scranton's son by his first wife, Eliza Wilcox, resided in this palatial Victorian residence at the corner of Madison Avenue and Vine Street. The residence was subsequently bought by the Orthodox Jewish congregation Machzikeh Hadas for use as a synagogue. The congregation later relocated, and the building was demolished and replaced by a Lackawanna College dormitory.

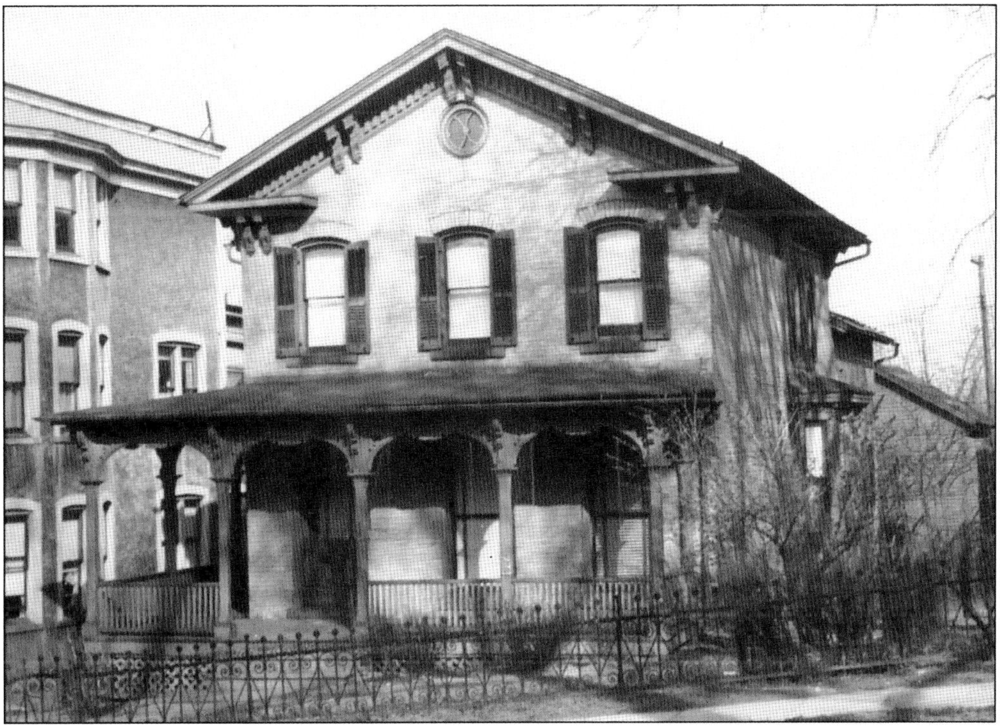

This residence at 406 Monroe Avenue was the home of William L. Hackett, a local real estate developer. The modest style of the Hackett residence was once ubiquitous in the lower Hill Section. Unfortunately, few examples of it exist today, including the Hackett residence, which was demolished long ago. Its former site is now the location of the University of Scranton's Pilarz and Montrone residence halls.

This large home at the corner of Monroe Avenue and Vine Street was the longtime manse of the Second Presbyterian Church. The ministers of this prominent congregation and their families resided here until the 1920s, when the congregation merged with First Presbyterian Church. The home was later sold but still stands today as a private residence.

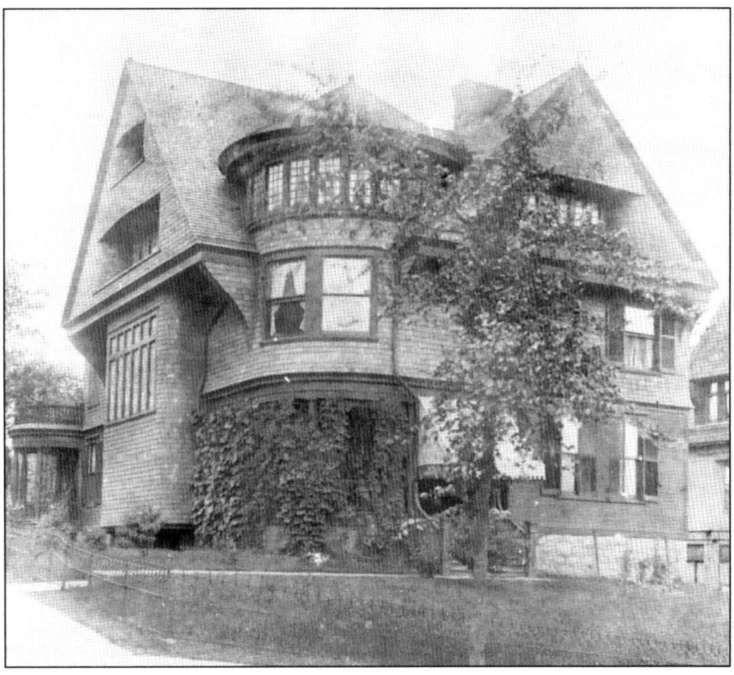

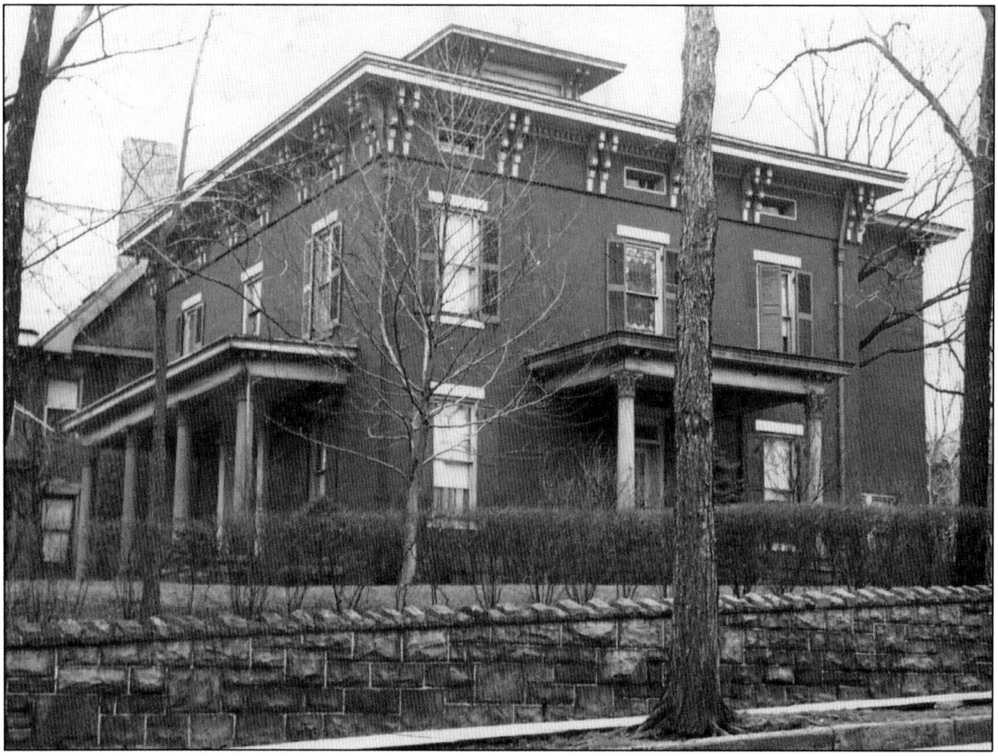

Willoughby W. Watson, a partner in the Scranton law firm Watson, Diehl & Watson, lived in this home at 504 Monroe Avenue. Watson's home has since been demolished, and two modern homes now occupy its former site.

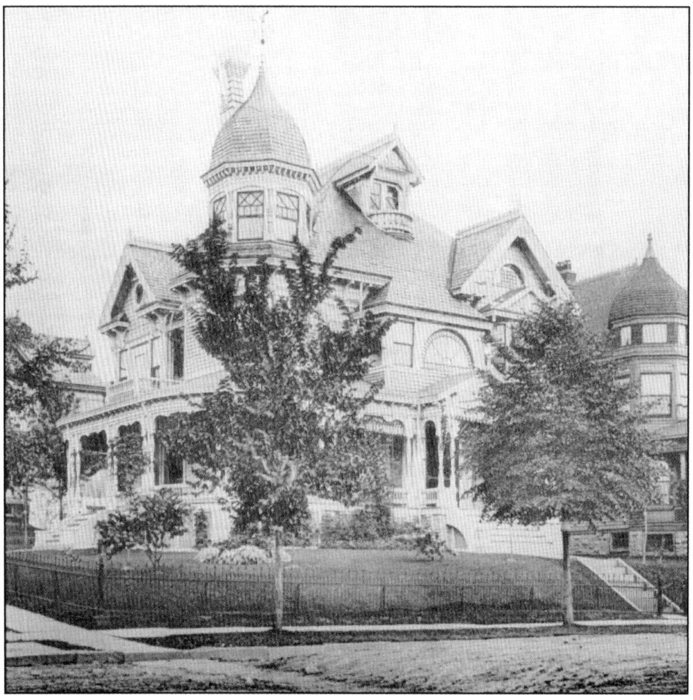

Shown here is the home of J.W. Peck, located at the corner of Monroe Avenue and Olive Street. J.W. Peck was a relative of the prominent Peck family, who owned and operated the Peck Lumber Company. The Peck residence was torn down many years ago, and its former site is now occupied by the Scranton Hebrew Day School.

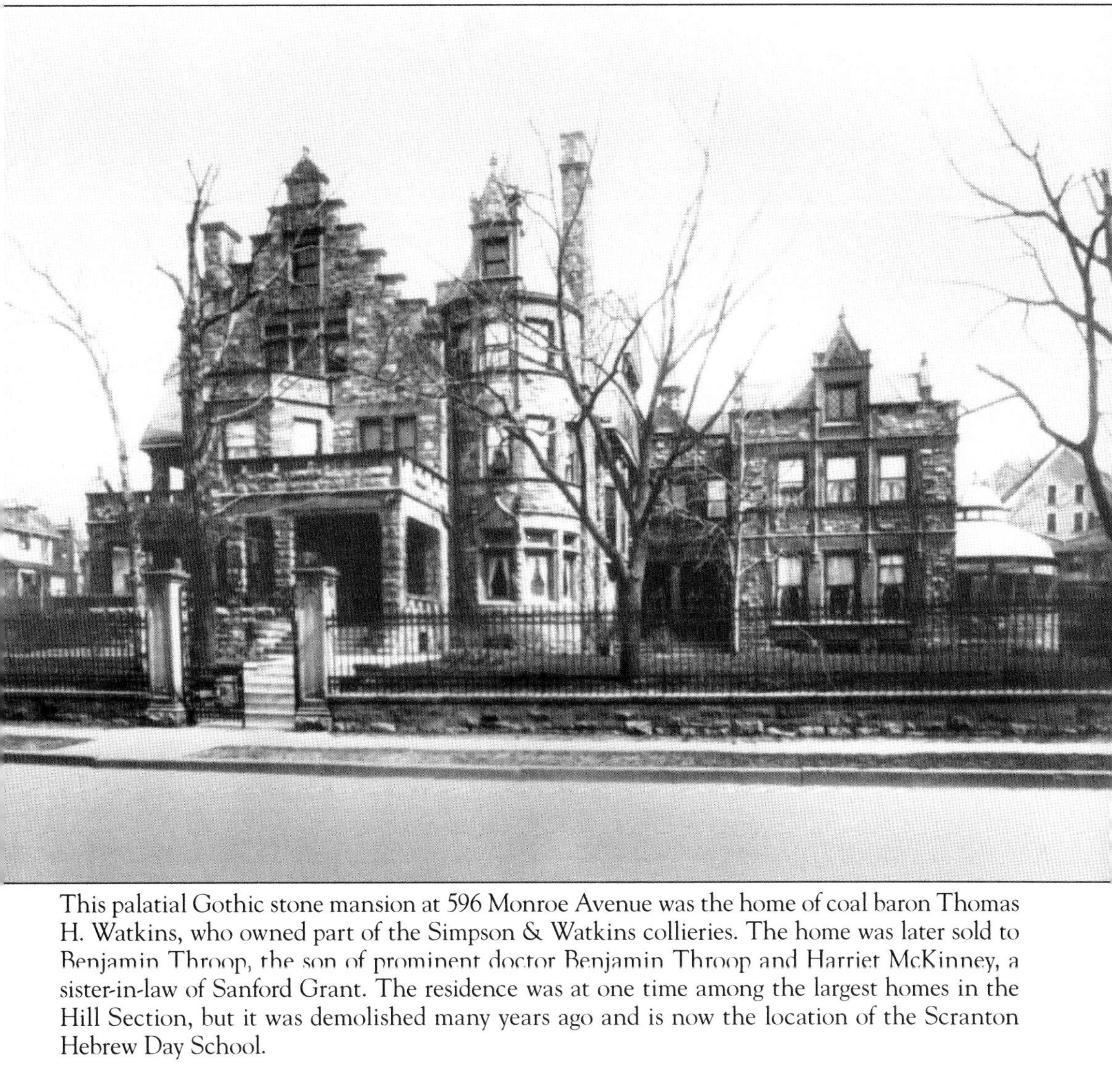

This palatial Gothic stone mansion at 596 Monroe Avenue was the home of coal baron Thomas H. Watkins, who owned part of the Simpson & Watkins collieries. The home was later sold to Benjamin Throop, the son of prominent doctor Benjamin Throop and Harriet McKinney, a sister-in-law of Sanford Grant. The residence was at one time among the largest homes in the Hill Section, but it was demolished many years ago and is now the location of the Scranton Hebrew Day School.

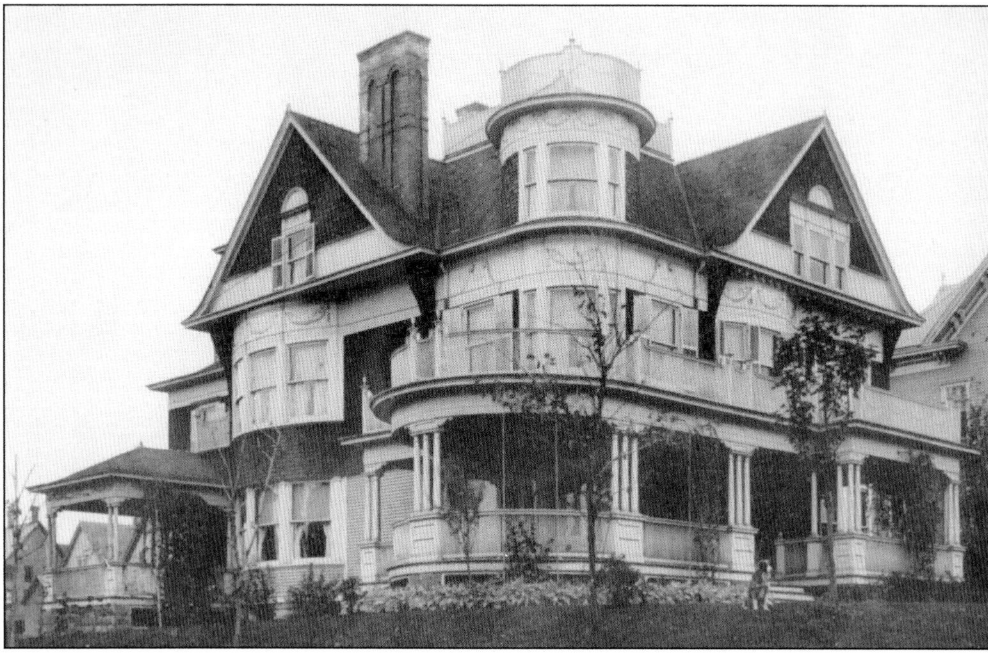

Cyrus D. Jones, a tea and coffee magnate, lived in this Queen Anne home at the corner of Monroe Avenue and Olive Street. Lackawanna Iron and Coal executive E.P. Kingsbury had previously resided there, and C.S. Woolworth, cofounder of the F.W. Woolworth Company, later occupied the residence. Later, the mansion served as the Rabbi Guterman Shul before being demolished and replaced with the Orthodox Jewish congregation Machzikeh Hadas's new synagogue.

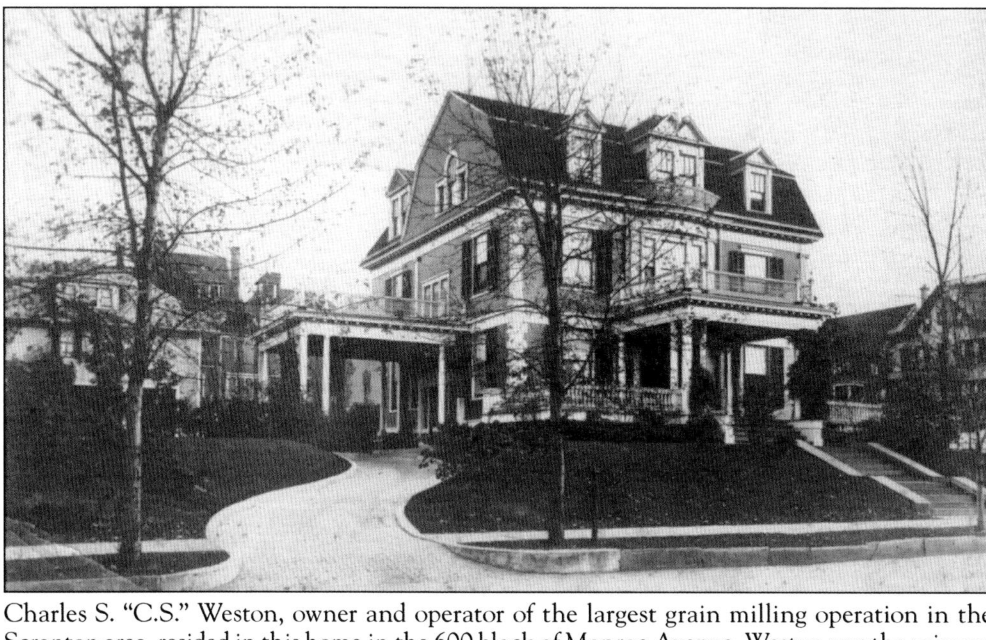

Charles S. "C.S." Weston, owner and operator of the largest grain milling operation in the Scranton area, resided in this home in the 600 block of Monroe Avenue. Weston was the primary benefactor behind the construction of Scranton's Weston Park and Weston Field. The Weston family eventually sold their milling company to their in-laws, the Connells, but their home still stands today as a private residence.

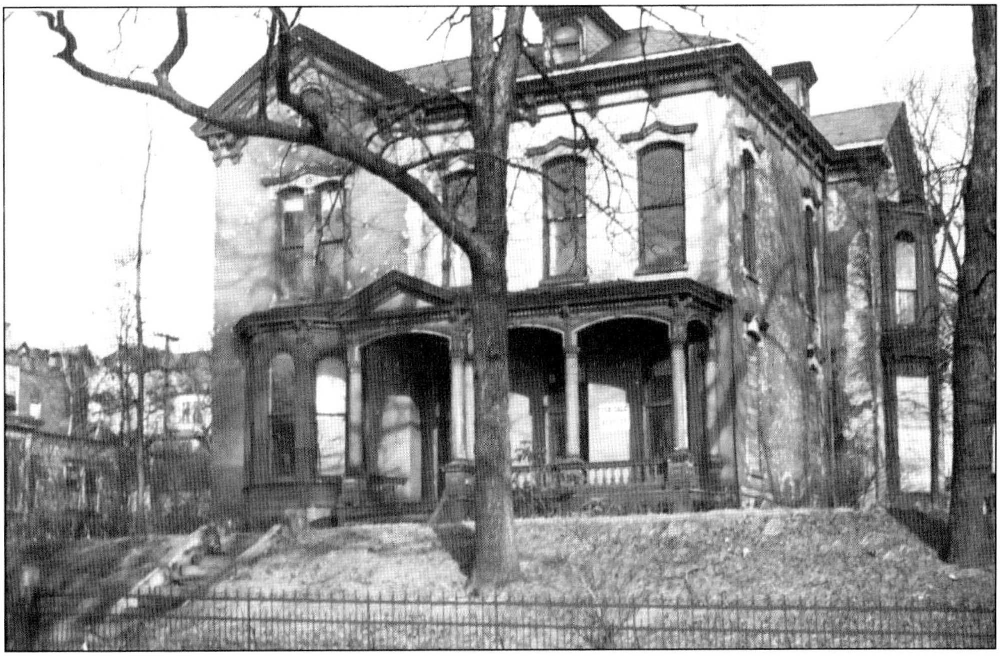

Coal baron Edward Moffat and his wife, A.R. Moffat, lived in this home at 306 Quincy Avenue. As owner of the Moffat Coal Company, the Moffat family was prominent in the local coal industry. This image shows the home shortly before it was demolished in the 1950s. Today, the University of Scranton's lower quad dormitories occupy its former site.

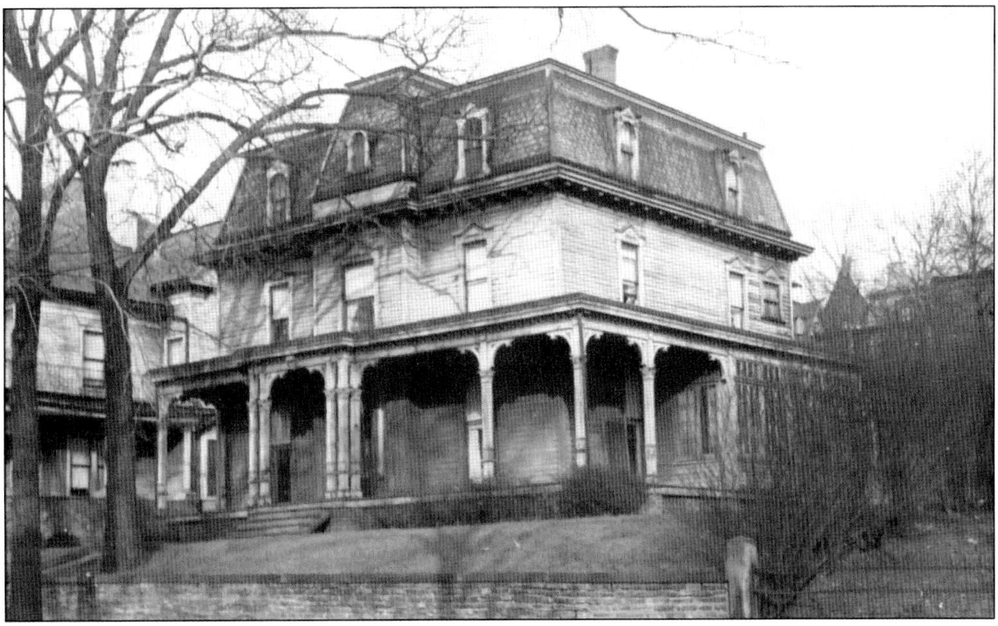

Irish immigrant and hardware store owner Thomas F. "T.F." Leonard built this Victorian home at 312 Quincy Avenue in the 1870s. Leonard's daughter Mabel and son-in-law attorney William F. Shean later occupied the home. The Shean family resided in the home until Mabel and William's deaths in 1944 and 1949, respectively. The home was then demolished and replaced by the University of Scranton's lower quad dormitories.

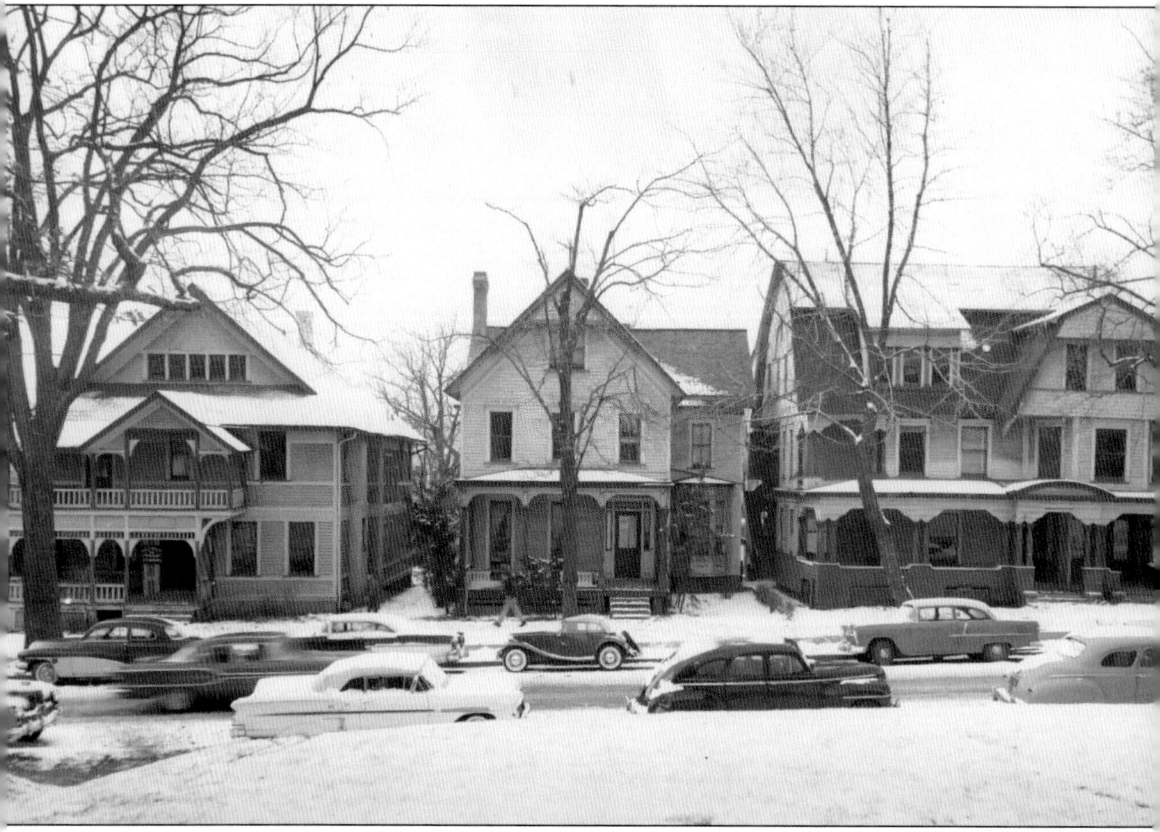

This image of the odd side of the 300 block of Quincy Avenue shows a typical Hill Section Street scene from the 1950s. At the time, these homes were being used as University of Scranton student housing, but they all used to be private residences. From left to right, the homes seen here were the onetime residences of Henry A. Knapp, a lawyer and vice president of the Scranton Trust Company; Henry V. Logan, a local physician; and C.D. Sanderson, an area stockbroker. All of these homes have been demolished, and the former sites are now the location of the University of Scranton's Dione Green. (Courtesy of the University of Scranton.)

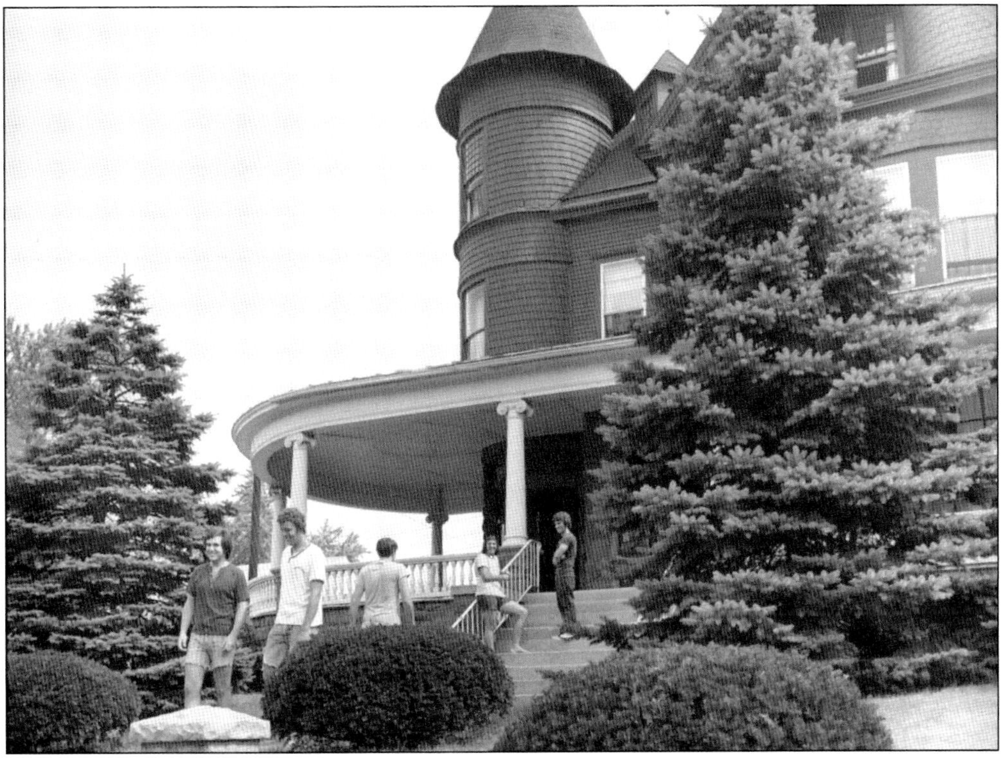

Irish immigrant, brewery magnate, and hotelier Patrick Joseph Casey and his wife, Bridget O'Malley, owned this home at 330 Clay Avenue. The Caseys resided here for many years with their nine children. The University of Scranton subsequently acquired the property and renamed it McGowan House. As depicted here, it is now used as student apartments. (Courtesy of the University of Scranton.)

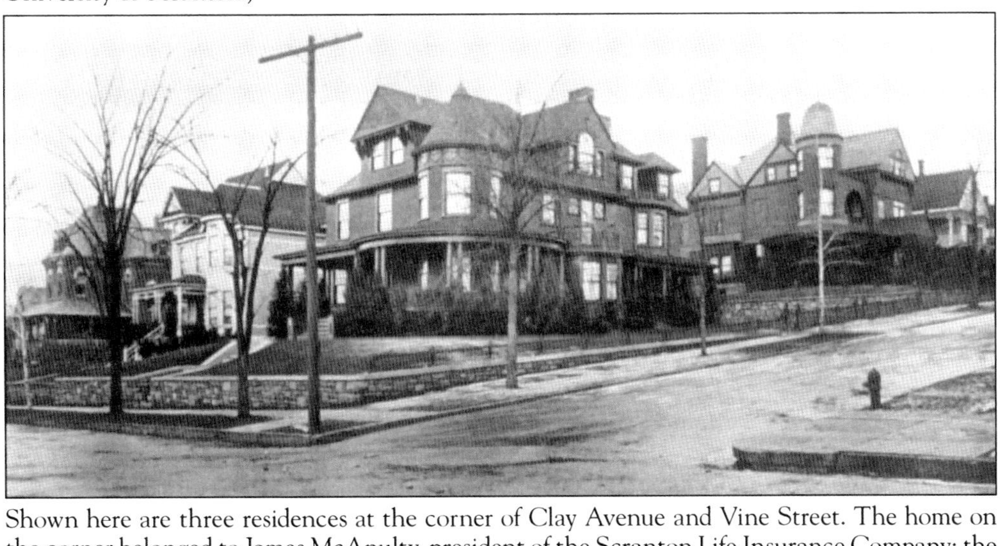

Shown here are three residences at the corner of Clay Avenue and Vine Street. The home on the corner belonged to James McAnulty, president of the Scranton Life Insurance Company; the home on the left belonged to Henry A. Connell, president of the Connell Coal Company; and the home on the right belonged to Luther Keller, president of the National Limestone Company. Beth Shalom Synagogue now occupies their former sites.

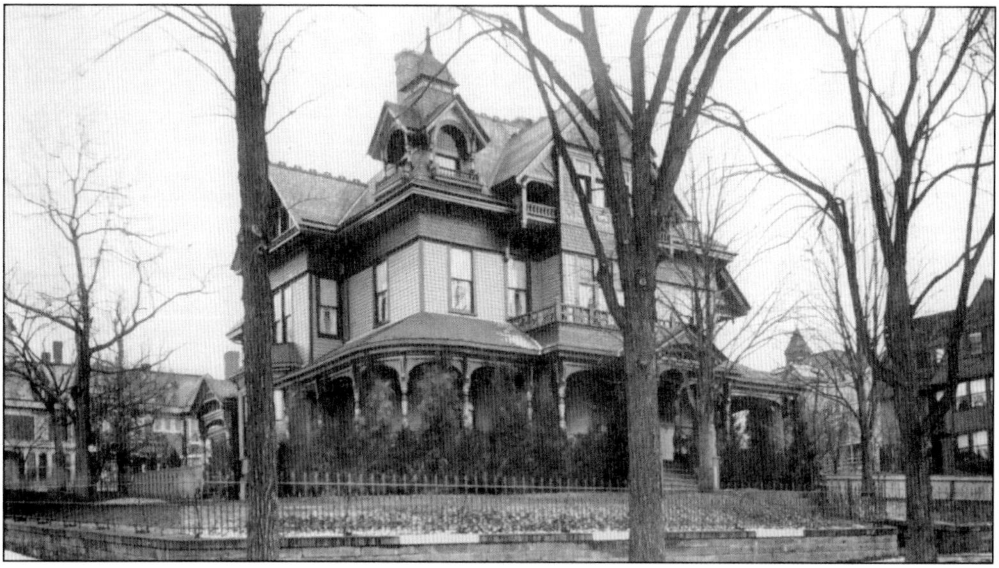

Millionaire tycoon William Connell resided in this home at the corner of Clay Avenue and Vine Street. This residence was relatively modest considering Connell's tremendous wealth and accomplishments. It could be argued that Connell and his many influential family members could be on par with the Scranton family in terms of local significance. The home was later demolished, and the Jewish Home of Northeastern Pennsylvania occupies the site.

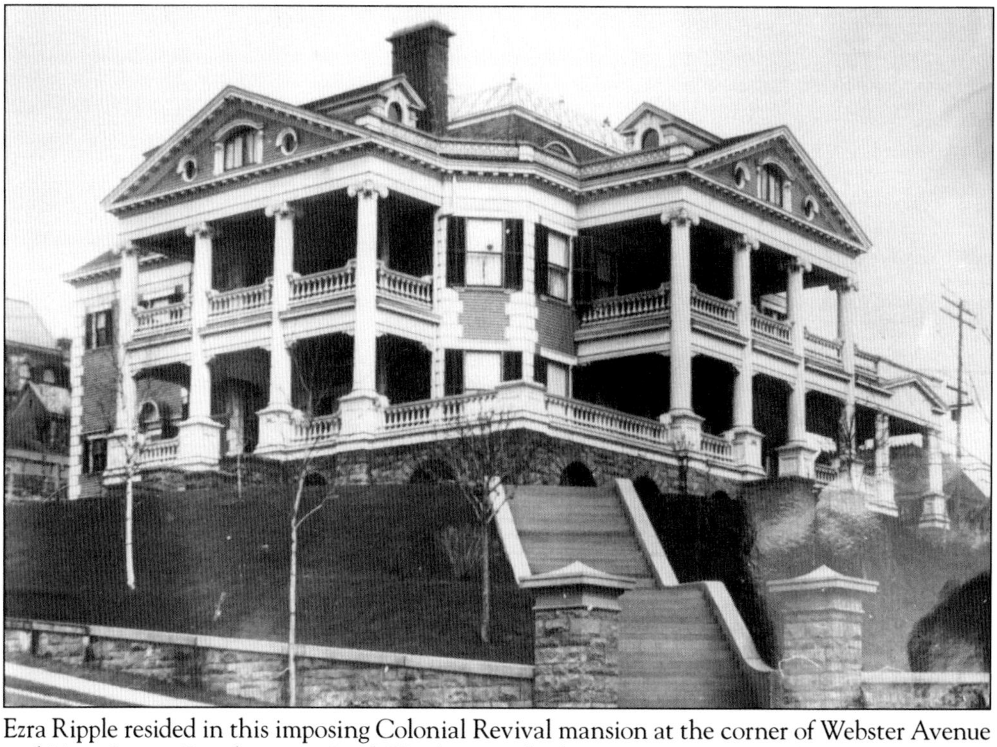

Ezra Ripple resided in this imposing Colonial Revival mansion at the corner of Webster Avenue and Vine Street. Ripple was a Civil War hero and a business associate of the Connell family. The Ripple mansion was demolished after World War II, and its former site is now the location of the Webster Towers high-rise.

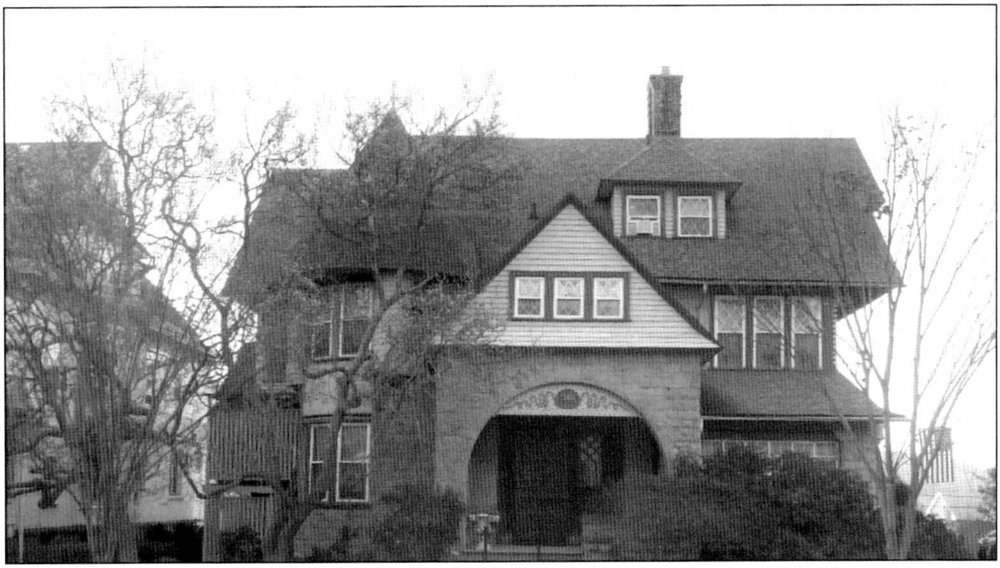

This Queen Anne home at 543 Clay Avenue was originally built by David Taylor, an associate of Scranton's Cleland-Simpson Company department store, better known as the Globe Store. The home was then acquired by George W. Clarke of the well-known Clarke Brothers Store. The home has since undergone extensive renovations and still stands today as a private residence.

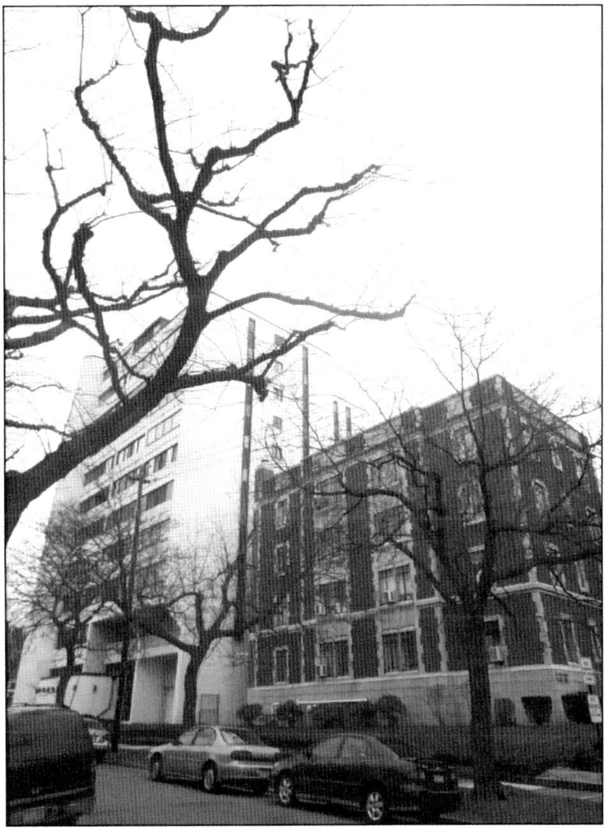

The Clay Avenue Apartments and the Plaza 550 condominiums seen here are two of the largest and most well-known residential high-rises in all of Scranton. The Clay Avenue Apartments, seen in the foreground, were built in the 1920s, and Plaza 550, seen in the background, was developed by the Weinberger family in the early 1970s. The Plaza 550 condominiums are among the most luxurious in Scranton, with unrivaled views. (Author's collection.)

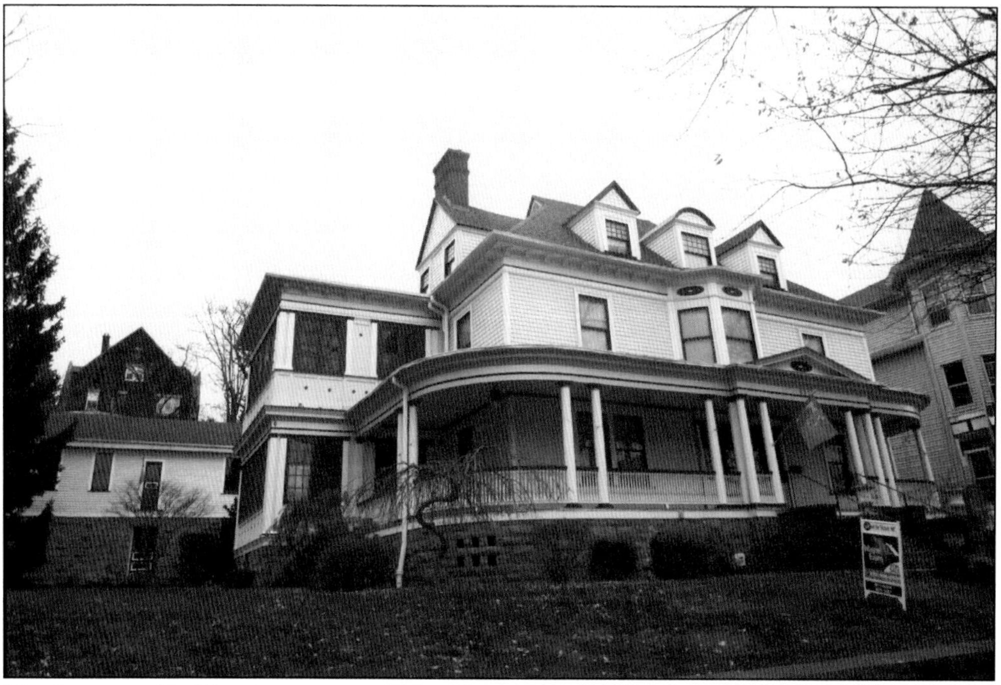

This home at 612 Clay Avenue was the residence of A.J. Casey, brother and business partner of P.J. Casey. The Casey residence has a large wraparound porch and a carriage house, which was a common feature of early Hill Section residences. A.J. Casey's daughter Pauline later donated the home to the Diocese of Scranton for use as a convent. The home eventually reverted to private hands.

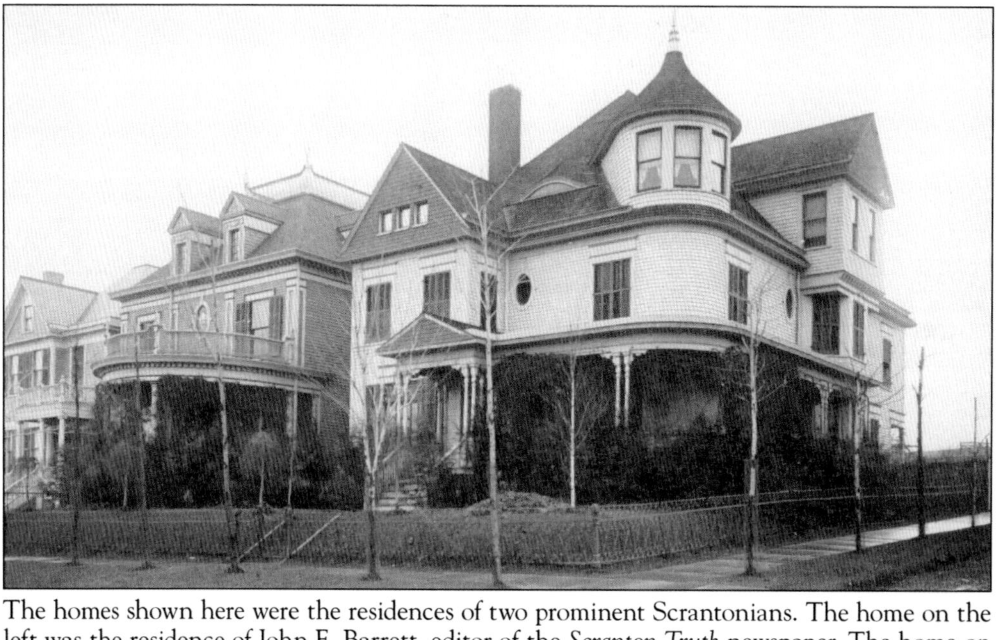

The homes shown here were the residences of two prominent Scrantonians. The home on the left was the residence of John E. Barrett, editor of the *Scranton Truth* newspaper. The home on the right was the residence of James J. Jordan, a local insurance broker. Both homes still stand today and are used as private residences.

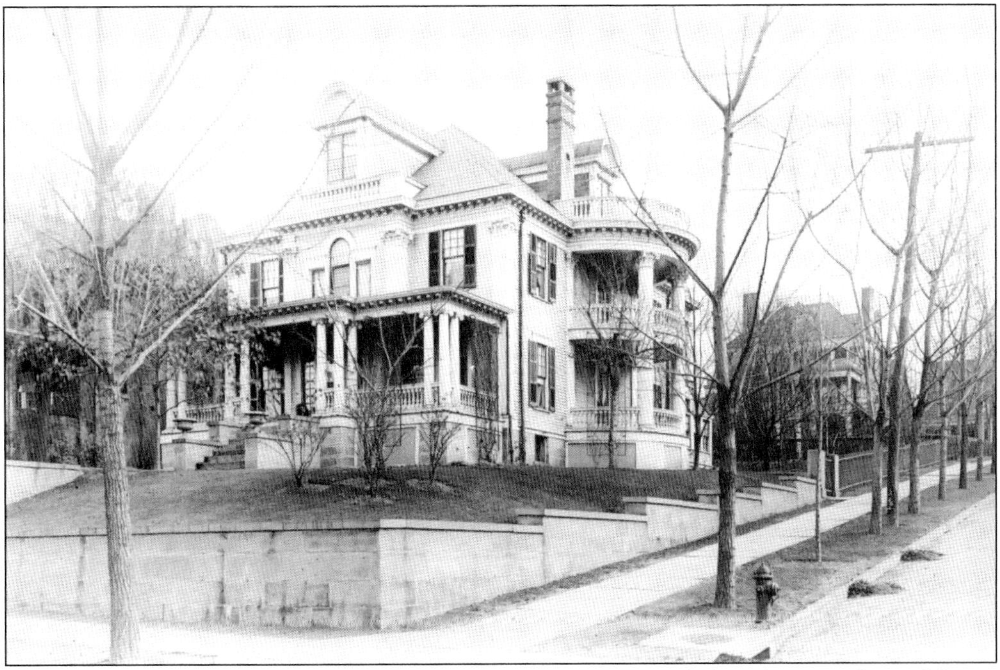

John F. Mears, president of the Anthracite Trust Company, resided in this Neoclassical home at 800 Clay Avenue. The home still appears much as it did when the Mears family resided here, and it is still used as a private residence. (Courtesy of Jack Hiddlestone.)

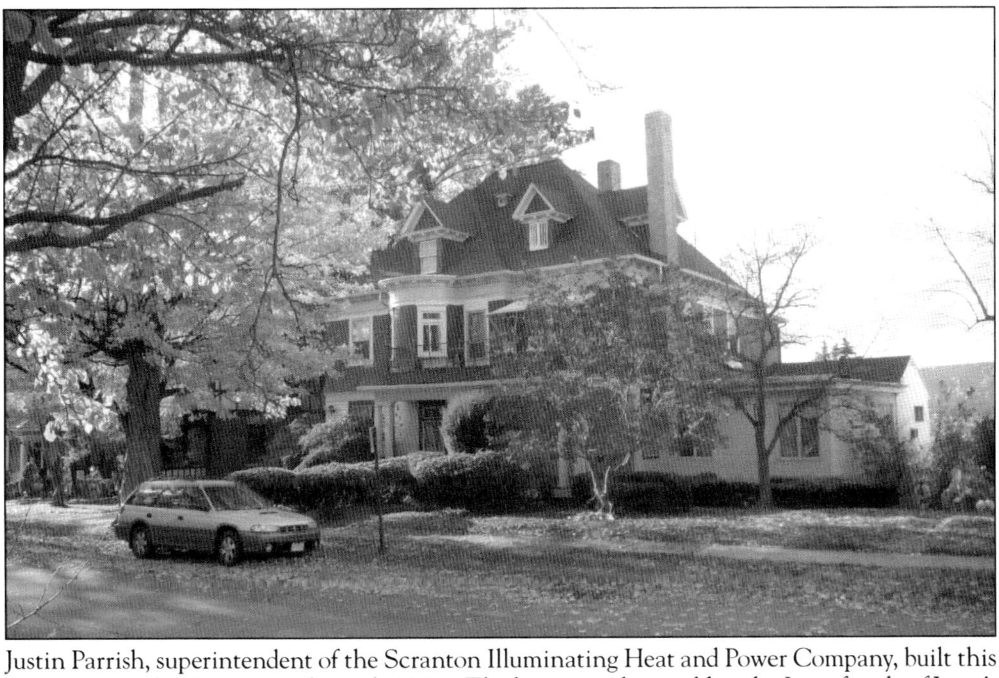

Justin Parrish, superintendent of the Scranton Illuminating Heat and Power Company, built this home at 827 Clay Avenue in the early 1890s. The home was later sold to the Levy family of Levy's Shoe Store, which in turn sold it to Mort and Adele Pollack in the early 1950s. Over the years, the Pollacks, who owned the Community Bake Shop, renovated and expanded the home. Adele Pollack continues to reside at this address. (Author's collection.)

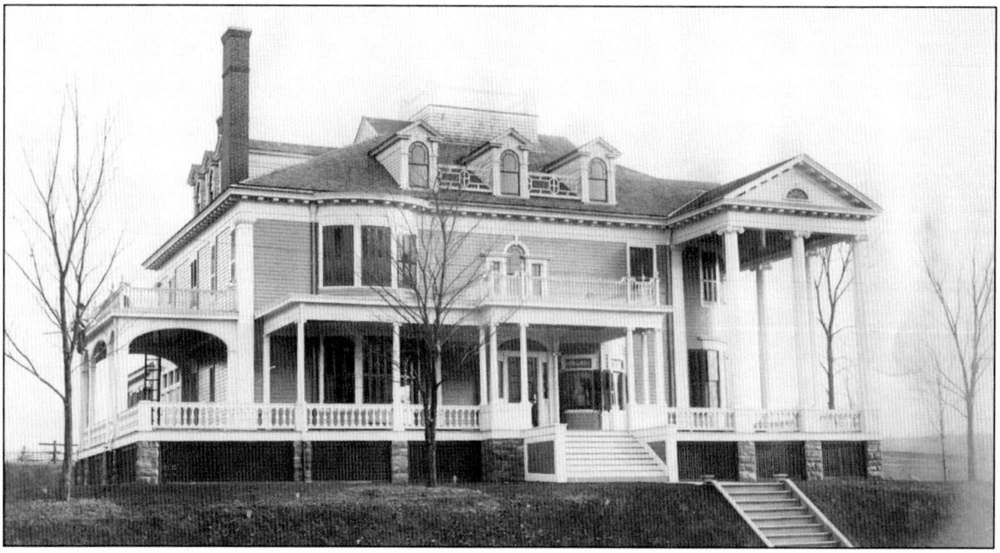

This mansion at 840 Clay Avenue was originally the home of Pennsylvania Coal Company president George B. Smith. The home was later occupied by Harry Weinberg, the president of the Scranton Transit Company, and his wife, Jeanette, who were generous philanthropists. The residence still stands today but has been heavily remodeled for use as apartments.

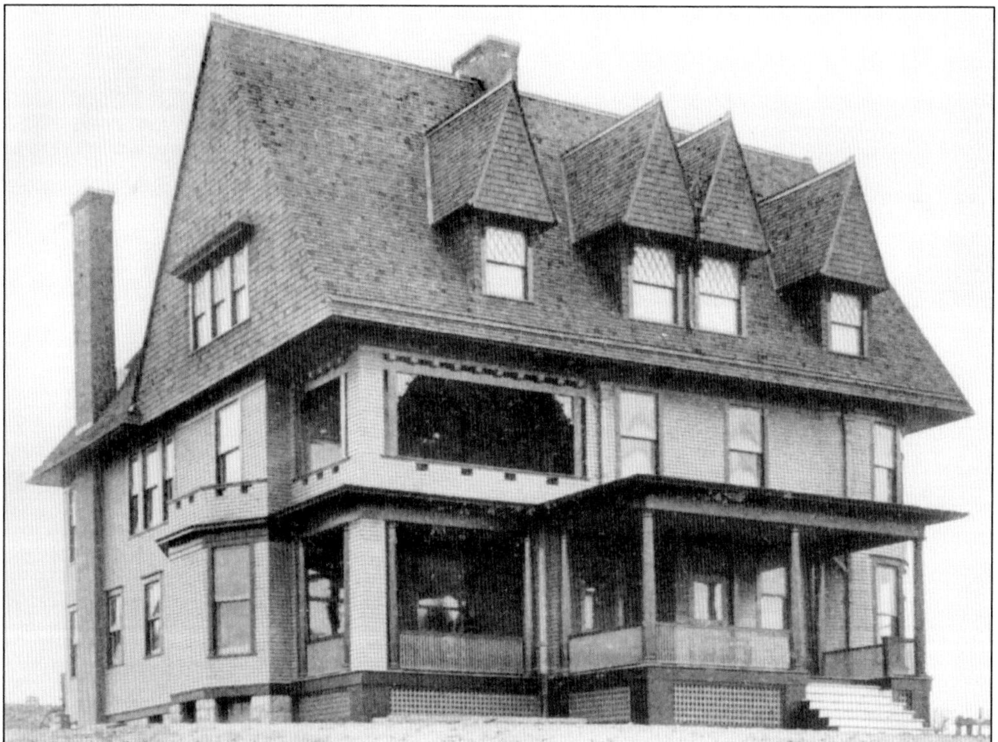

This home at 842 Clay Avenue was originally the residence of E.P. Kingsbury, an executive of the Lackawanna Iron and Coal Company. Benjamin Samter, cofounder of Samter's Store, resided here before selling the home to the Smulowitz family, owners of the Stegmaier Brewery. The home has been slightly altered but is still used as a private residence.

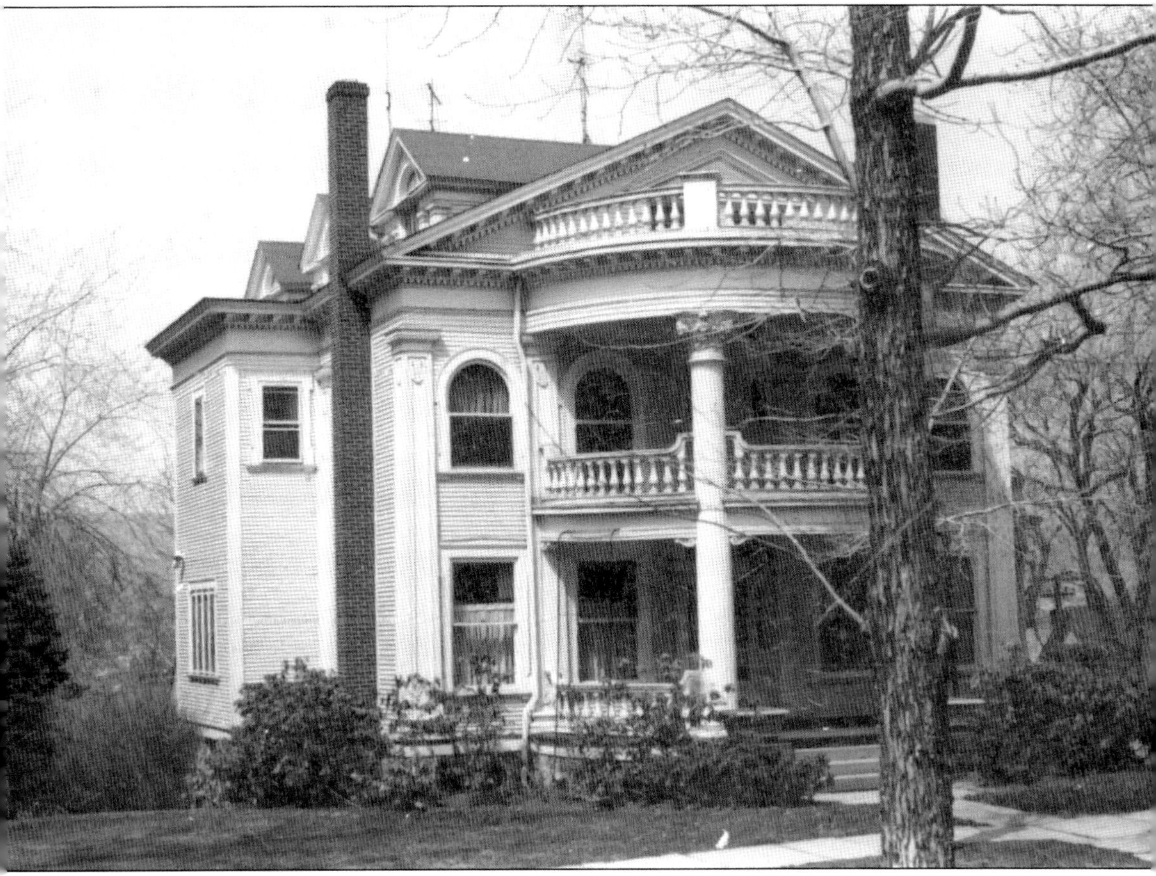

E.J. Lynett, founder of the *Scranton Times*, originally built this home at 841 Clay Avenue. The Lynett family later sold the home to plumbing and real estate magnate Harold Weinberger and his wife, Rosalyn. Descendants of the Weinberger family continue to reside in the home, which has some of the most impressive views in the entire Hill Section. (Courtesy of Nancy J. Weinberger.)

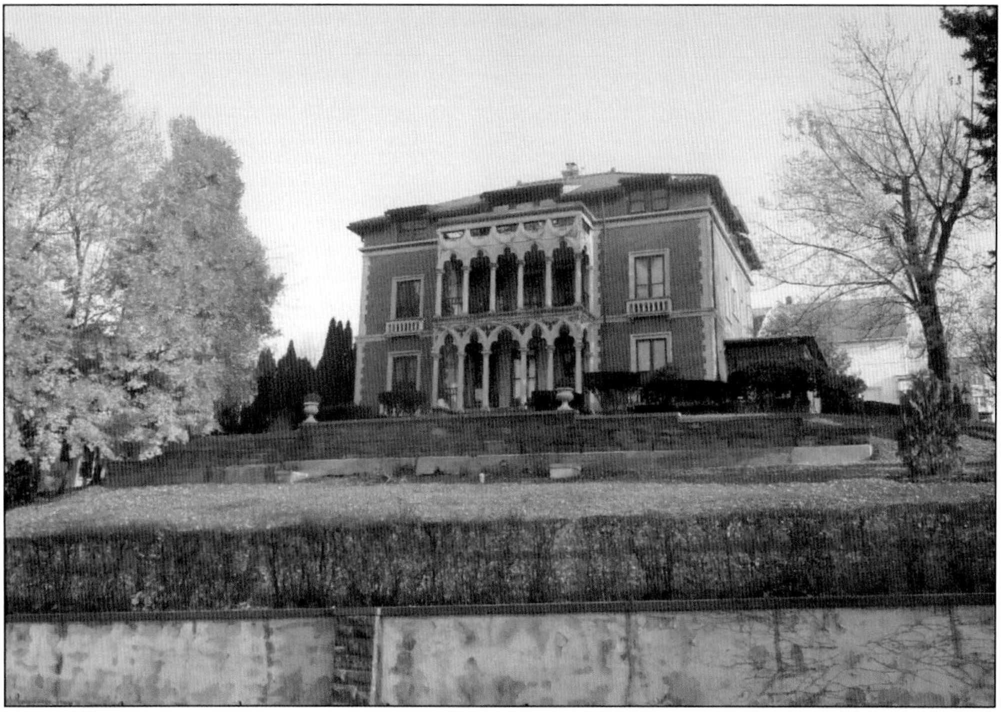

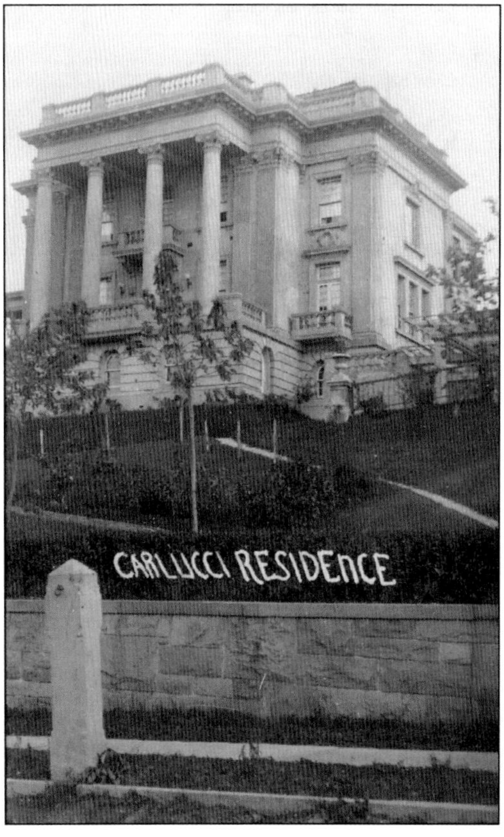

This Venetian Gothic mansion located at 1000 Clay Avenue was originally the residence of Anthony J. Cassese, a wholesale grocer, steamship agent, and cousin of the Carlucci family. The mansion was later sold to the Cusick family of Standard Brewing, which in turn sold it to Angelo and Rose Fiorani, owners of the WPTS radio station. In recent years, this home has been renovated into apartments. (Author's collection.)

Frank Carlucci, owner of the Carlucci Stone Company, built this mansion at 1048 Clay Avenue. In 1912, undertaker and brewery owner Patrick F. Cusick purchased the residence. Cusick's brother-in-law and business associate James F. Bell then acquired the home shortly before a fire ravaged it in the 1930s. Later, the mansion's ruins were abandoned, and they became an unofficial playground for Hill Section children.

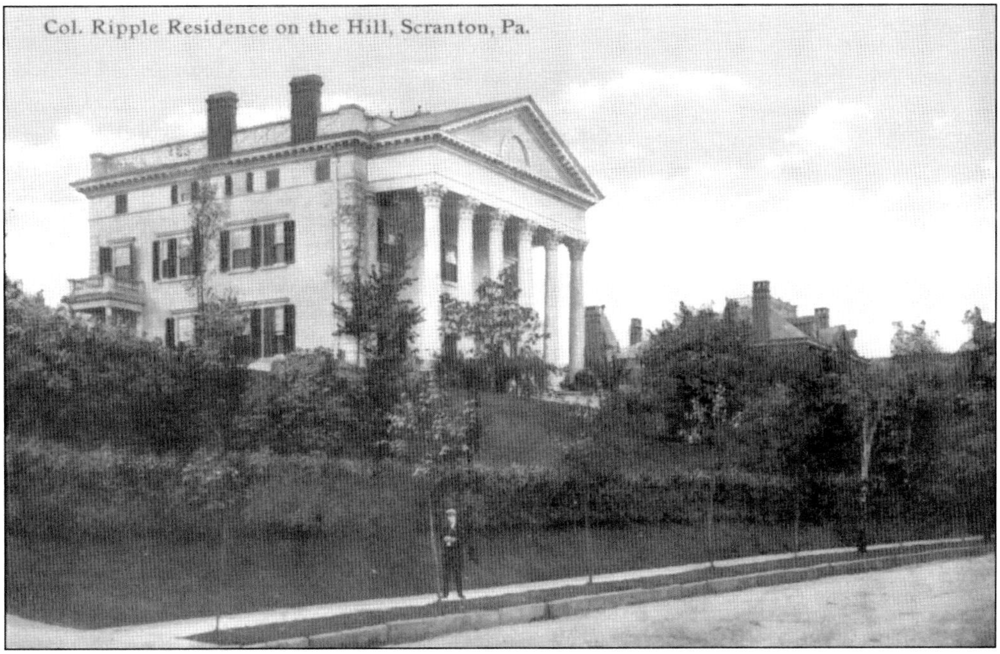

This Colonial home at 616 Webster Avenue was built by coal baron William H. Taylor, who only briefly resided in it before selling it to George Jermyn, son of John Jermyn. The home was commonly referred to as Hillside due to its position near the top of the Hill Section's highest hill. The home no longer stands, and its former site has been divided among the surrounding private residences.

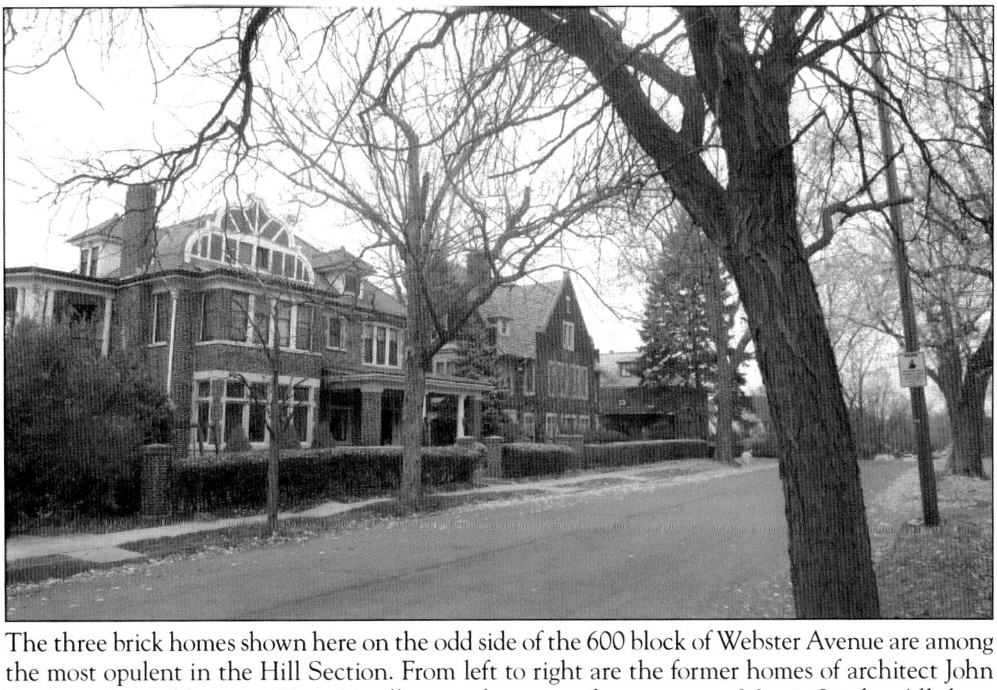

The three brick homes shown here on the odd side of the 600 block of Webster Avenue are among the most opulent in the Hill Section. From left to right are the former homes of architect John Duckworth, coal baroness Rose Vandling, and garment factory owner Martin Linder. All three of these homes, built in the 1920s, still stand today as private residences. (Author's collection.)

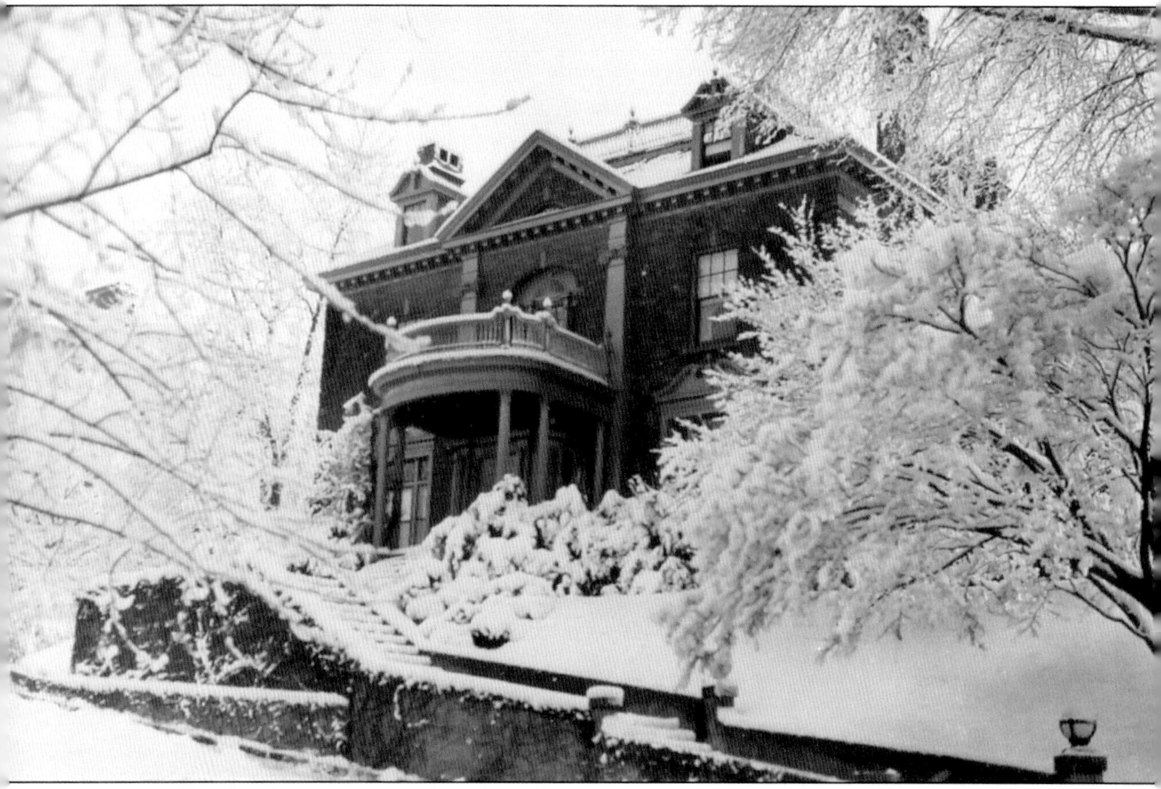

The yellow brick Georgian Colonial residence at 610 North Webster Avenue depicted in this majestic winter scene was originally the residence of Fredrick Platt, an in-law and business associate of the Scranton family. Fredrick Platt was also the owner of the Scranton Electric Manufacturing Company, which made railway equipment. As a result, he was able to procure a miniature turntable for his family's automobiles in the home's driveway, which is still operational today. Judge Robert D. Mariani and his wife, Sallyann, later acquired the home in 1988. The family has since restored the home and continues to live there today.

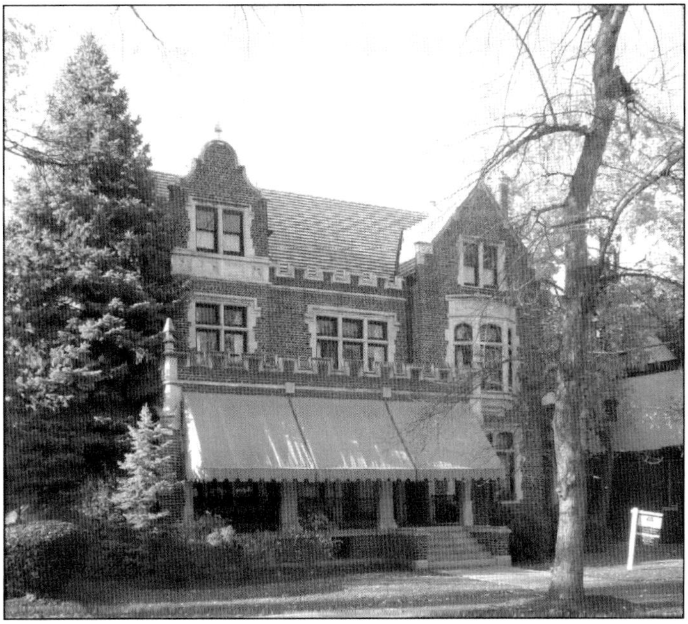

German immigrants J. George Hufnagel and his wife, Augusta Gutknecht, built this Flemish-influenced Gothic mansion, known as "the Castle," at 815 Webster Avenue. Hufnagel made a substantial fortune through a partnership with the Robinson family's E. Robinson Brewery. After being subdivided into apartments for many years, the Castle was restored to its former glory by a local technology company that uses it as a guesthouse. (Author's collection.)

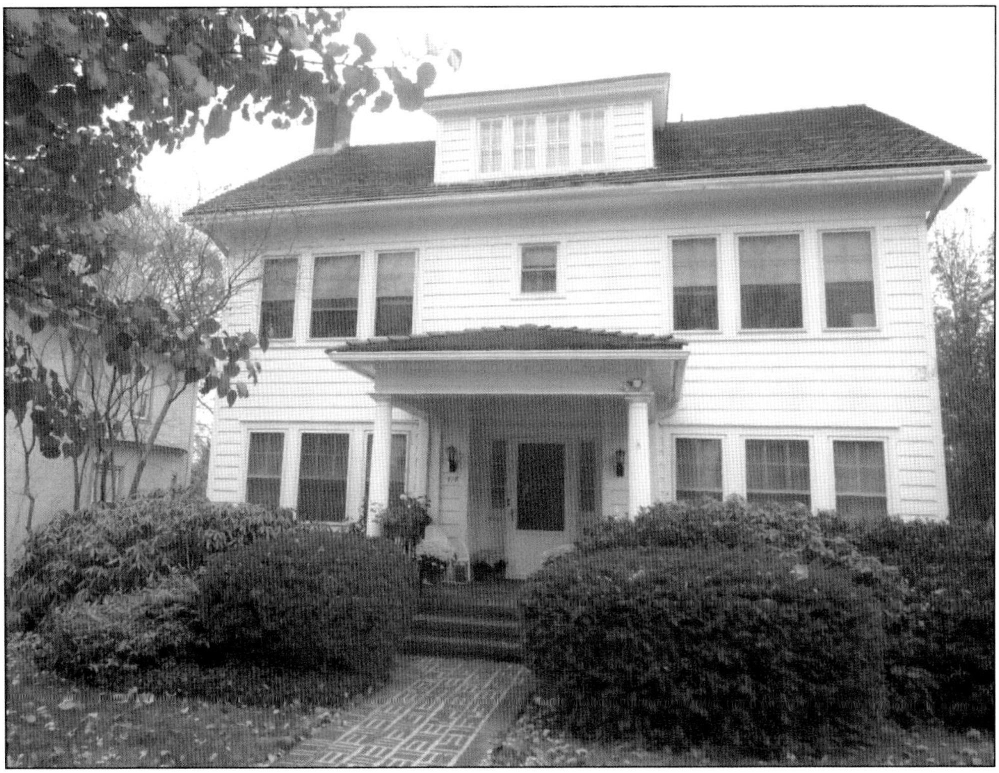

Architectural engineer Tudor Williams, who designed many Hill Section homes, built this Colonial home for himself at 718 Taylor Avenue in 1918. In 1952, Richard and Jane Oppenheim of Oppenheim's Department Store purchased the home, which is said to be the most well built in the Hill Section. The Oppenheim family continues to own and live in this historic residence. (Author's collection.)

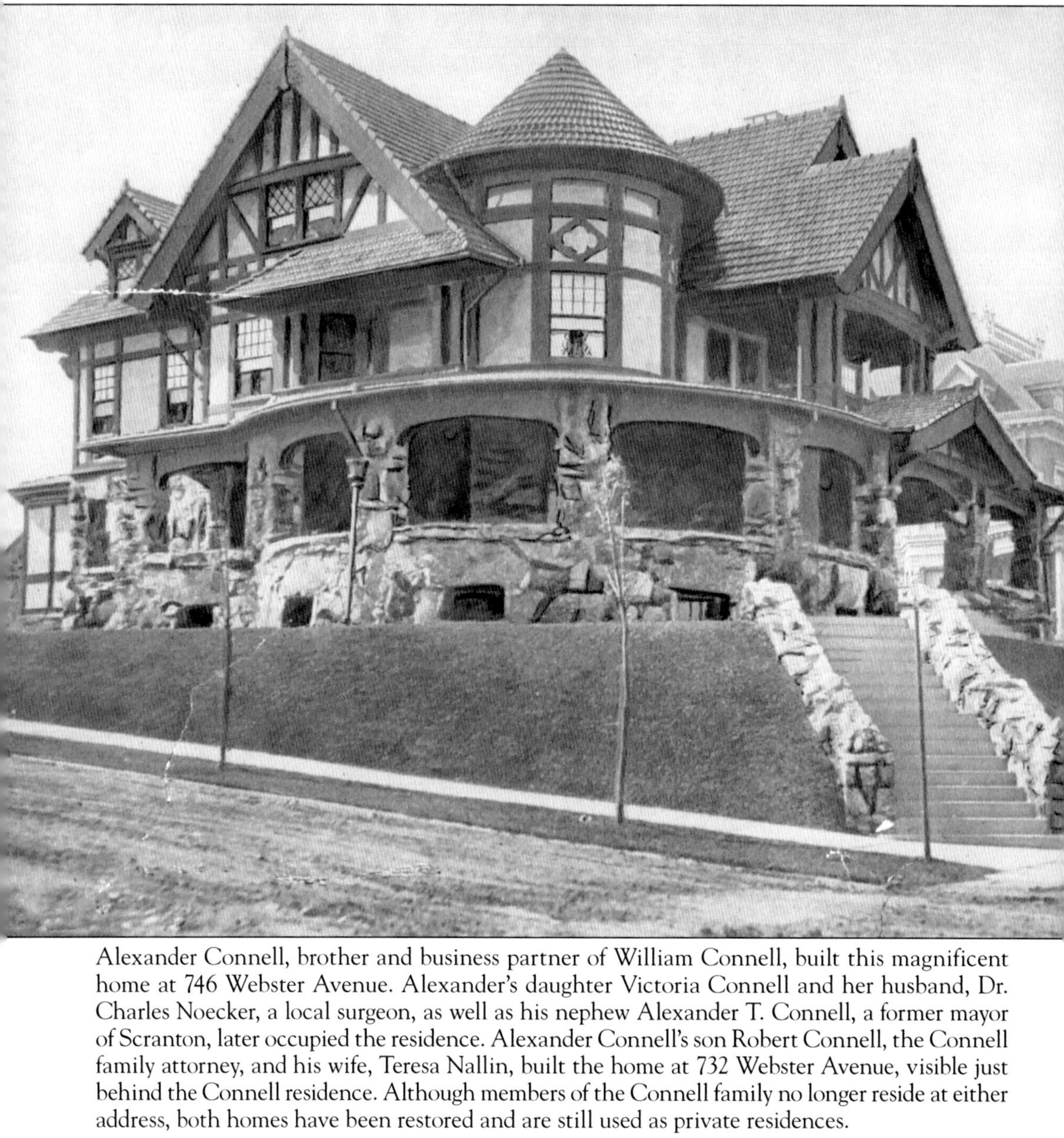

Alexander Connell, brother and business partner of William Connell, built this magnificent home at 746 Webster Avenue. Alexander's daughter Victoria Connell and her husband, Dr. Charles Noecker, a local surgeon, as well as his nephew Alexander T. Connell, a former mayor of Scranton, later occupied the residence. Alexander Connell's son Robert Connell, the Connell family attorney, and his wife, Teresa Nallin, built the home at 732 Webster Avenue, visible just behind the Connell residence. Although members of the Connell family no longer reside at either address, both homes have been restored and are still used as private residences.

Two

People

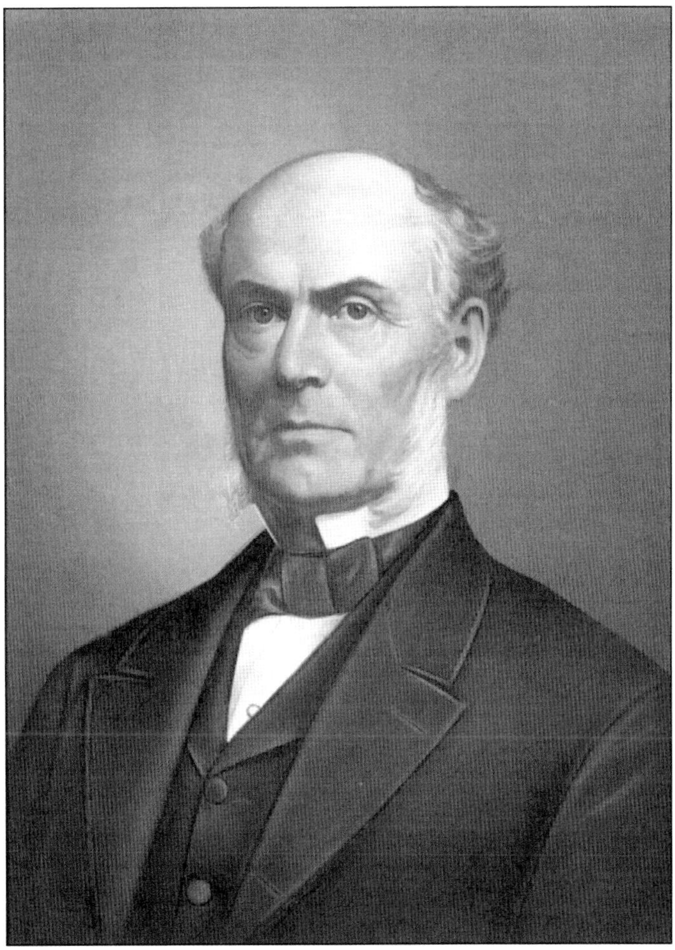

In 1813, Joseph Hand Scranton was born in Augusta, Georgia. He came to Scranton to invest in his cousin's iron furnace operation, and after many of his relatives left the city they had founded, Joseph became the family patriarch. Until his death in 1872, Joseph Hand Scranton greatly influenced the development of the city of Scranton, not only through his family's business empire, but also through civic organizations.

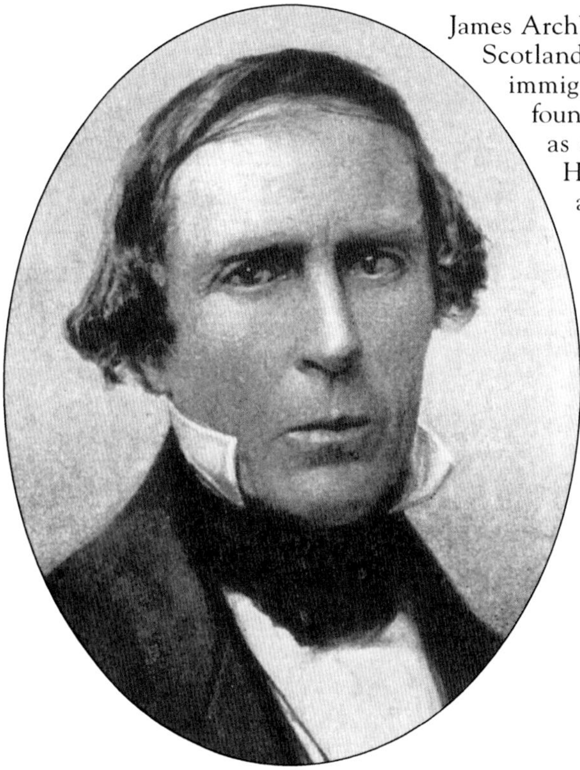

James Archbald was born in Little Cumbrey Isle, Scotland, in 1793. By the mid-1800s, he had immigrated to the United States, where he found work in northeastern Pennsylvania as a civil engineer for the Delaware & Hudson Railroad. Archbald later served as chief engineer for the DL&W Railroad and established a residence in the Hill Section. The borough of Archbald, north of Scranton, is named after him.

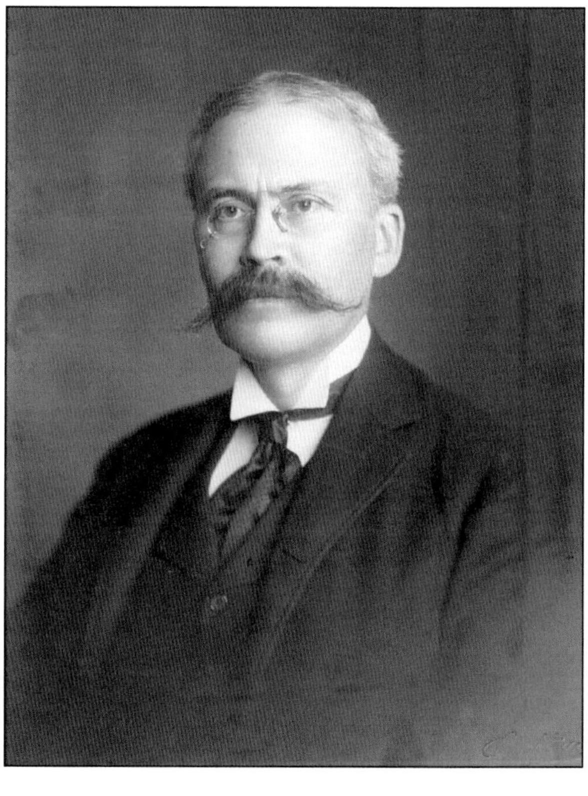

George H. Catlin was born in Shoreham, Vermont, in 1845. He relocated to Scranton after marrying Mary Woodrow Archbald. He was a lawyer and vice president of the Third National Bank. Following Mary's death, Catlin married Helen Walsh and built a new home at 232 Monroe Avenue in 1912. Upon his death in 1935, George H. Catlin willed his home to the Lackawanna Historical Society.

Austin Blair was the son of banker James Blair, who had followed the Scrantons to Pennsylvania from Belvidere, New Jersey. James Blair was an original shareholder in the Lackawanna Iron and Coal Company and DL&W Railroad and was the founder and president of the Scranton Saving's Bank. Austin Blair inherited much of his father's wealth and followed him into the banking business.

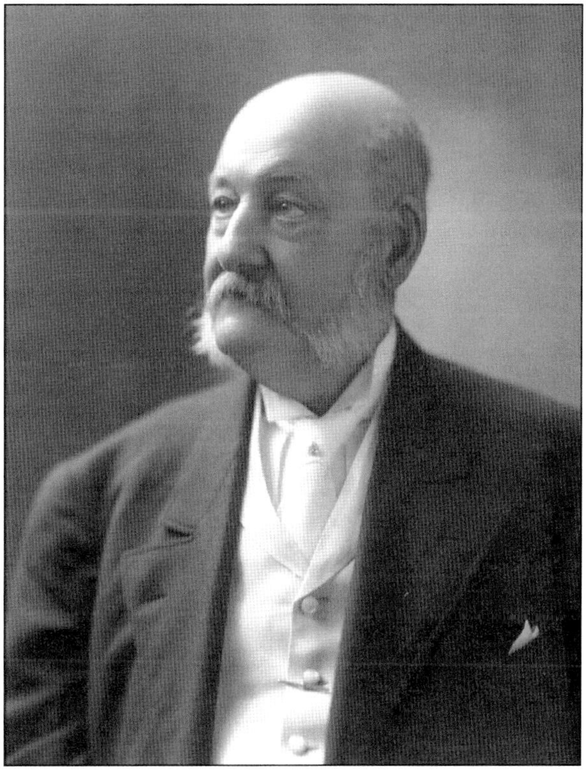

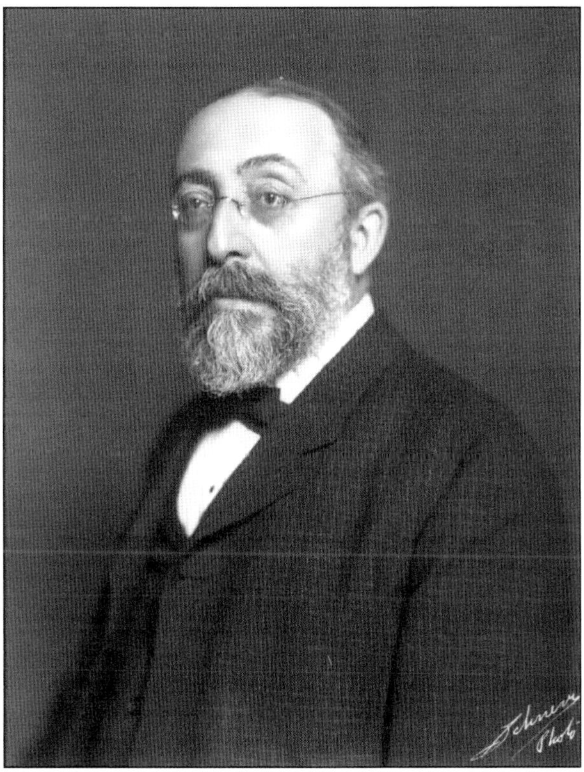

Henry Belin Jr.'s great-grandfather John Belin first came to the United States in 1791 after the Haitian Revolution forced him from his plantation in the French colony of Saint-Domingue. Members of the Belin family subsequently developed personal connections with the E.I. DuPont de Nemours Powder Manufacturing Company. In 1863, Henry Belin Jr. took over DuPont's Pennsylvania Corporation and established his residence in the Hill Section.

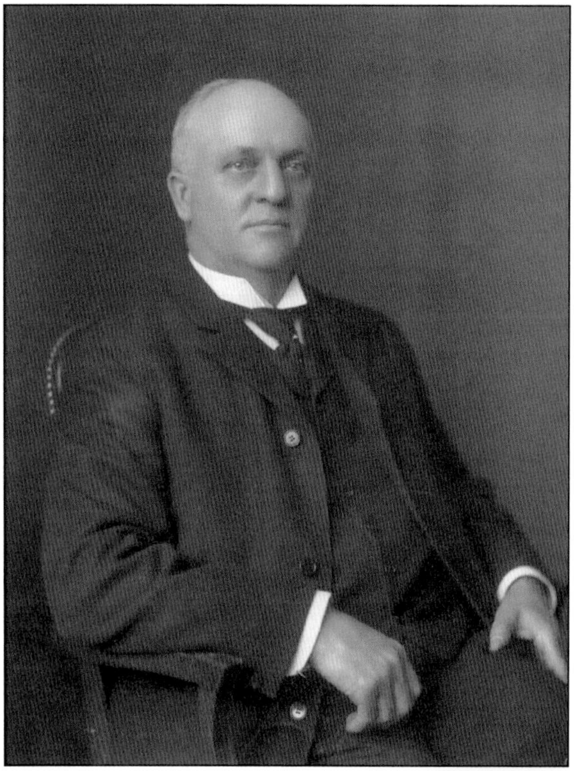

Reese Brooks was born near Slocum's Hollow in 1846. He served in the Union army at the Battle of Gettysburg and later founded the prominent banking and brokerage house Brooks & Company. Brooks and his family resided at 535 Monroe Avenue and were noted philanthropists, using their largesse to endow numerous community endeavors, including the educational Brooks Mine in Nay Aug Park.

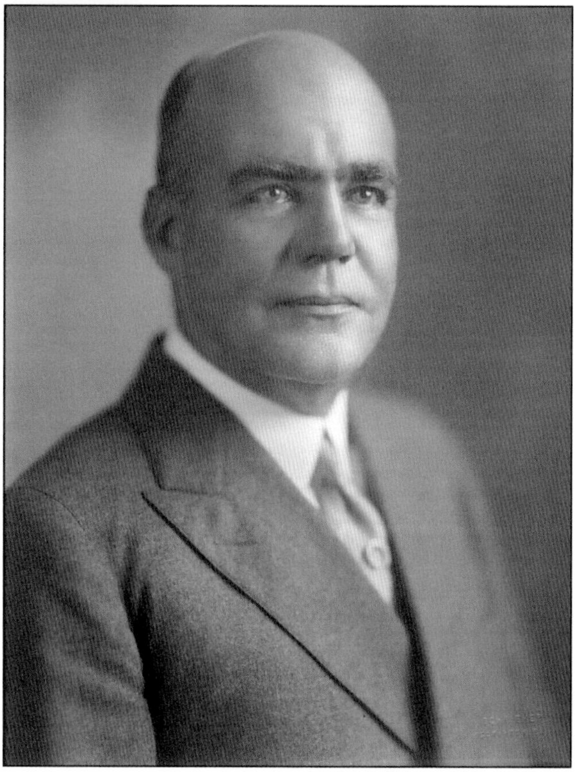

In 1877, Mortimer Bartine Fuller was born in Scranton to Edward Laton and Helen Silkman Fuller. Edward Fuller was a partner of railroad tycoons Jay and George Gould. Mortimer B. Fuller attended Princeton University before succeeding his father as president of the International Salt Company. The Fullers lived for many years at 634 Jefferson Avenue and were longtime members of the Second Presbyterian Church.

John Jermyn was born in Suffolk, England, in 1825. He immigrated to Slocum's Hollow in 1847 and subsequently made a fortune in the coal mining industry. He used these profits to invest in many other enterprises, including the luxurious Hotel Jermyn in Scranton's downtown. John Jermyn resided in a grand Hill Section mansion with his wife and 10 children until his death in 1902.

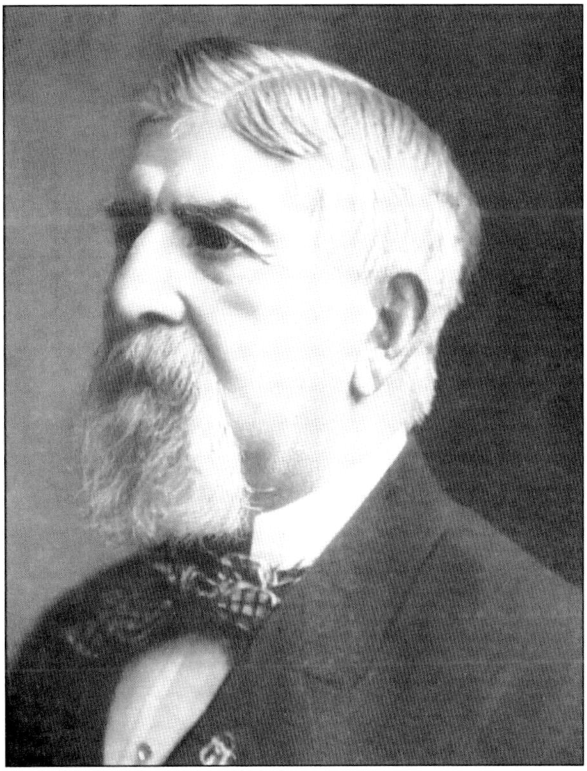

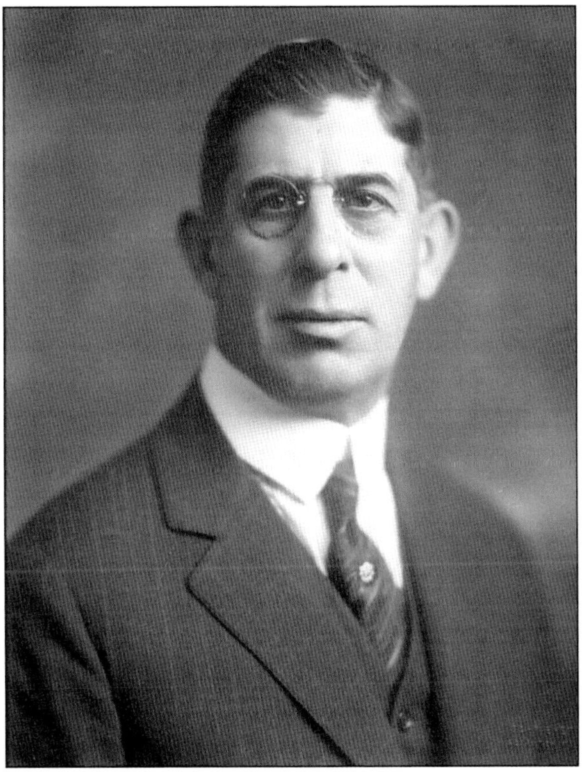

Edmund Beson "E.B." Jermyn, son of John Jermyn, was born in 1867. Jermyn was elected mayor of Scranton from 1913 to 1917 and from 1925 to 1931. During this time, he presided over many successes, including the founding of the Nay Aug Zoo. E.B. Jermyn, who resided in the Hill Section for most of his life, died on November 14, 1934, ironically one day after his family's rival hotelier, P.J. Casey.

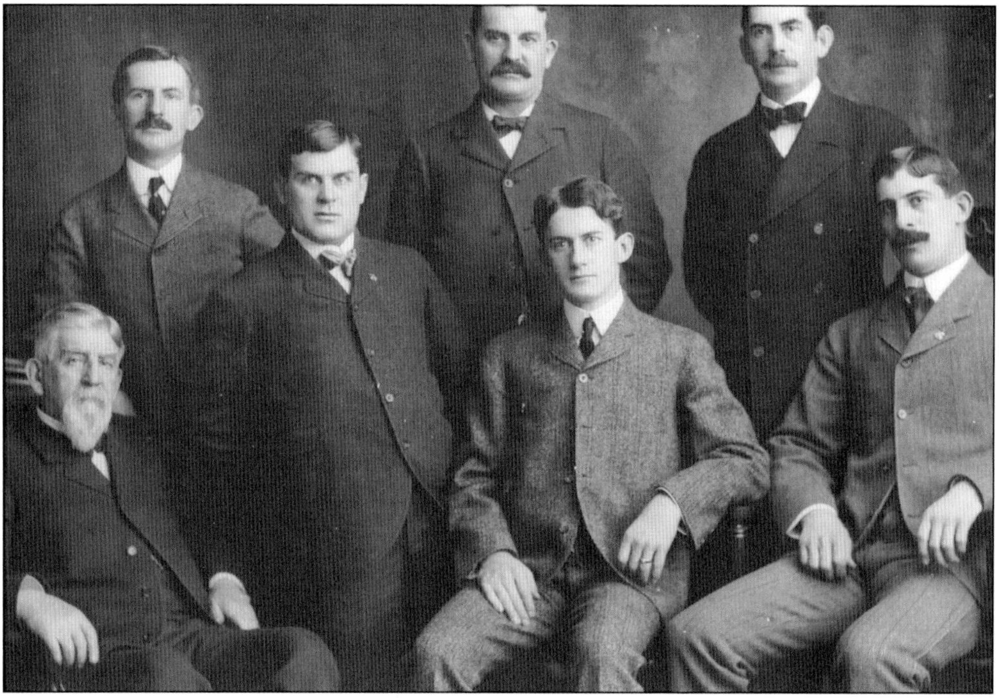

Pictured here are John Jermyn and his sons. From left to right are (first row) John, Walter, Rollo, and Edmund; (second row) George, Joseph, and Frank. The Jermyn family figured prominently into the history of the Hill Section and the entire Scranton region through their extensive business and political interests.

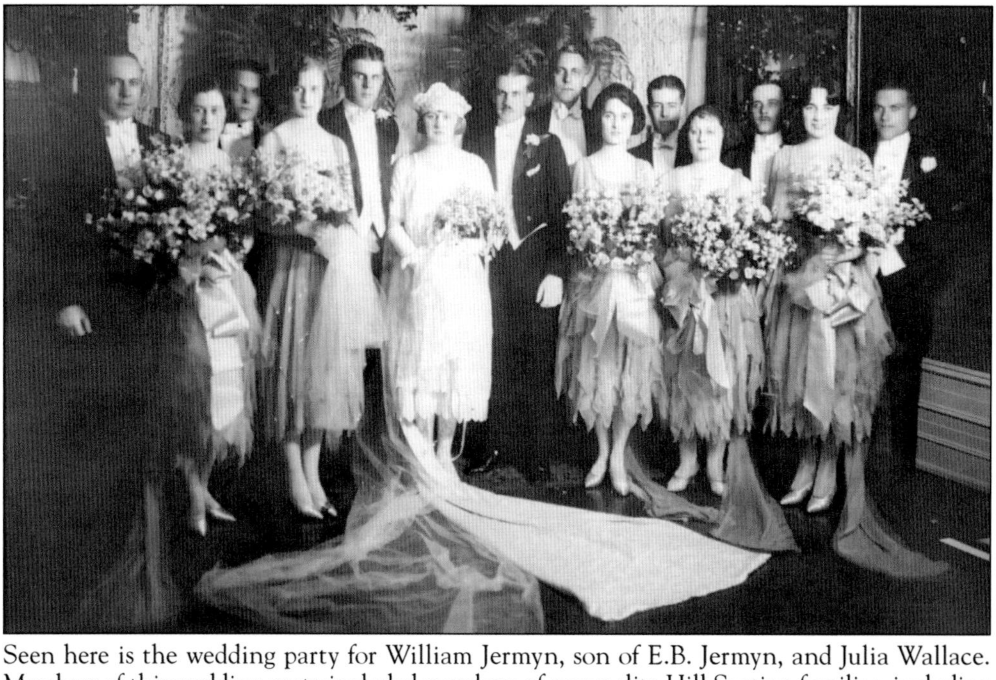

Seen here is the wedding party for William Jermyn, son of E.B. Jermyn, and Julia Wallace. Members of this wedding party included members of many elite Hill Section families, including the Mears and the Robinsons.

Andrew Joseph "A.J." Casey was born in Sligo, Ireland, in 1852. He immigrated to Scranton in 1866. There, he built a wholesale liquor business, and later, he and his younger brother P.J. founded a brewery known as Casey Brothers. A.J. and P.J. Casey later cofounded the luxurious Hotel Casey in downtown Scranton. A.J. Casey resided with his family in the Hill Section until his death in 1928.

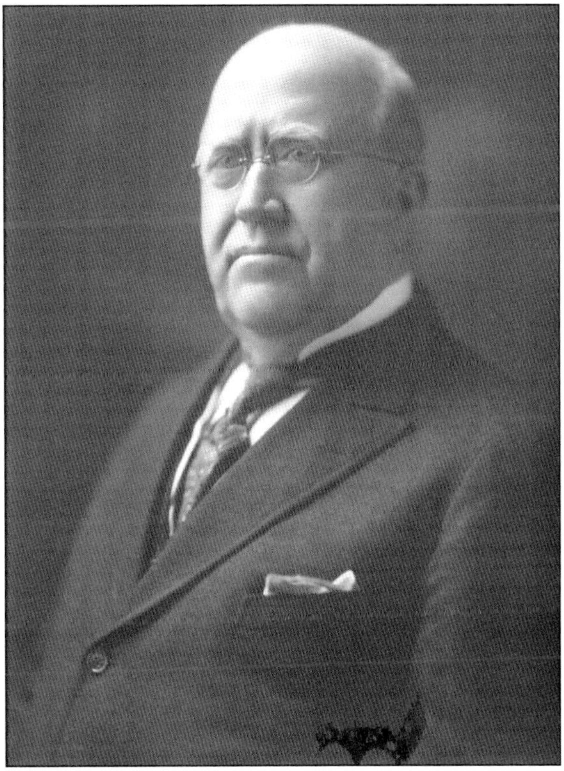

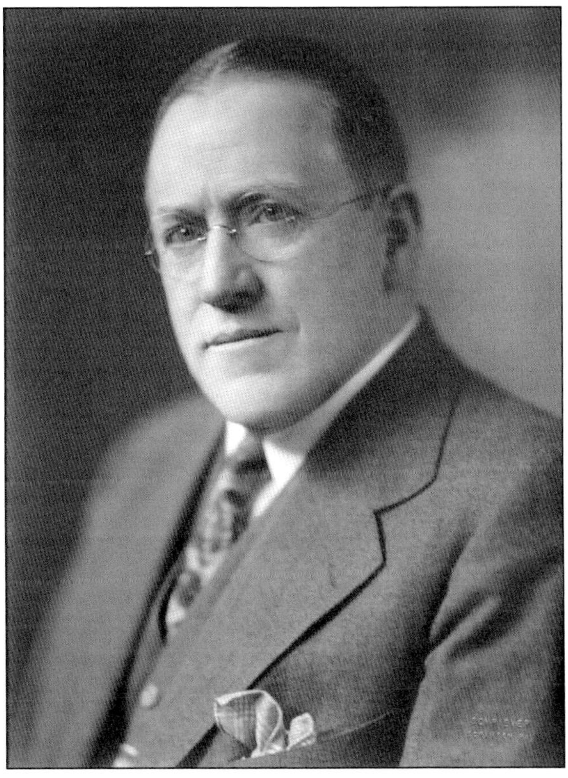

Patrick Joseph "P.J." Casey was born in Sligo, Ireland, in 1868 and immigrated to Scranton in 1883. He partnered with older brother A.J. to cofound Casey Brothers wholesale liquor business and brewery, as well as the grand Hotel Casey. P.J. Casey resided in the Hill Section until his death on November 13, 1934, just one day before the death of rival hotelier E.B. Jermyn.

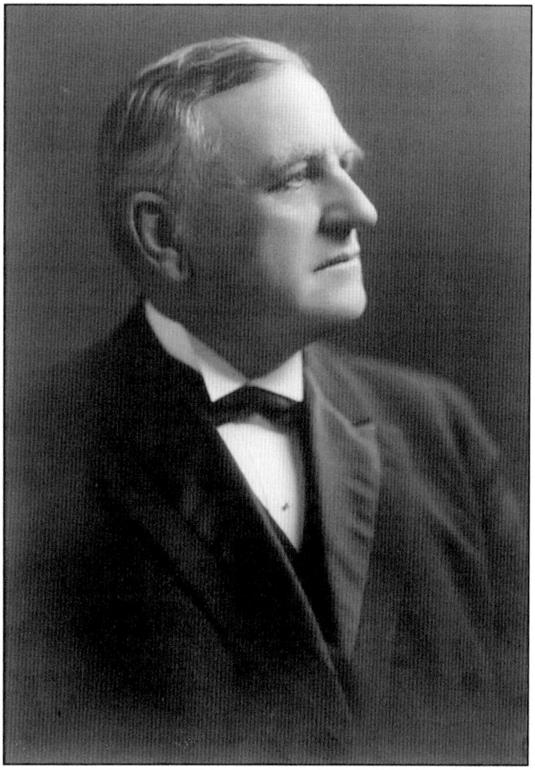

Luther Keller was born in the Scranton area in 1850. He eventually made a fortune in the lime, cement, brick, and clay industries. Keller also held an interest in Scranton's Third National Bank and area textile enterprises. Luther Keller was a Hill Section resident and resided in a home at 515 Clay Avenue for many years.

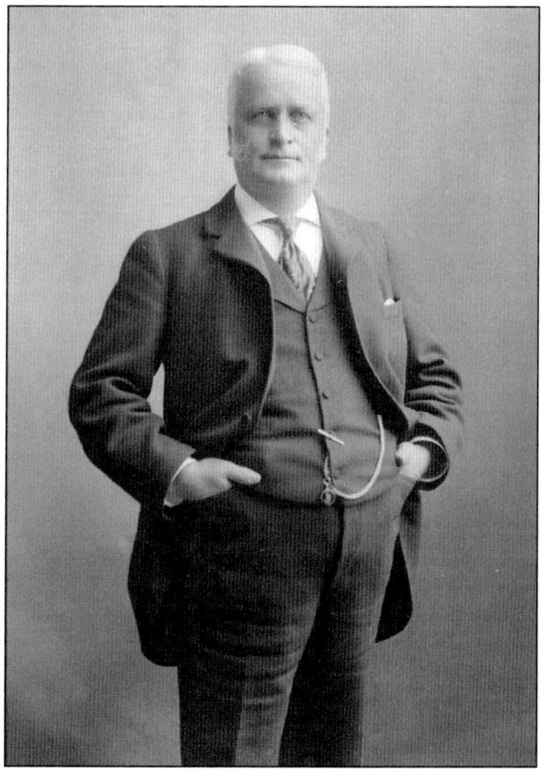

Col. Henry Martyn Boies was married to Elizabeth L. Dickson, daughter of industrialist Thomas Dickson. Colonel Boies made his fortune managing his father-in-law's Dickson Manufacturing Works and the Boies Steel Wheel Company. Colonel Boies was a noteworthy philanthropist and served on the Pennsylvania Board of Public Charities. After the colonel's death in 1903, his son David continued his father's legacy and maintained the family's residence at 600 Clay Avenue.

Cyrus D. Jones was born in Stamford, Connecticut, in 1852. He later moved to Scranton and cofounded the Grand Union Tea Company with his brothers in 1877. The business was vertically integrated and diversified with substantial interest in the coffee trade. Cyrus D. Jones built a large home at 901 Olive Street and was a longtime member of the Elm Park Methodist Church.

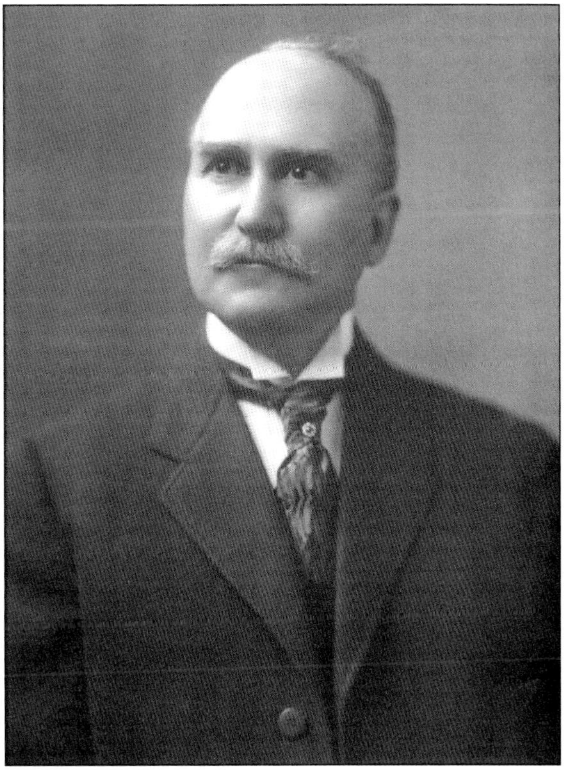

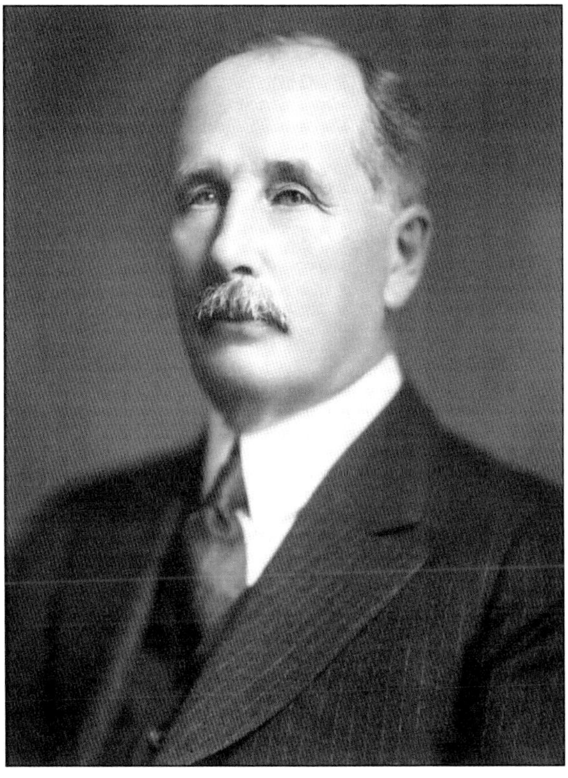

Charles Sumner "C.S." Woolworth cofounded the famous F.W. Woolworth's Company with his brother F.W. Woolworth. In 1880, the brothers opened their second five-and-dime store in Scranton and eventually built a massive retail empire. Following F.W.'s death in 1919, C.S. took over Woolworth's executive operations. Although Woolworth's was headquartered in New York City, C.S. Woolworth always resided in Scranton's Hill Section.

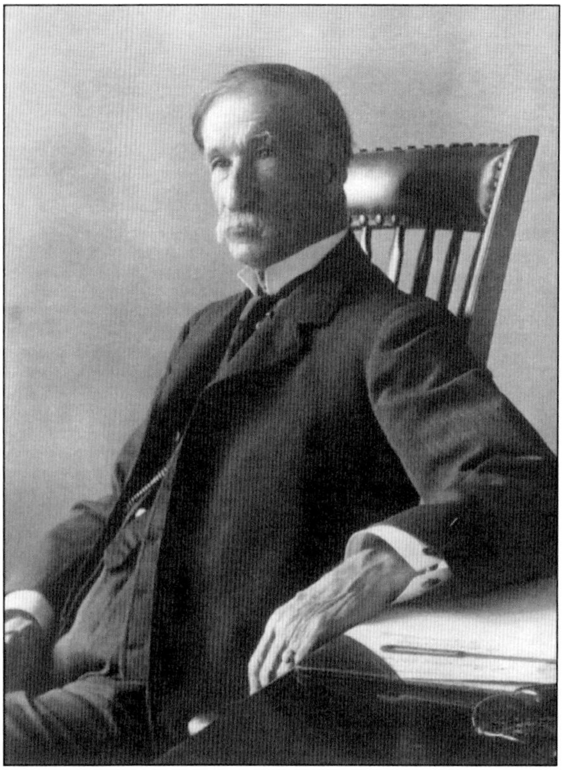

William Connell was born in Nova Scotia in 1827. Connell, along with his brothers Alexander, James, and Thomas, immigrated to the Scranton area, where he entered the coal industry, founded the Third National Bank, and became a millionaire. From 1896 to 1902, Connell served in the Pennsylvania Legislature. He was a major benefactor of the Elm Park Methodist Church and resided with his family at 1117 Vine Street.

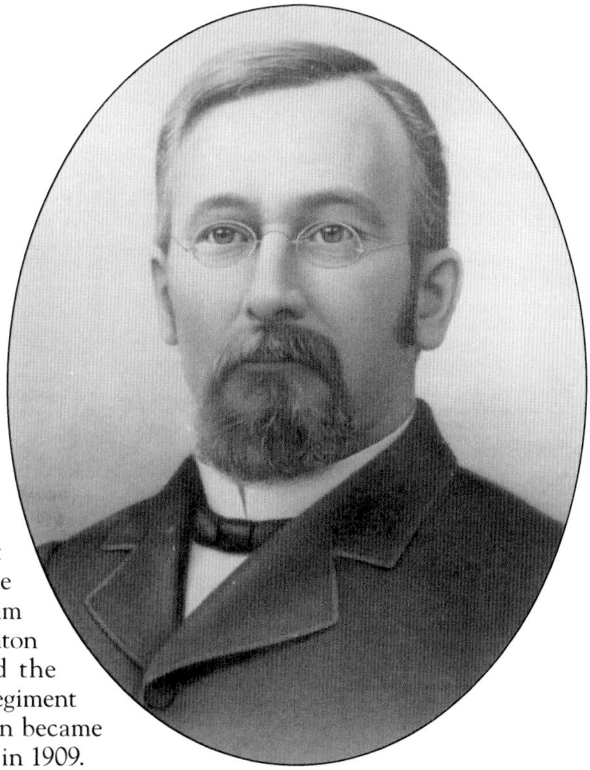

Ezra Ripple was born in Mauch Chunk, Pennsylvania, in 1842. He was a Civil War hero and a prisoner of war at Andersonville, Georgia. Ripple became a longtime business associate of William Connell and served as mayor of Scranton from 1886 to 1890. In 1892, he led the Pennsylvania National Guard's 13th Regiment during the Homestead labor riots, then became postmaster of Scranton until his death in 1909.

William L. Connell was born to the James Connell branch of the Connell family in Scranton in 1862. Connell, who was a staunch Republican, worked for numerous family enterprises and owned the *Scranton Republican* (later, *Scranton Tribune*) newspaper. William L. Connell served as mayor of Scranton twice, from 1893 to 1896 and from 1901 to 1903. Connell resided at 303 Clay Avenue for many years.

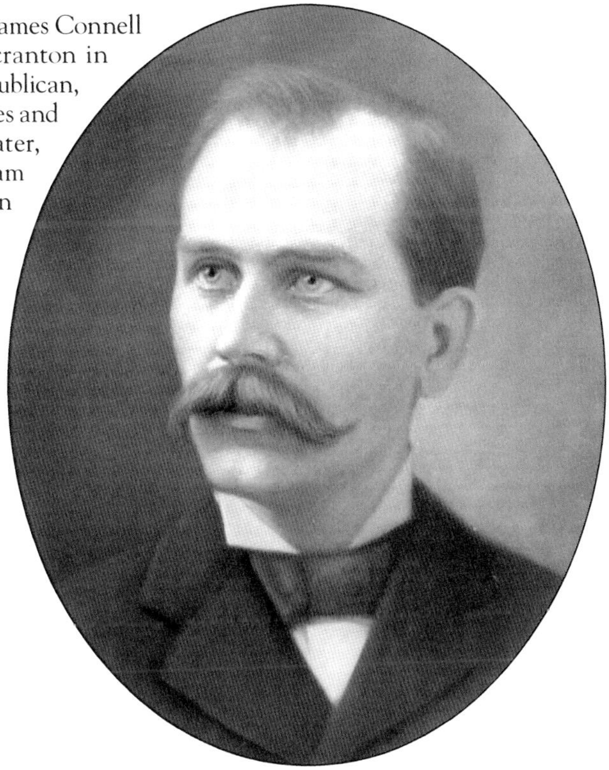

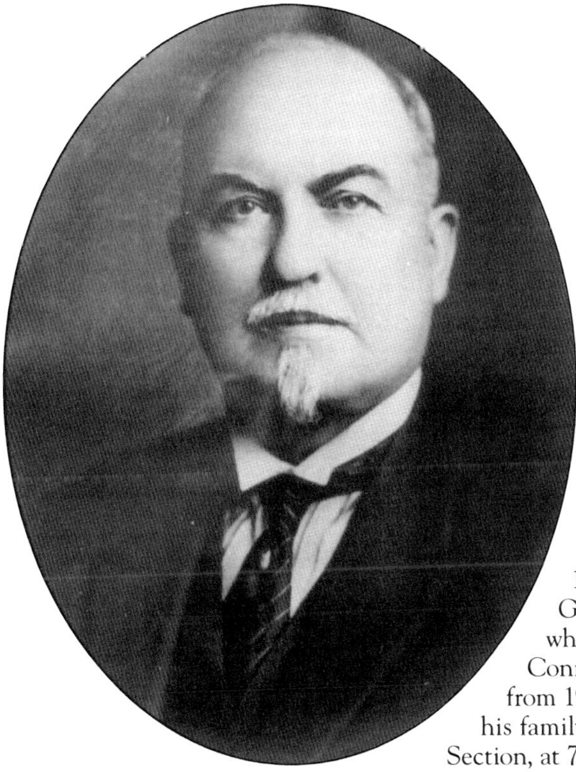

Alexander T. Connell was born to the Thomas Connell branch of the Connell family in Minooka, Pennsylvania, in 1861. He was a prospector in the Yukon Gold Rush but later returned to Scranton, where he was elected to the state legislature. Connell was elected mayor of Scranton twice, from 1902 to 1906 and from 1918 to 1922. Like his family members, Connell resided in the Hill Section, at 746 Webster Avenue.

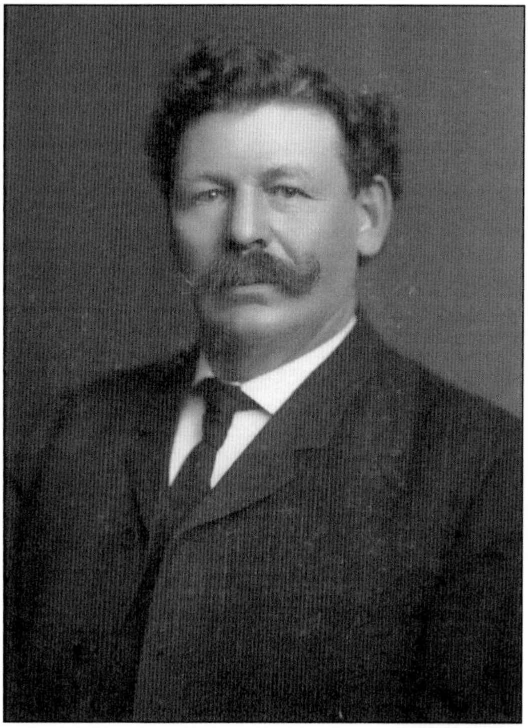

Frank Carlucci I was a Hill Section resident and owner of the Carlucci Stone Company, which provided the stone for the immigration facilities at Ellis Island. His grandson Frank Carlucci III served as Ronald Reagan's secretary of defense from 1987 to 1989.

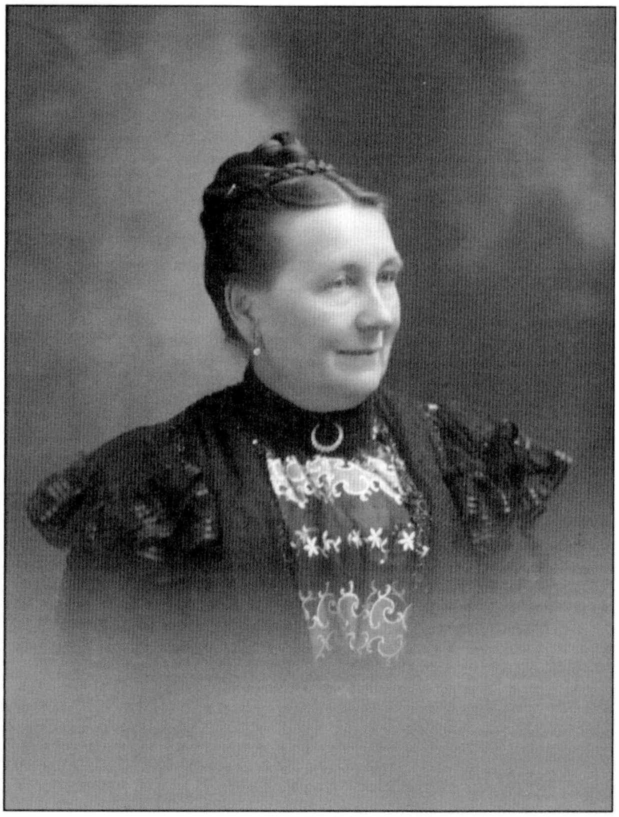

Mina Schimpff Robinson was born in Lautrecken, Bavaria, and immigrated to the United States as a child. She later married Phillip Robinson of E. Robinson's Brewery. When Phillip Robinson died at a young age, Mina became the company's chief executive. Eventually, the brewery merged with other breweries, including that of the Casey family, to form Pennsylvania Central Brewery, where Mina secured important positions for her sons.

Samuel Samter was born in New York City in 1851. By 1872, Samter had made his way to Scranton, where he and his brother Benjamin founded a clothing store called Samter Brothers (later, Samter's) at the corner of Lackawanna and Penn Avenues in Scranton's downtown. The store prospered for years as one of Scranton's largest retail stores. Samuel Samter was a generous benefactor of Temple Israel and resided at 701 Webster Avenue.

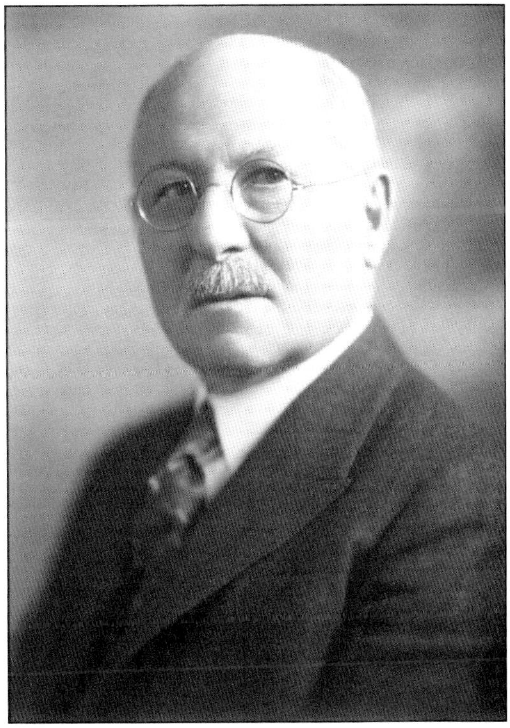

Pictured here is the Oppenheim family. From left to right are Richard, Constance, and Ellis, with a portrait of Isaac E. "I.E." Oppenheim visible behind them. I.E. Oppenheim founded the Scranton Dry Goods Company (Oppenheim's) in 1912 and eventually settled at 1117 Myrtle Street in the Hill Section. Under the guidance of I.E.'s sons Richard and Ellis, Oppenheim's became one of the area's leading department stores. (Courtesy of the Oppenheim family.)

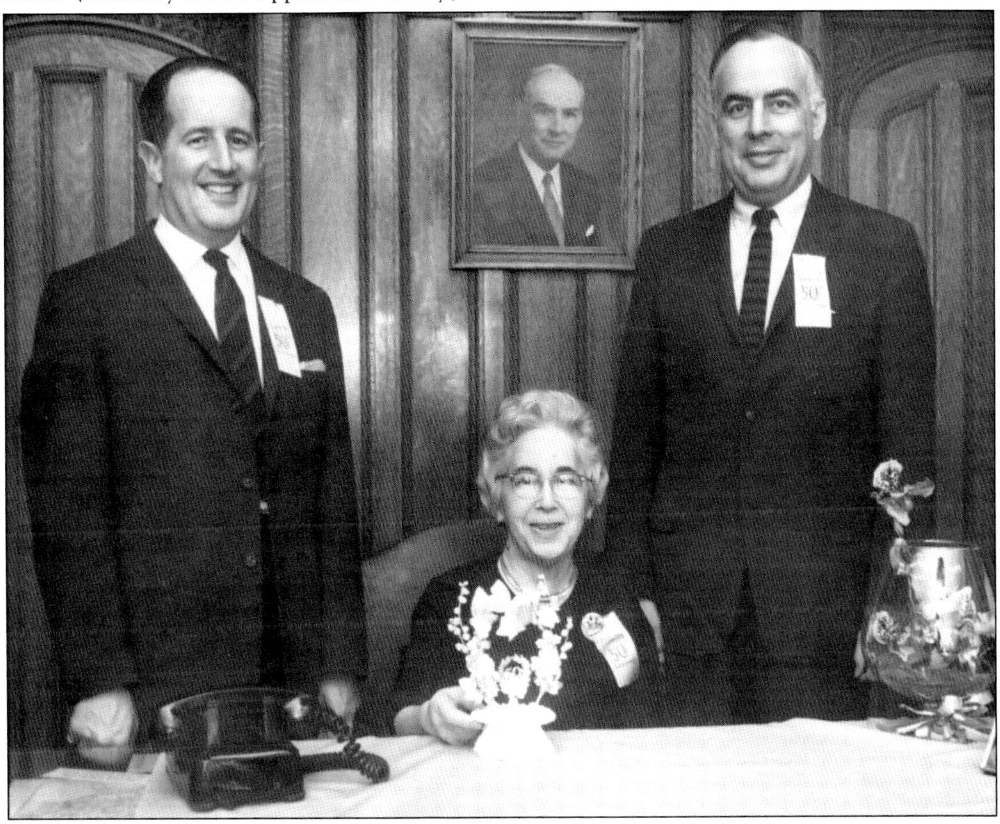

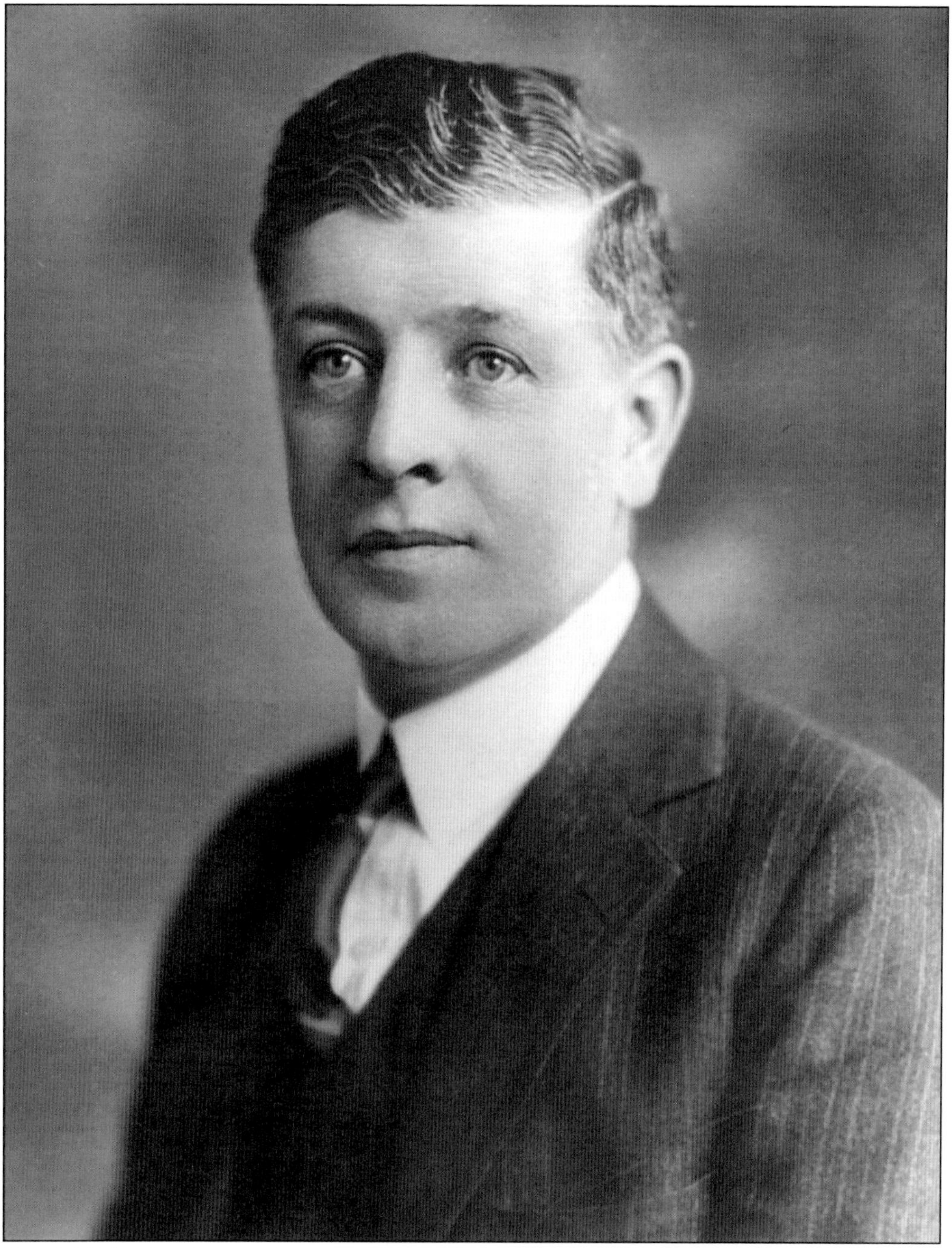

Patrick J. Boland was born in Scranton in 1880. He attended St. Thomas College and was subsequently elected to several positions in local government. In 1930, Boland was elected as a Democrat to the US House of Representatives for the 11th District of Pennsylvania. In 1935, he became house majority whip, a position that made him instrumental in the passage of New Deal legislation, particularly the Social Security Act of 1935. In 1942, Boland was still majority whip when he died of a heart attack in Washington, DC. A special election was held to fill the remainder of his term, and his widow, Veronica Barrett, was elected as the first congresswoman from Pennsylvania. The Boland family resided in the 700 block of North Irving Avenue for many years.

William F. Shean was born in Syracuse, New York, in 1873. He subsequently moved to Scranton and became a lawyer with the firm Cawley & Shean. He then founded the *Catholic Light* newspaper before marrying Mabel Leonard and taking over the hardware business of her father, T.F. Leonard. William Shean later moved into the Leonard home on Quincy Avenue, where he nurtured a family who is still active in the Hill Section. (Author's collection.)

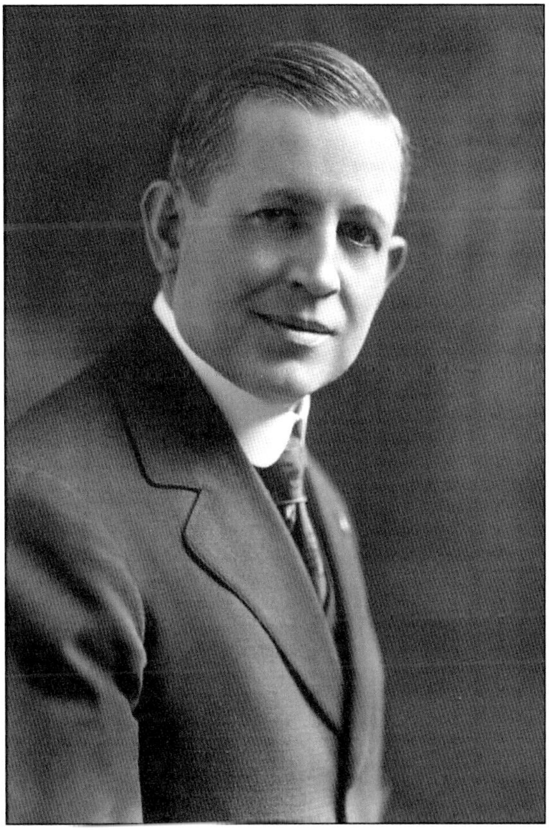

Shown here at their Quincy Avenue home are the sons and son-in-law of William F. Shean. From left to right are Thomas "Leonard" Shean, John "Jack" Shean, Edward "Ed" Shean, William F. "Bill" Shean Jr., and Bert Lynch, Dorothy Shean Lynch's husband. (Author's collection.)

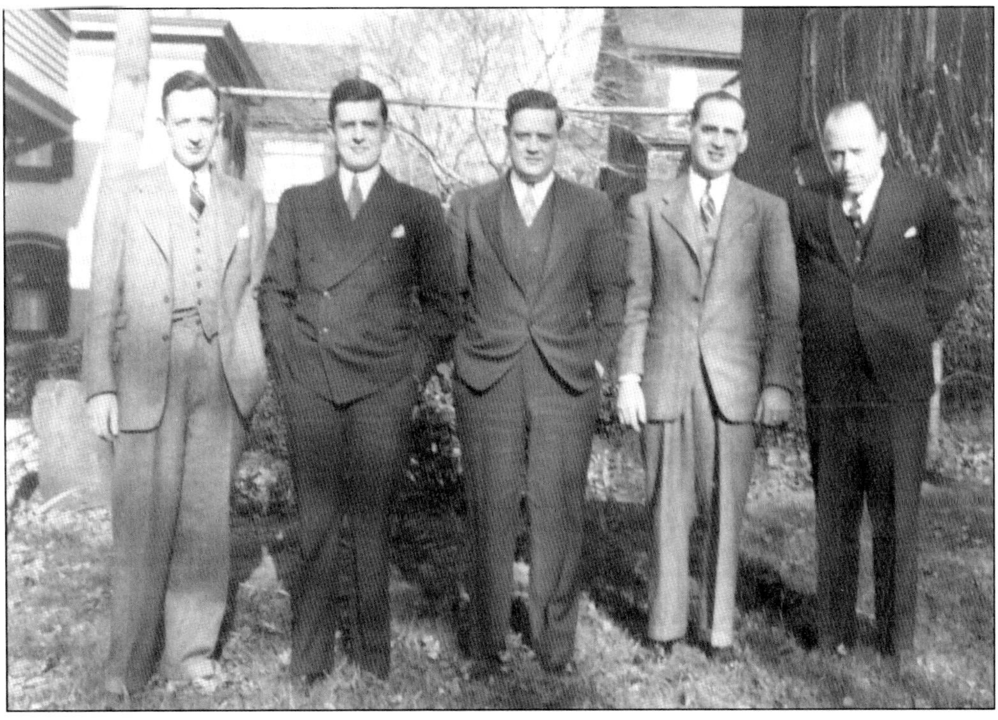

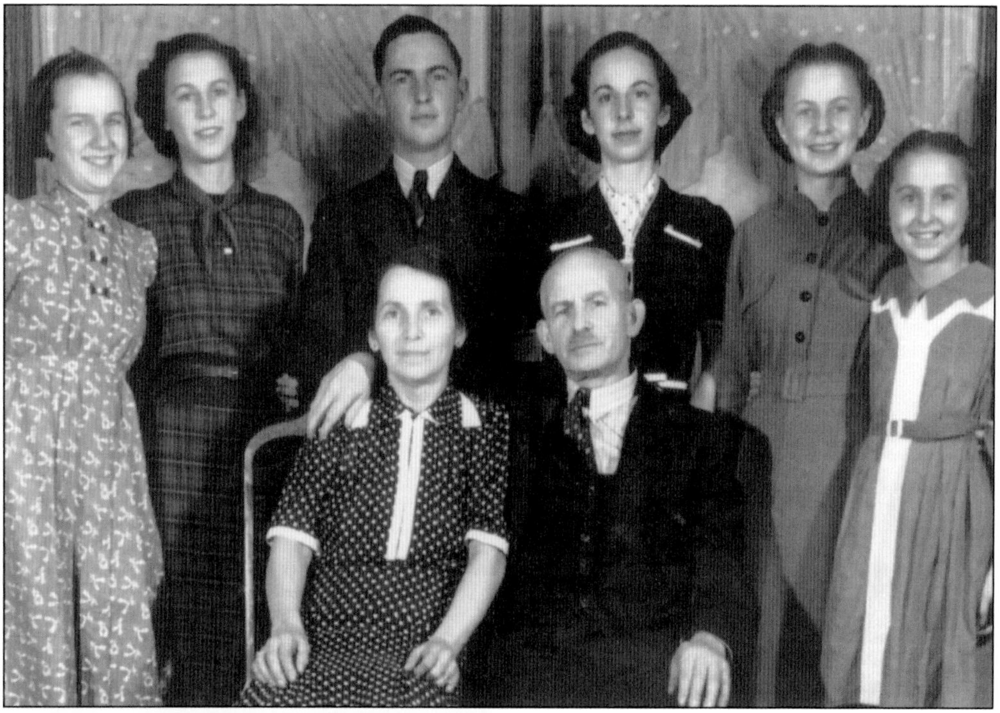

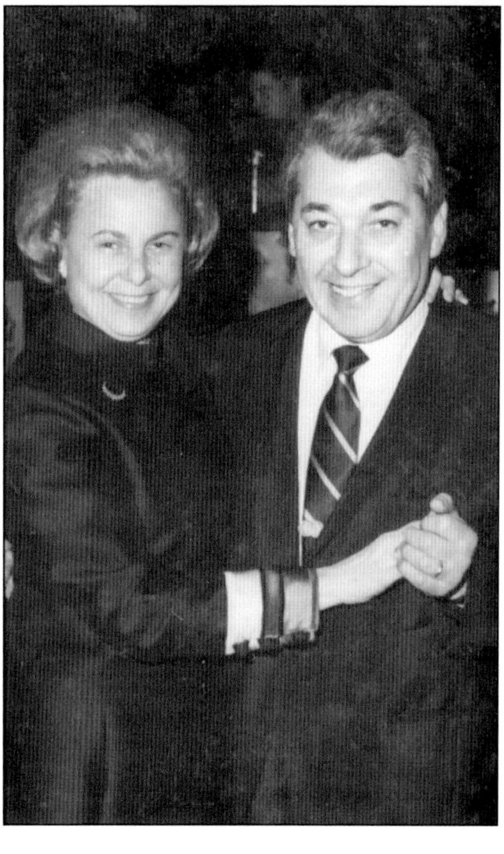

Pictured here in the 1930s is the Gildar family. From left to right are (first row) Ida and Morris; (second row) Bernice, Sylvia, Harold, Annette, Rosalyn, and Lillian. The Gildar family was among the earliest Jewish residents of the Hill Section and lived on Madison Avenue for many years. (Courtesy of Nancy J. Weinberger.)

Pictured here are Rosalyn "Rozzie" (Gildar) and Harold "Heshy" Weinberger. After World War II, Harold took over his father's plumbing business, G. Weinberger Mechanical, and greatly expanded its scope. He was also involved in numerous real estate projects with his brothers and was a director of the Third National Bank. The Weinbergers lived on Clay Avenue for many years and were involved in numerous organizations, including Temple Israel and the JCC. (Courtesy of Nancy J. Weinberger.)

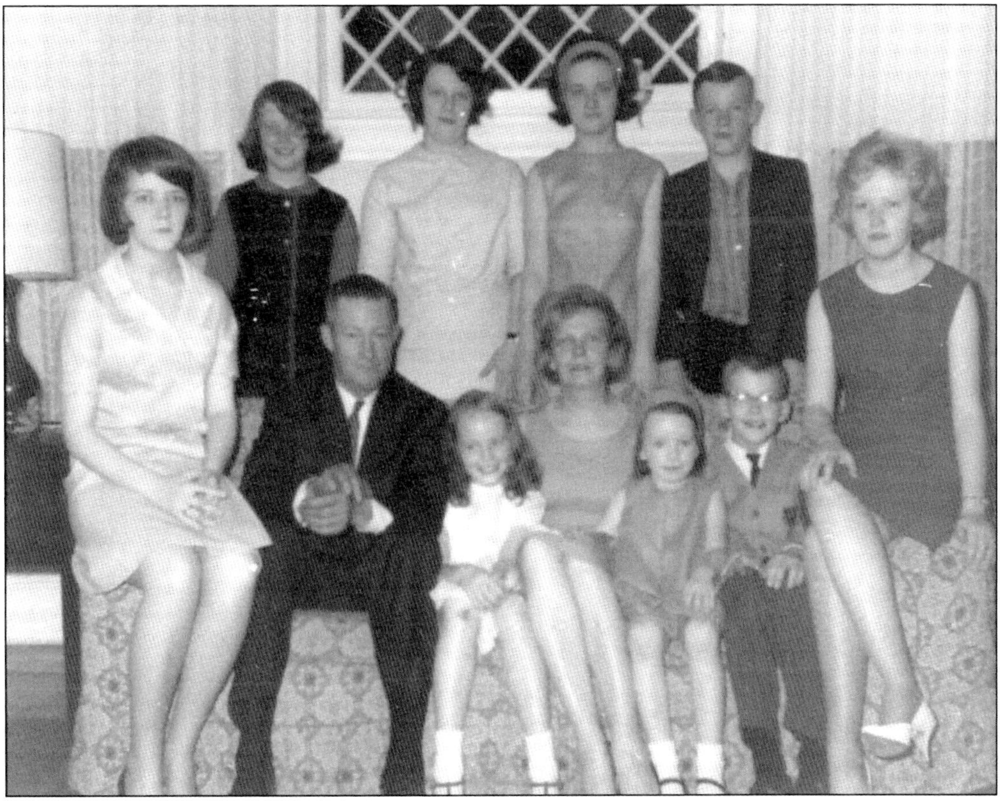

Represented here is a large Irish Catholic Hill Section family. Frank Oliver Sr., a city inspector, and his wife, Margaret Chase, a clerk at Mercy Hospital, resided at 919 Pine Street, where they raised nine children. Pictured here is the entire Oliver family. From left to right are (first row) Marylou, Frank Sr., Ann "Nancy," Margaret, Christine, Frank Jr., and Joan; (second row) Elizabeth, Patricia, Margaret "Peggy," and James "Chuck." (Author's collection.)

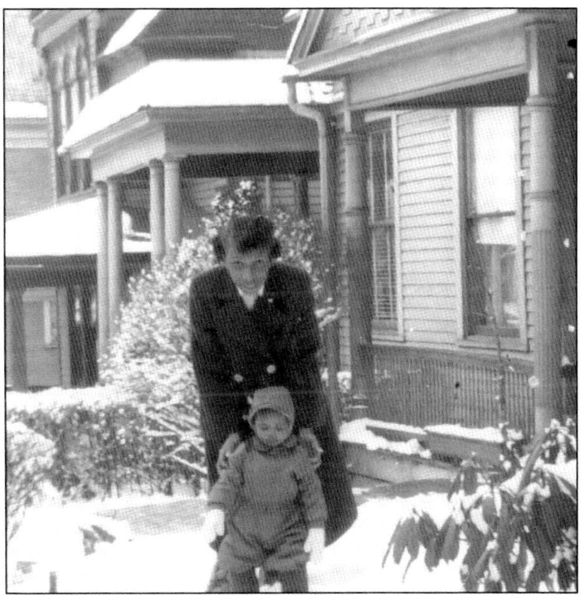

Pictured here are Dorothy Smith and her son Granville "Pud" Smith Jr. Granville Smith Sr. was an affluent African American business owner who bought G.W. Brown Trucking from businesswoman Louise Tanner Brown in the late 1940s. The Smiths lived in a stately residence at 921 Pine Street for many years. (Courtesy of Granville Smith Jr.)

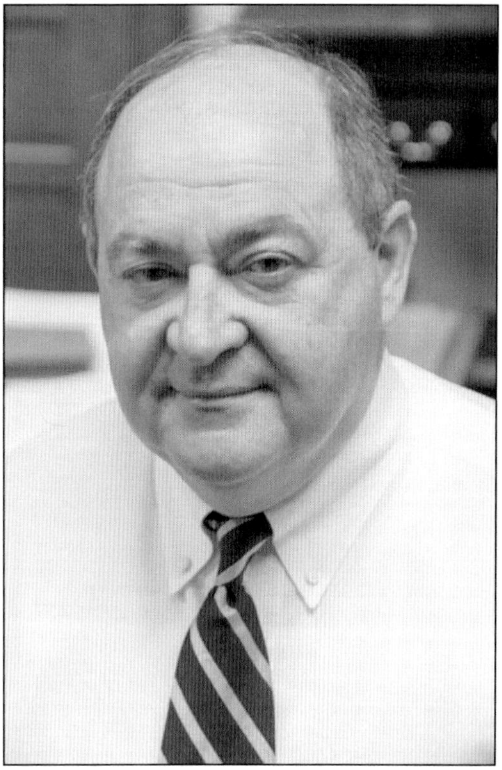

Robert D. Mariani is a federal judge of the Middle District of Pennsylvania. After privately practicing law in Scranton for many years, Judge Mariani was nominated to his current post by Pres. Barack Obama in 2010 and confirmed by the US Senate in 2011. Judge Mariani currently lives in the historic Platt residence on Webster Avenue, which he has taken great pains to restore. (Courtesy of Judge Robert D. Mariani.)

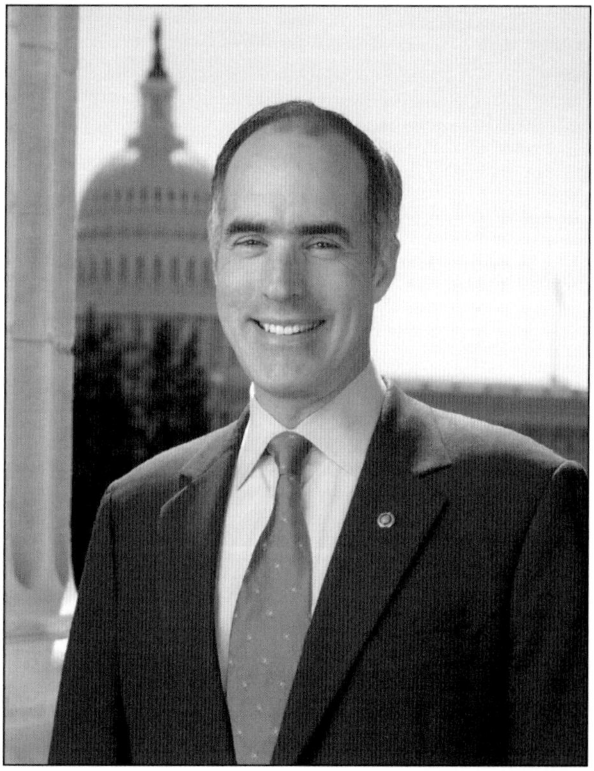

Sen. Robert P. "Bob" Casey Jr. was elected as a Democrat from Pennsylvania in 2006. Senator Casey previously served as Pennsylvania's auditor general and state treasurer. Casey is the oldest son of the late governor Robert P. Casey. Bob Casey is a graduate of the College of the Holy Cross and received his law degree from the Catholic University of America. He resides with his family in Scranton's Hill Section. (Courtesy of the office of Sen. Robert P. Casey.)

Three

Religious and Community Organizations

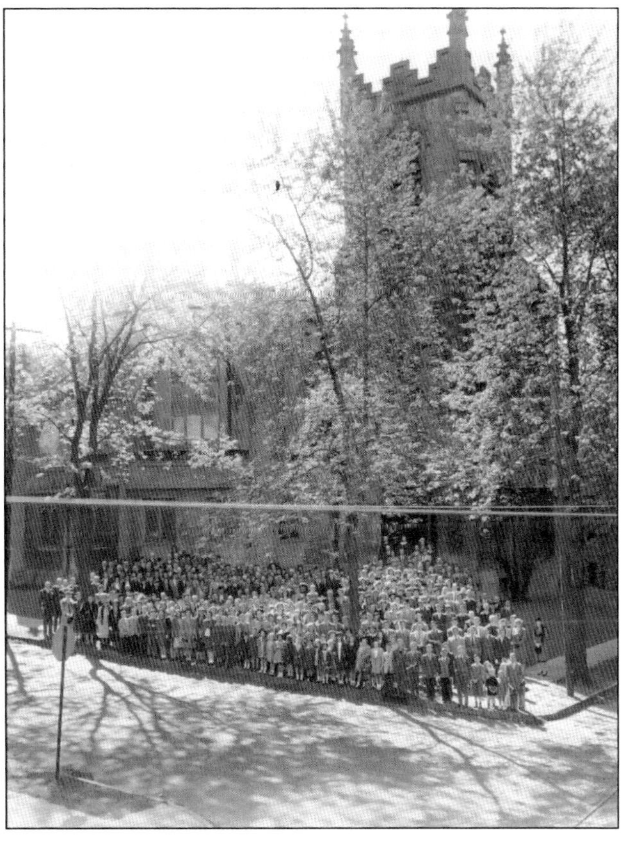

Covenant Presbyterian Church's origins can be traced to the First Presbyterian Church, founded on North Washington Avenue in 1848. In 1903, the congregation relocated to the corner of Madison Avenue and Olive Street, where it built a new structure. In 1926, the congregation merged with the Second Presbyterian Church and became the Westminster Presbyterian Church. Subsequently, it merged with the Green Ridge Presbyterian Church and adopted its present name.

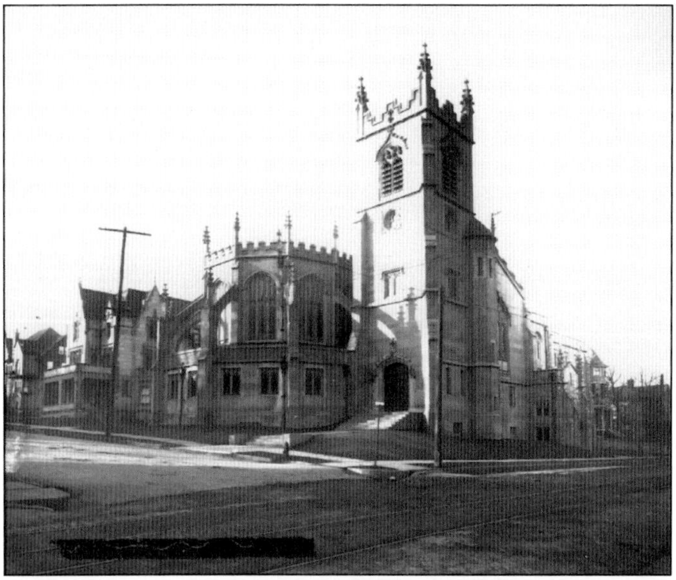

The Covenant Presbyterian Church at the corner of Madison Avenue and Olive Street is an impressive example of Gothic architecture, complete with flying buttresses. In 1903, W.W. Scranton, son of Joseph H. Scranton, laid the cornerstone of the church, built by Stipp Construction. The manse located behind the church was constructed in 1898, and an addition along Madison Avenue was later erected.

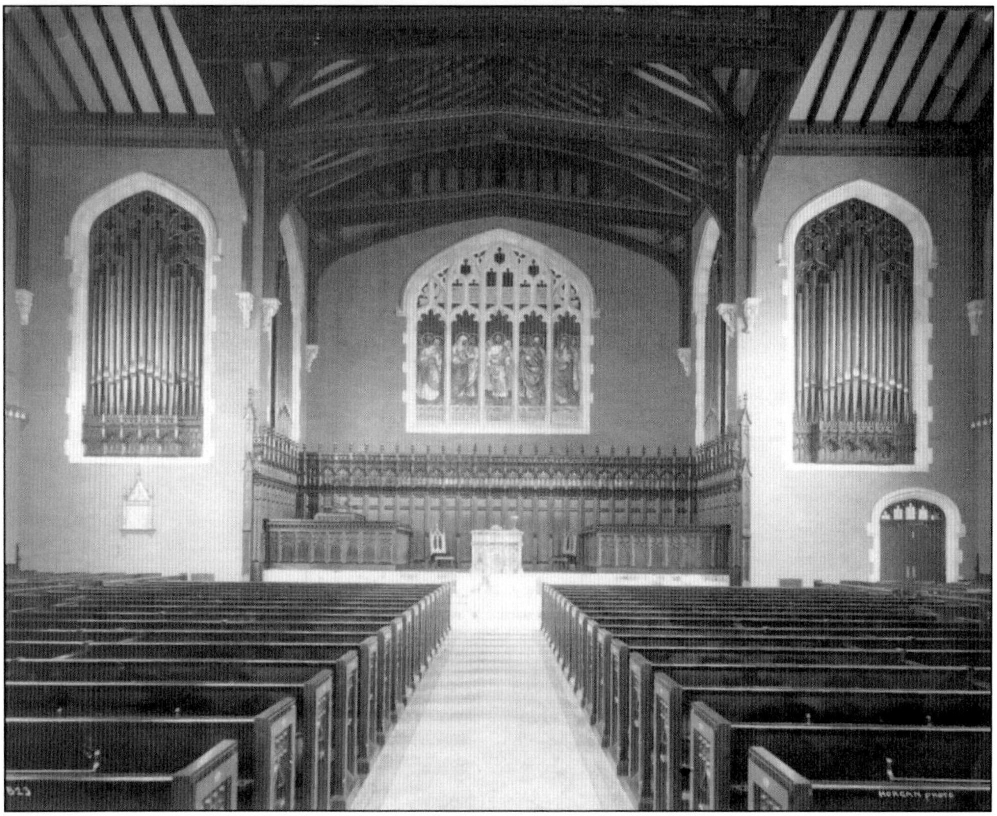

This interior view of Covenant Presbyterian Church depicts the beautiful craftsmanship of the church's sanctuary. Each of the church's pews was reserved for benefactors. The first pew to the right of the altar was reserved for the Scranton family, who also endowed one of the sanctuary's magnificent stained-glass windows. Other stained-glass windows were endowed by the Platt family. (Courtesy of Covenant Presbyterian Church.)

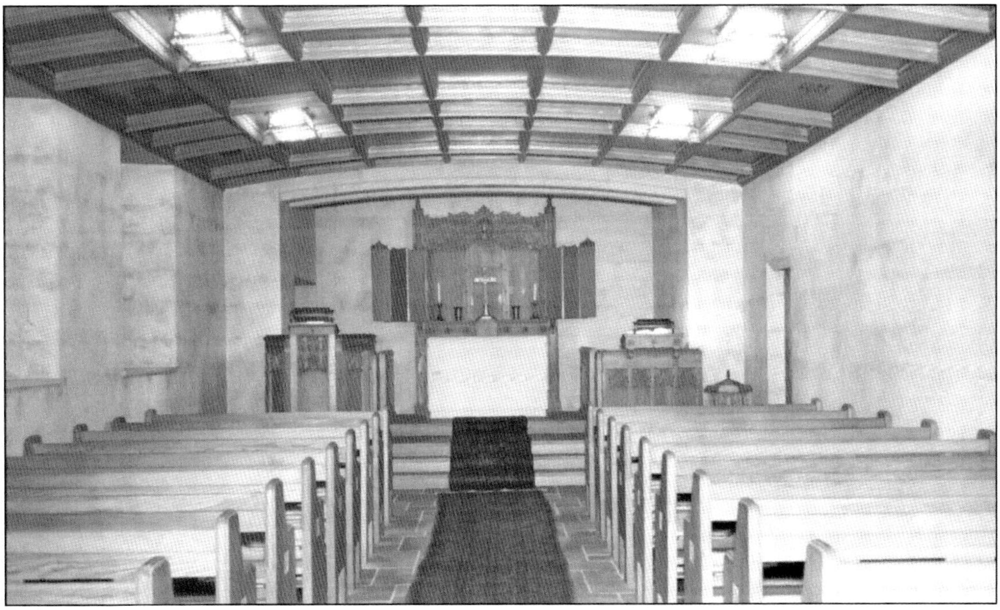

The chapel of Covenant Presbyterian Church, located beneath the main sanctuary, was endowed by the Schautz family in 1948. The Schautz family was among the first settlers of Petersburg, and they were the owners of Grove Textiles, located near Petersburg Corners. They were also the main benefactors of Schautz Stadium and Park, adjacent to the Grove Textiles factory. (Courtesy of Covenant Presbyterian Church.)

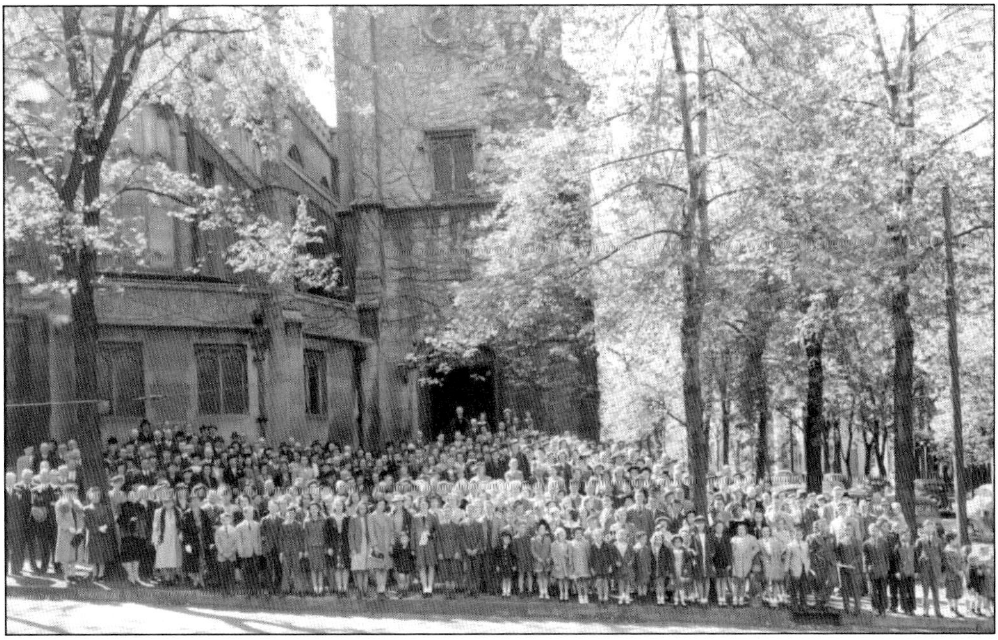

Congregation members gather outside Westminster Presbyterian Church in 1944. For years, Westminster Presbyterian Church reigned as one of the most important Presbyterian churches of not only the Hill Section but also the entire Scranton area. Even during the Great Depression and war years, Westminster's services were always well attended by Hill Section residents. (Courtesy of Covenant Presbyterian Church.)

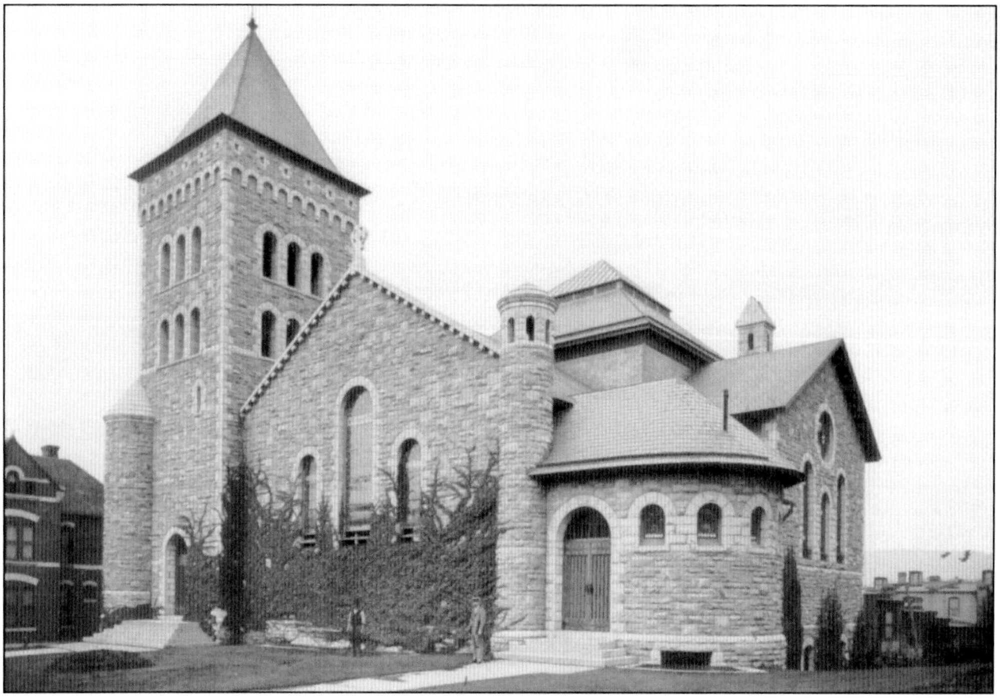

The Second Presbyterian Church was founded in 1874. Much like the First Presbyterian Church, it was originally organized by Hill Section families, who also funded its construction in the 400 block of Jefferson Avenue. After the 1926 merger of the First and Second Presbyterian Churches, the Jefferson Avenue church became St. John's Lutheran Church, then St. Matthew's Evangelical Lutheran Church, which it still is today.

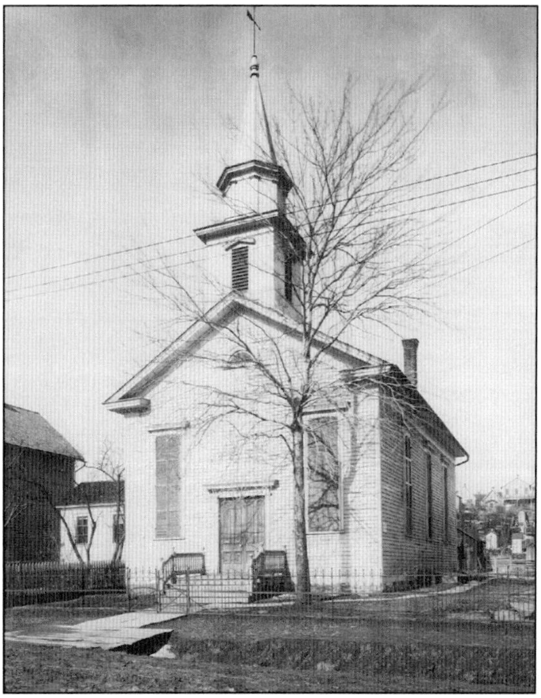

The original structure of the Petersburg Presbyterian Church, pictured here, was located at the corner of Wheeler Avenue and William Street. The congregation later built a new church in the 900 block of Prescott Avenue, closer to Petersburg Corners. The Petersburg Presbyterian Church closed in the postwar years, but its Prescott Avenue church was repurposed for use as offices, then as a Hindu temple.

John Raymond Memorial Universalist Church was located at the corner of Madison Avenue and Vine Street. The Romanesque building was constructed in 1906 with an impressive 2,600-pound stained-glass window called "Christ the Teacher." In 1987, the Universalists sold the church to the University of Scranton, which moved the stained-glass window to Hyland Hall and transformed the structure into the Smurfit Fine Arts Center.

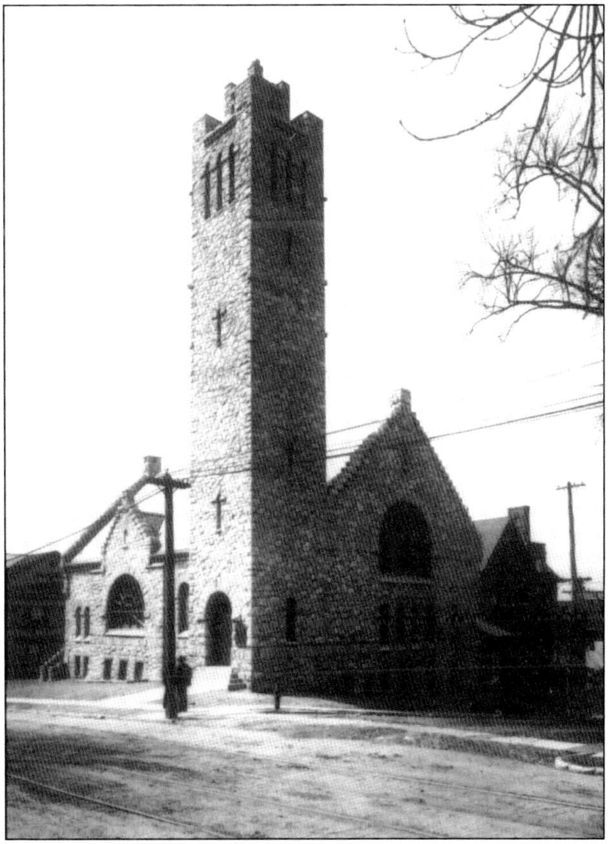

A local Methodist congregation established the Elm Park Methodist Church in 1893. The church was built and burned down twice in 1893, so the current building, pictured here, is actually the third Elm Park Church. Each time, William Connell led a group of citizens in their efforts to rebuild the church. It was later proven that a disillusioned church sexton had lit both fires.

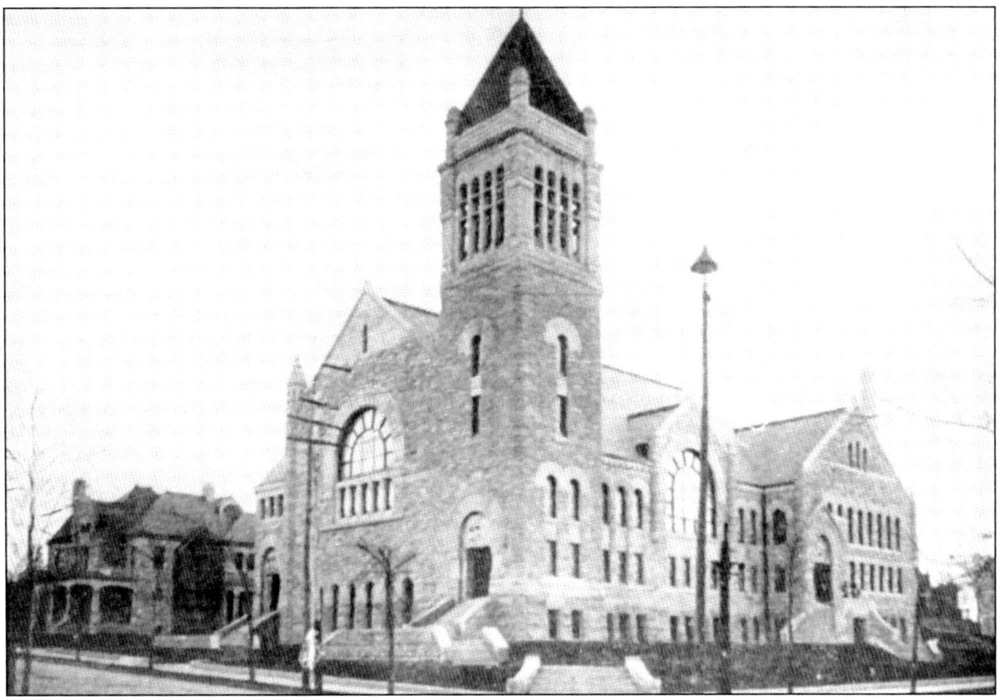

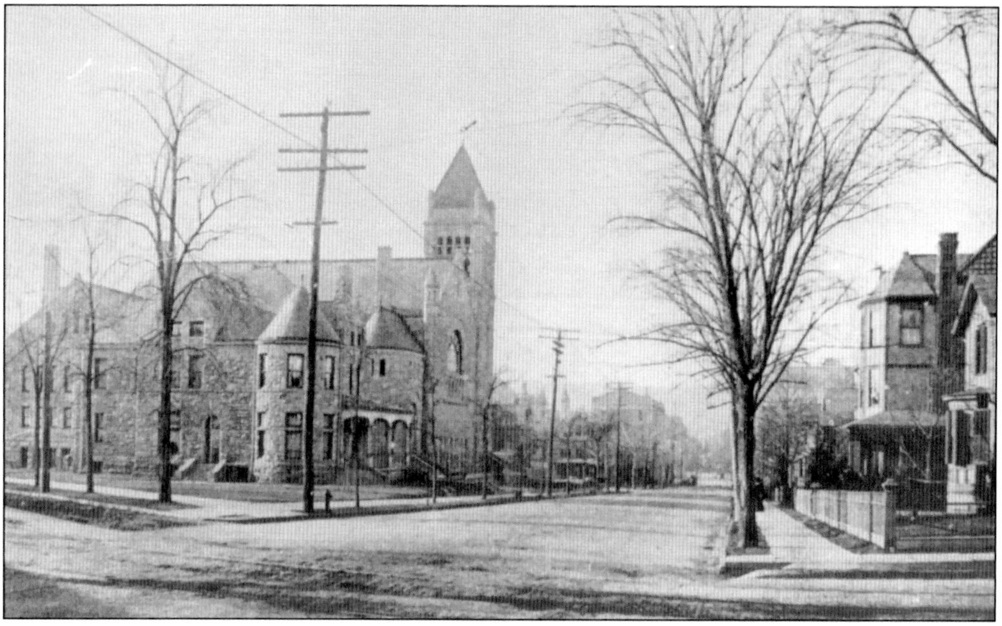

The Elm Park Methodist Church is among the most impressive structures in Scranton. The church and its parsonage occupy an entire city block, between Jefferson and Madison Avenues and Spruce and Linden Streets. The church, which straddles the border between Scranton's downtown and the Hill Section, is an iconic part of Scranton's skyline, with bells that can be heard throughout the city.

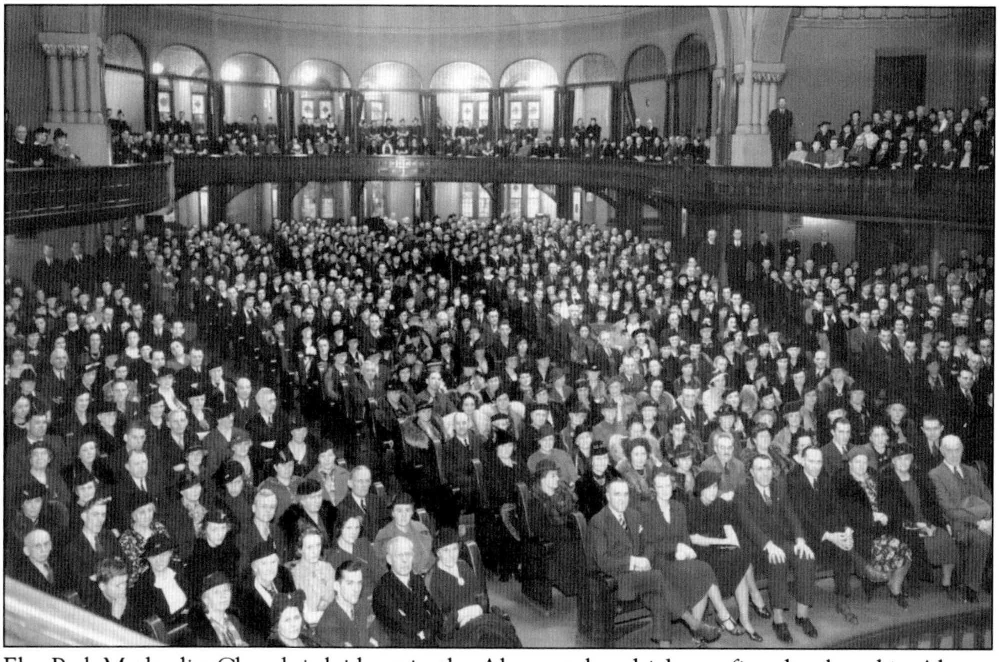

Elm Park Methodist Church is laid out in the Akron style, which was first developed in Akron, Ohio. Akron-style churches became very popular among Protestant congregations in the late 19th century. The interior of Elm Park is a perfect example of this style, with its spacious auditorium, gallery, and sanctuary.

The Victorian Gothic Immanuel Baptist Church, pictured here, was built in 1910 on land previously owned by Bartholomew Leonard, brother and business partner of T.F. Leonard. The University of Scranton purchased the church in 1986 and subsequently transformed it into the Houlihan McLean Center for performance music.

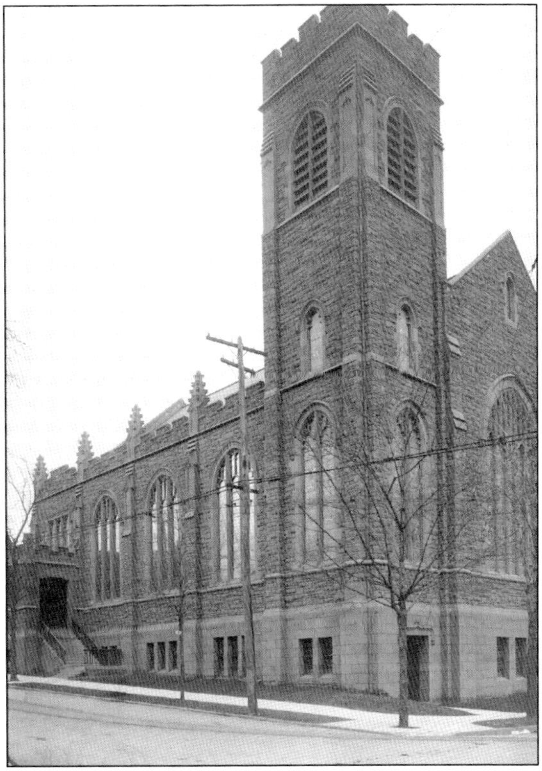

Pictured here is the Cathedral Chapel Catholic Church. Initially, there were not many Catholics in the Hill Section, and the Diocese of Scranton decided to build only a small chapel under the administration of St. Peter's Cathedral in downtown Scranton to serve the area. It was not until the 1950s when many more Catholics moved into the Hill Section that the chapel became Immaculate Conception Church. (Courtesy of Mary Catherine Smith.)

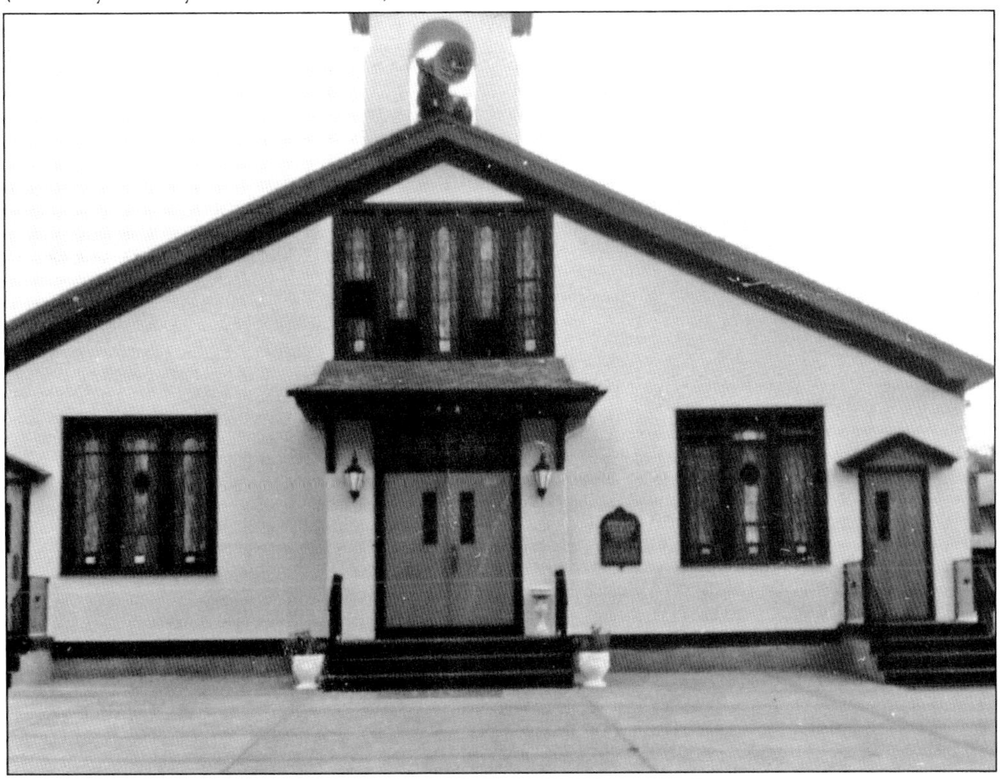

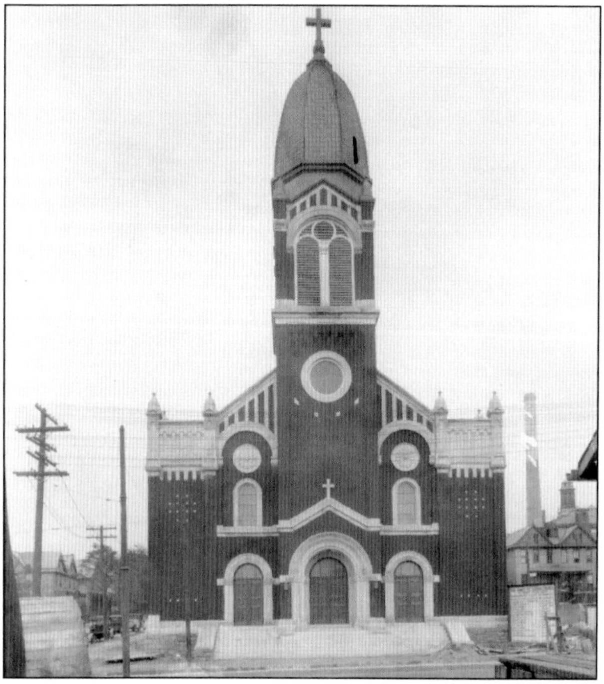

Holy Family Catholic Church is located at the corner of Washington Avenue and Gibson Street. Although only on the edge of the Hill Section, Holy Family served a great number of Hill Section residents. Holy Family was also a major part of the local Slovak community. The Diocese of Scranton closed the Holy Family Catholic Church in the 2000s, and the building has since been demolished.

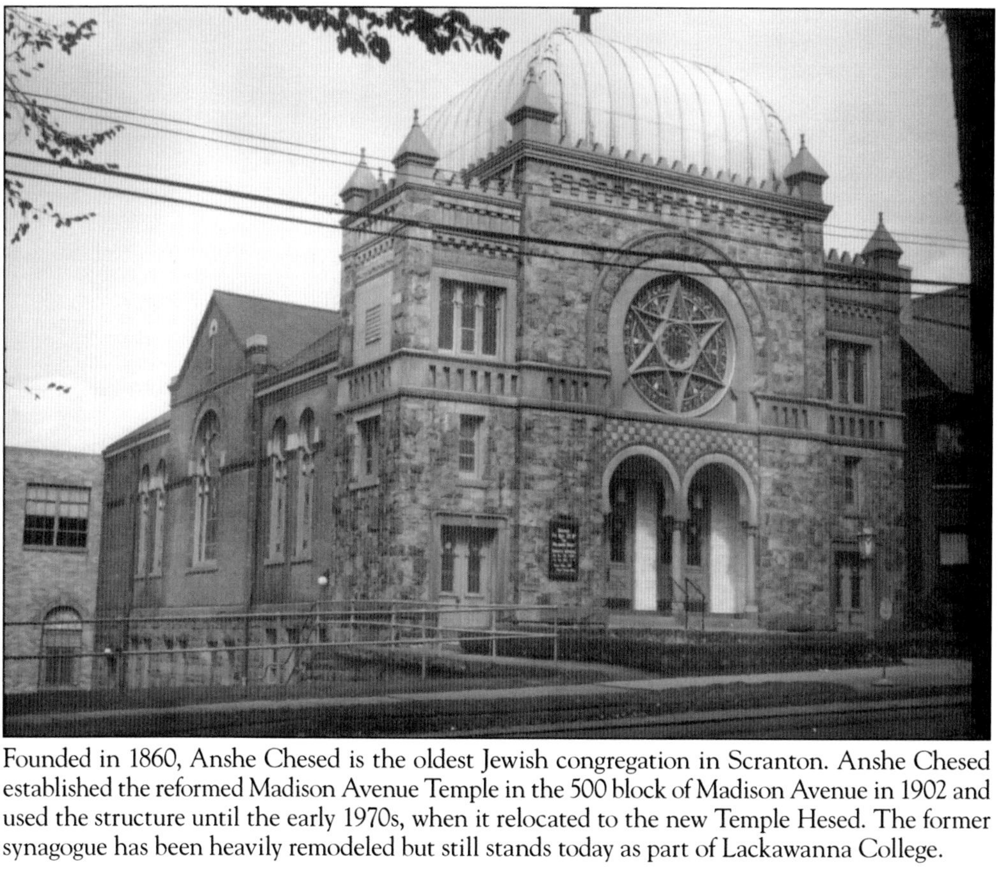

Founded in 1860, Anshe Chesed is the oldest Jewish congregation in Scranton. Anshe Chesed established the reformed Madison Avenue Temple in the 500 block of Madison Avenue in 1902 and used the structure until the early 1970s, when it relocated to the new Temple Hesed. The former synagogue has been heavily remodeled but still stands today as part of Lackawanna College.

Temple Israel is the largest conservative Jewish synagogue in Scranton. It was constructed on the former site of Calvary Reformed Church, at the corner of Monroe Avenue and Gibson Street, in 1926. For many years, Temple Israel was the heart of Scranton's thriving Jewish community. Temple Israel is still an active congregation based out of this historic structure. (Author's collection.)

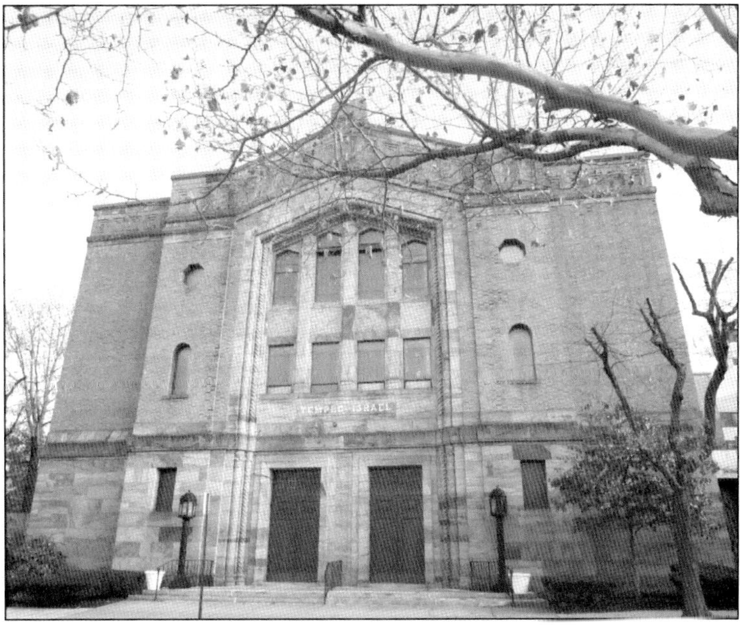

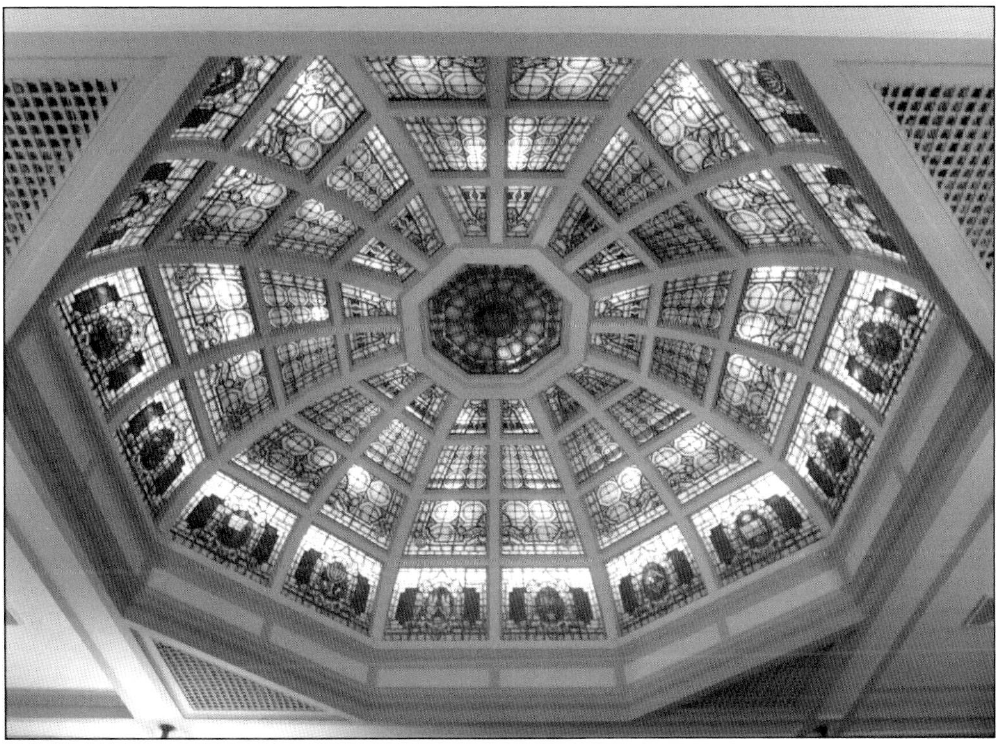

Temple Israel's sanctuary is located on the structure's second level, above the temple banquet hall and Weinberger Chapel. A stained-glass dome decorated with Jewish symbols illuminates the room, and yahrzeit boards that commemorate deceased temple congregants adorn its walls. (Author's collection.)

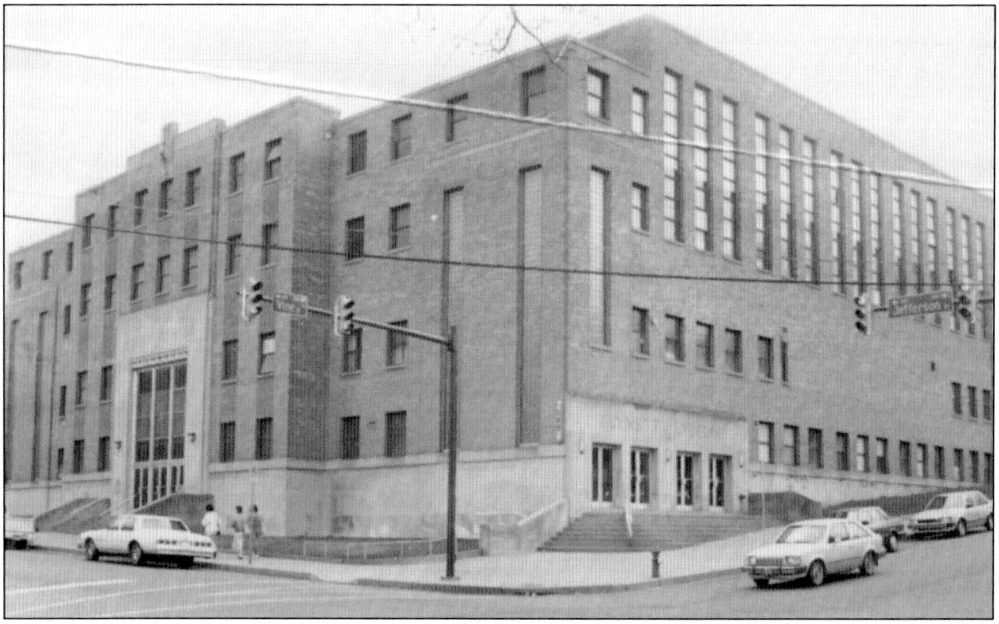

The Diocese of Scranton built the Catholic Youth Center (CYC) at the corner of Jefferson Avenue and Olive Street in 1949. The CYC was among the largest and most popular recreational complexes in the area, with a basketball court, 12 bowling lanes, swimming pool, health club, and auditorium. The CYC closed in the early 2000s, and its former structure is now Lackawanna College's student union building.

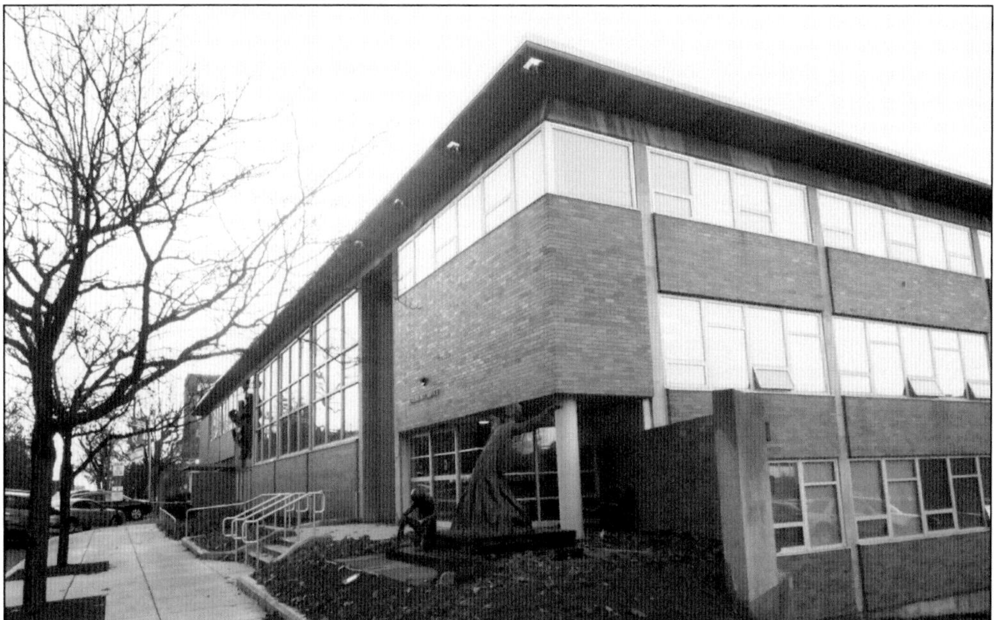

The Jewish Community Center (JCC) was built at the intersection of Jefferson Avenue and Olive Street in 1952 to serve the Hill Section's thriving Jewish community. The JCC is home to extensive recreational and educational space, as well as office space for local nonprofit organizations. The JCC is still one of Scranton's most important community organizations. (Author's collection.)

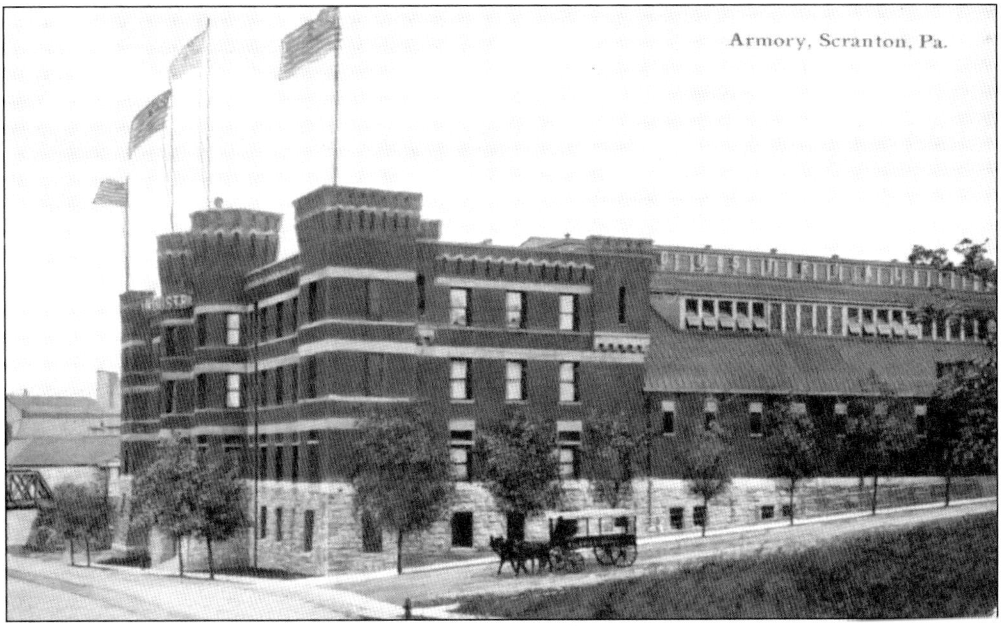

Designed by Lansing Holden, the Watres Armory was built at 900 Adams Avenue, along Myrtle Street, in 1901. The armory is named after Col. Lewis A. Watres, president of the Scranton Water Company, and was originally used by the 13th Regiment of the Pennsylvania National Guard. Armories like this were built in several locations throughout the area as community centers and arsenals in case of labor riots. (Courtesy of Jack Hiddlestone.)

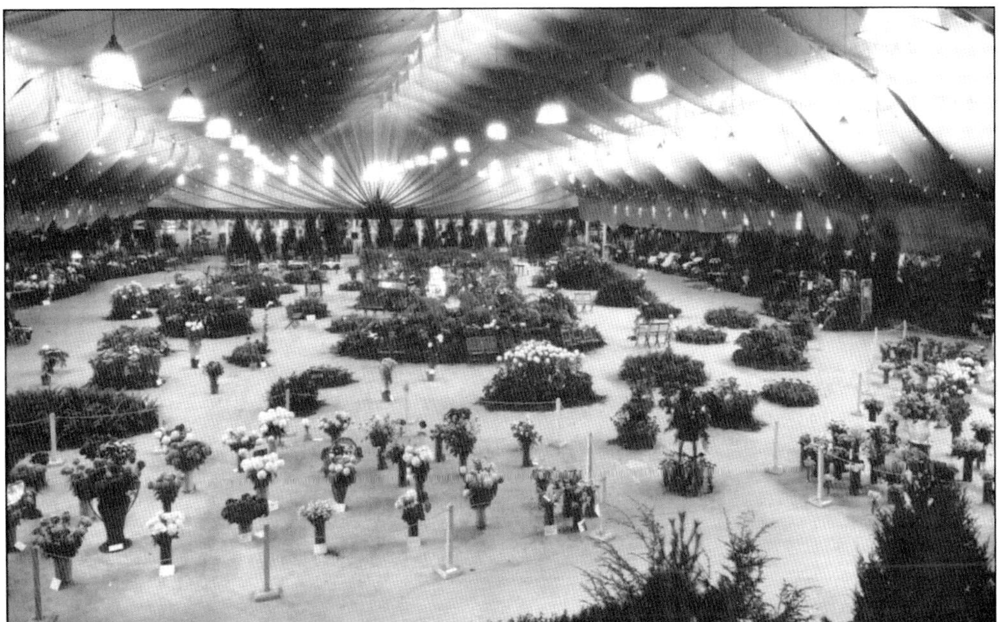

The Watres Armory is approximately 102,000 square feet and has a large auditorium, as seen here. The auditorium was used for numerous community events, such as military drills, industrial trade shows, and even roller-skating nights for local young people. In the early 2000s, the National Guard relocated to a new facility, and efforts are still being made to redevelop the structure.

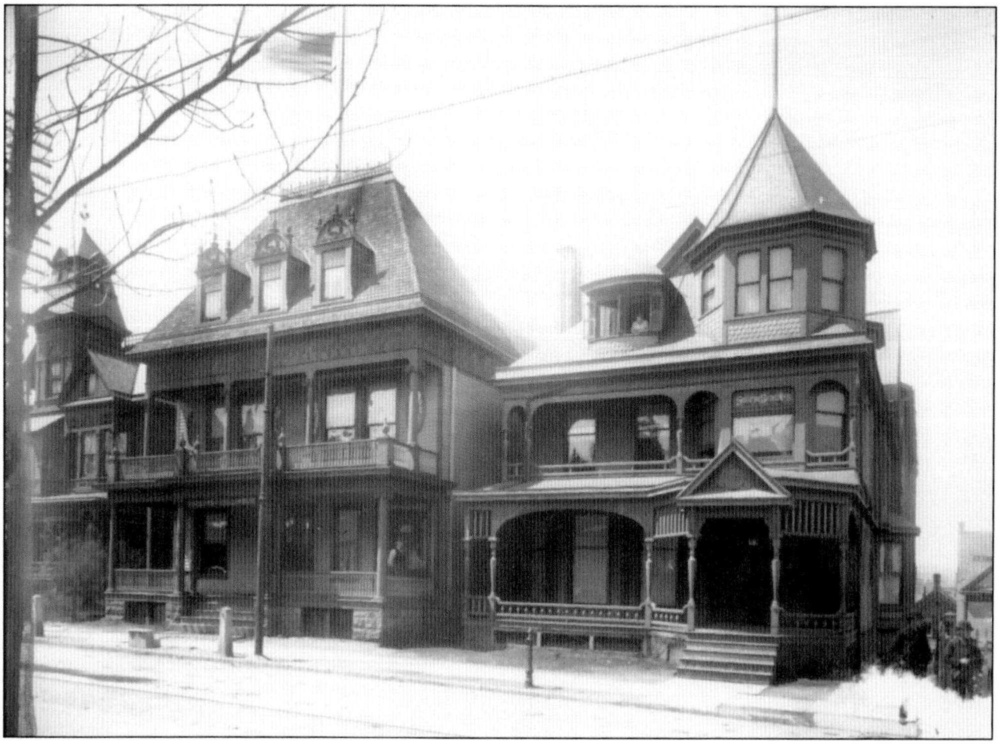

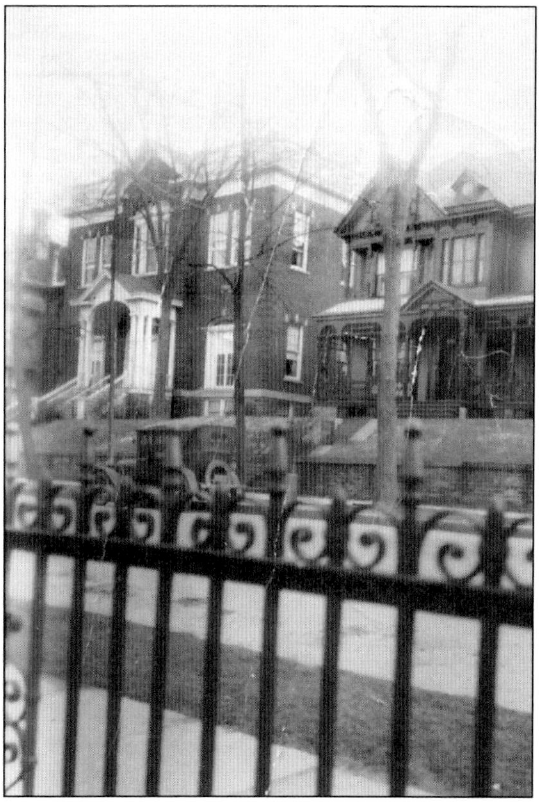

Pictured here are the headquarters of two civic organizations near the corner of Washington Avenue and Pine Street. The building at left was the local headquarters of the Knights of Columbus, a Catholic fraternal association, and the building at right was the headquarters of the Lackawanna Bicycle Club. Many of the Hill Section's most prominent residents were involved in one or both of these organizations.

In 1909, a group of prominent Scranton women founded a civically minded social organization known as the Century Club. In 1914, the Century Club building, pictured here at left, was constructed at 612 Jefferson Avenue on land donated by W.W. Scranton and his wife, Katherine. The Century Club continues to operate in this historic building over a century later.

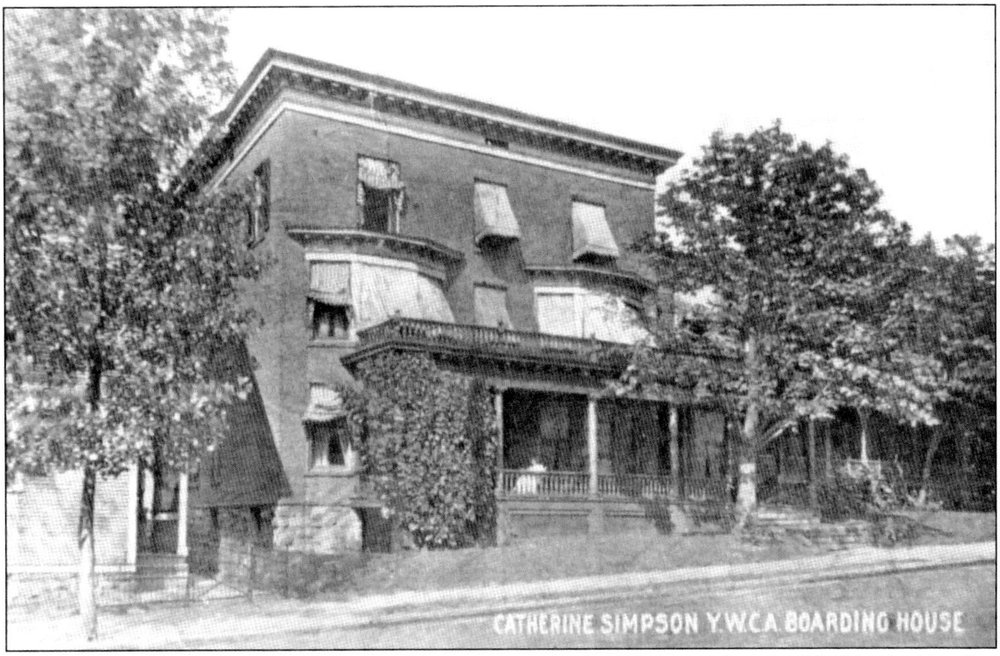

In 1906, Clarence Simpson built the Catherine Simpson YWCA, located in the 800 block of Linden Street, as a community center for the working women of Scranton in memory of his wife. In later years, the wife of Dr. L.A. Gates organized a new YWCA in downtown Scranton. The Kay Drug Company and the University of Scranton subsequently used the now demolished building.

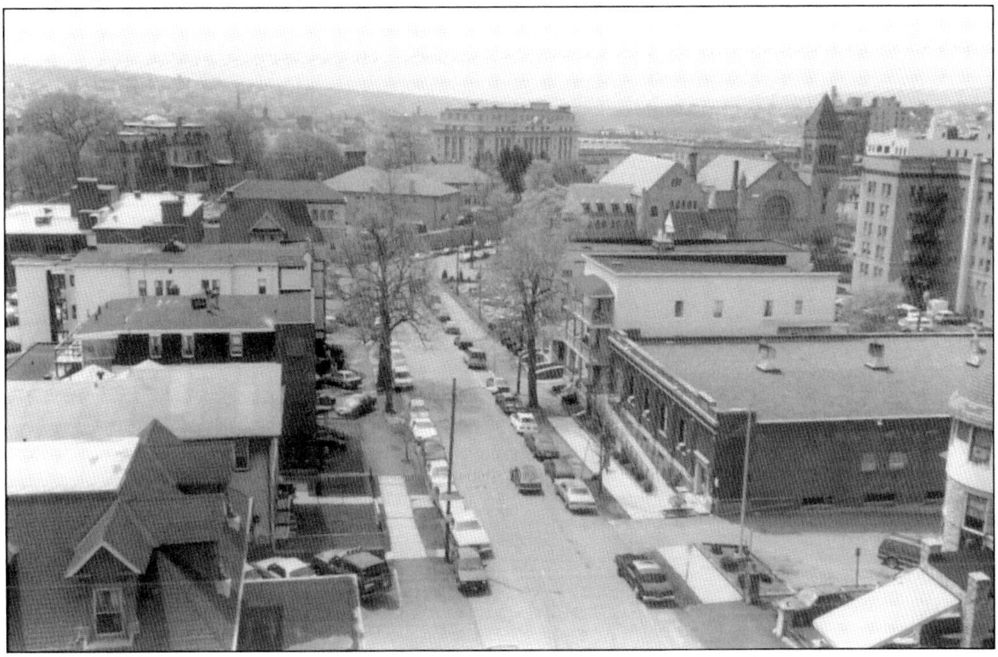

The large brick structure visible on the lower right of this aerial image is the former regional headquarters of the Girl Scouts of the USA. The Girl Scouts used their headquarters for various purposes over the years; in the early days of television, they even leased out part of it to the local ABC affiliate WNEP for their studios. The University of Scranton now owns the building.

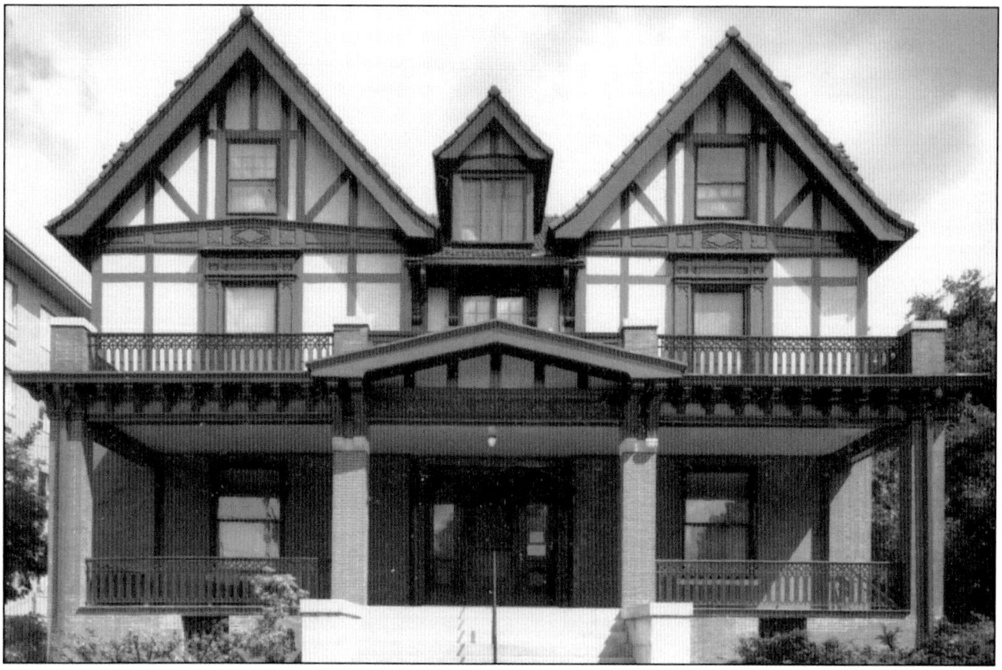

In 1886, the Lackawanna Historical Society was founded as the Lackawanna Institute of History and Science by a group of prominent area residents. In 1921, the organization, often noted as the oldest cultural institution in the county, changed its name to the Lackawanna Historical Society. After decades of meeting in various locations throughout Scranton, the society permanently established its home at the former residence of society benefactor George H. Catlin.

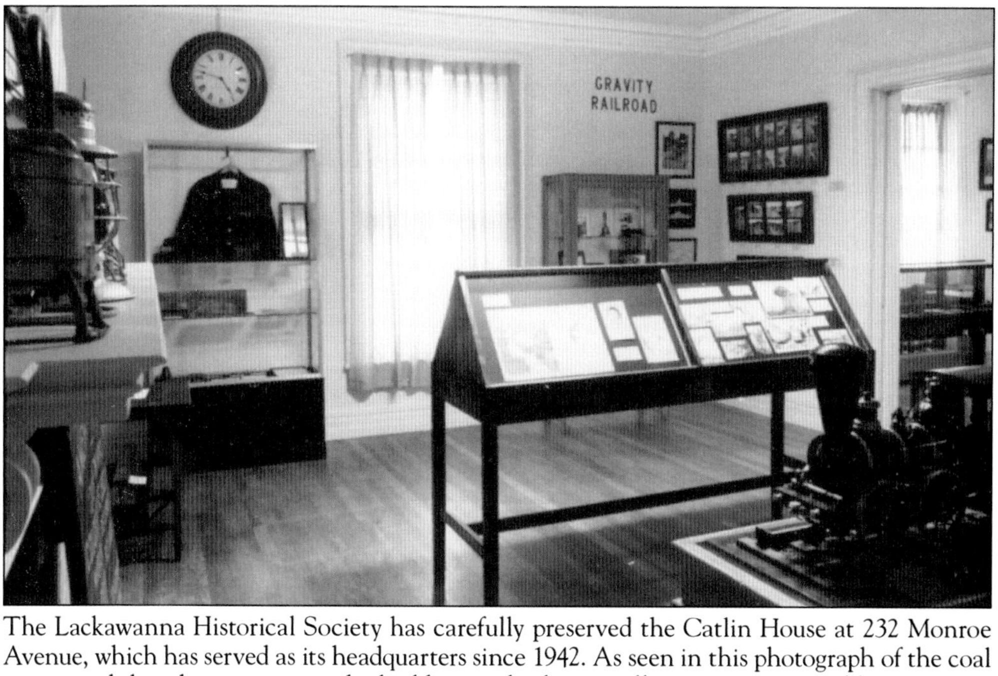

The Lackawanna Historical Society has carefully preserved the Catlin House at 232 Monroe Avenue, which has served as its headquarters since 1942. As seen in this photograph of the coal mining exhibit, the society uses the building to display its collections, present public programs, and house a local history research center.

The Lackawanna Historical Society has preserved the first floor of the Catlin House to look much like it did when George H. and Helen Walsh Catlin resided in the home. The parlor, pictured here during the holiday season, displays historical furnishings, including items that previously belonged to the Catlin and Archbald families.

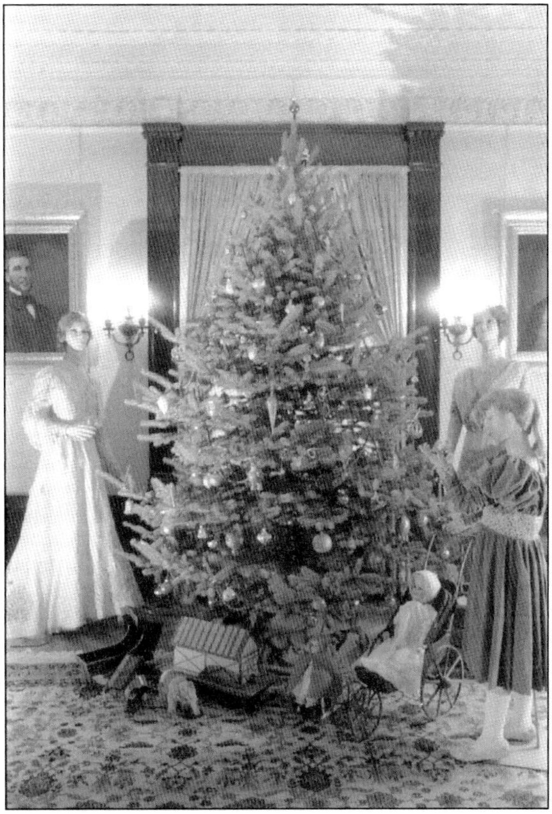

The fashion display on the second floor of the Catlin House is one of the Lackawanna Historical Society's most popular exhibits. Over the years, vintage wedding dresses, hats, and even women's lingerie have been featured. Many of these pieces were donated by the descendants of Hill Section residents.

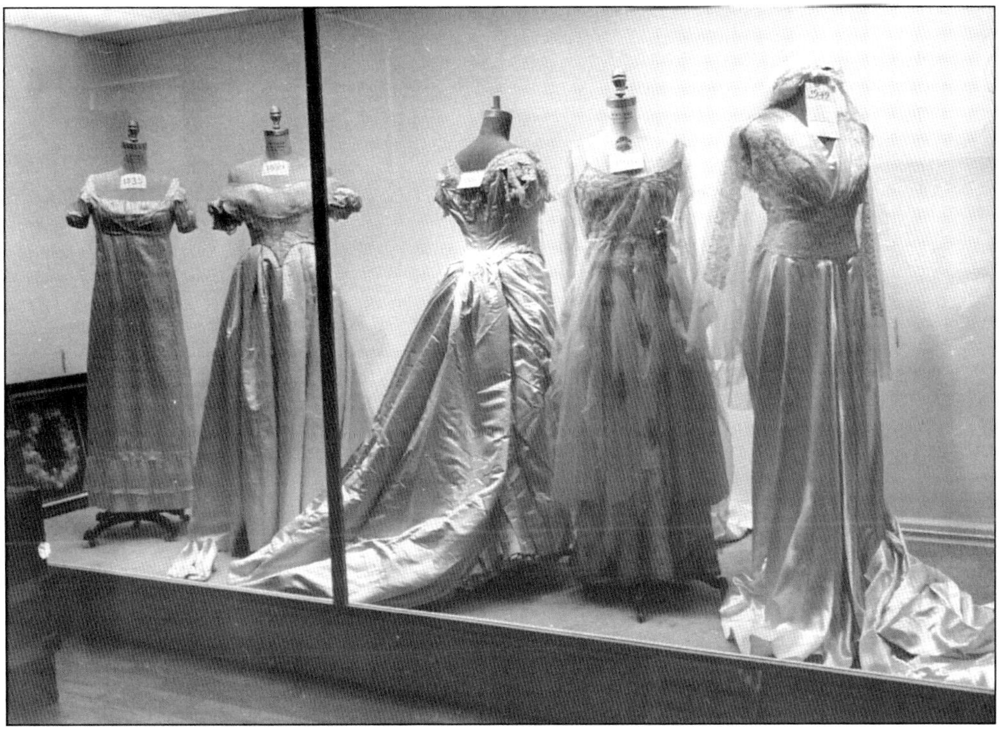

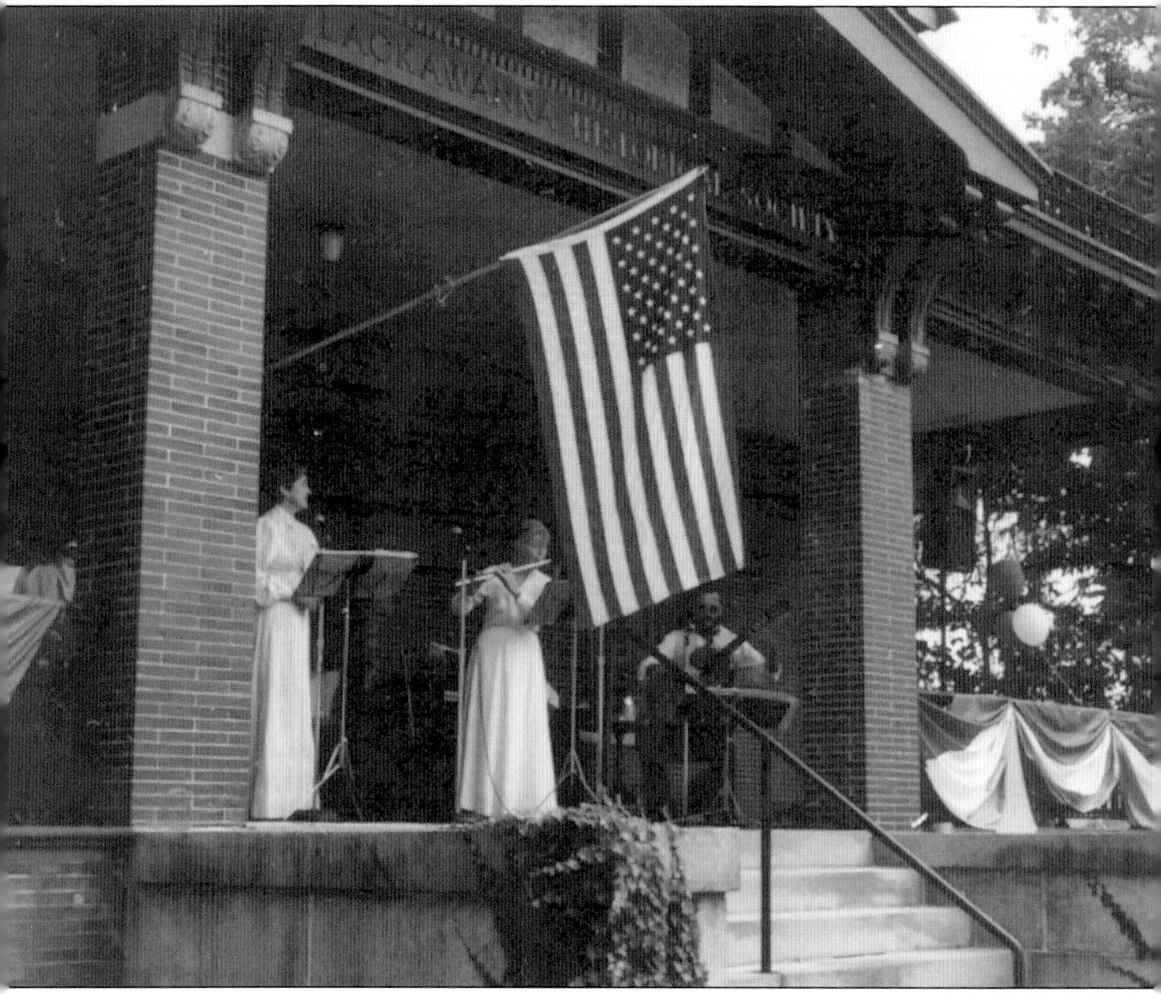

The Lackawanna Historical Society has supported numerous community activities, including Civil War reenactments and educational programs. In recent years, the society has sponsored the Historic Hill House Tour, which is a biannual event that provides tours of many of the Hill Section's historic residences.

Four

Commercial Enterprises

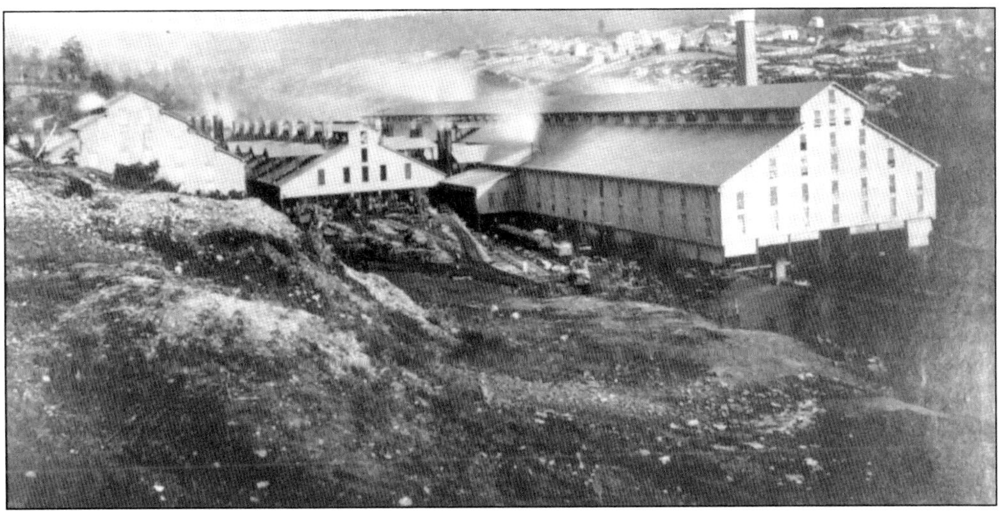

The Lackawanna Iron and Coal Company, Scranton's first major business, can trace its origins to the company founded in Slocum's Hollow, Pennsylvania, in 1840. Its founding members were William Henry, his son-in-law Selden T. Scranton, Selden's brother George Scranton, and Sanford Grant, all of Belvidere, New Jersey. The men had taken an interest in the area due to the plentiful anthracite coal and iron ore deposits.

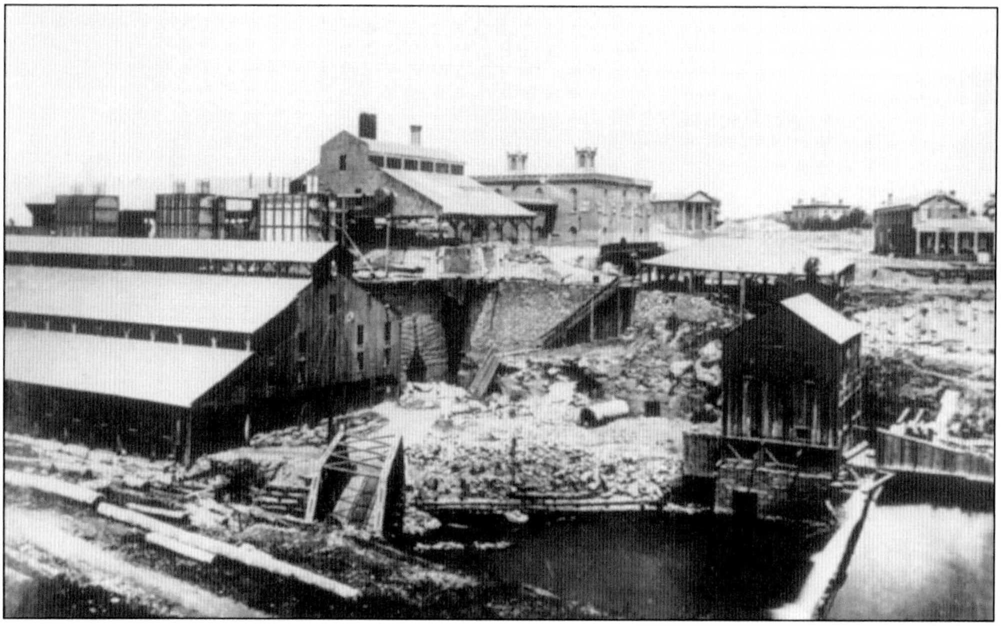

The main Lackawanna Iron and Coal Company blast furnaces seen here were located along the Roaring Brook, near the original center of Slocum's Hollow between Scranton's downtown, South Side, and Hill Section. Joseph H. Scranton solidified his family's control over the company that won its first major contract building T-rails for the Erie Railroad in 1847.

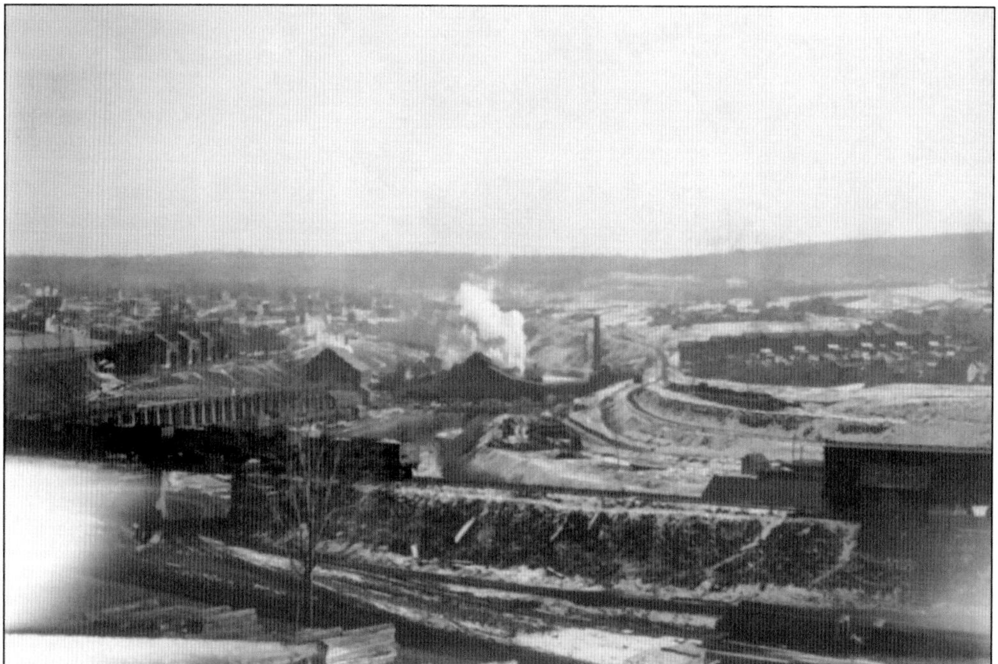

This image shows early development around the Lackawanna Iron and Coal Company's industrial facilities. The company originally owned 503 acres surrounding their facilities, and it subdivided the land for company housing known as Shanty Hill, visible on the left side of the image, and what became the Hill Section for more elite developments, seen on the right side of the image.

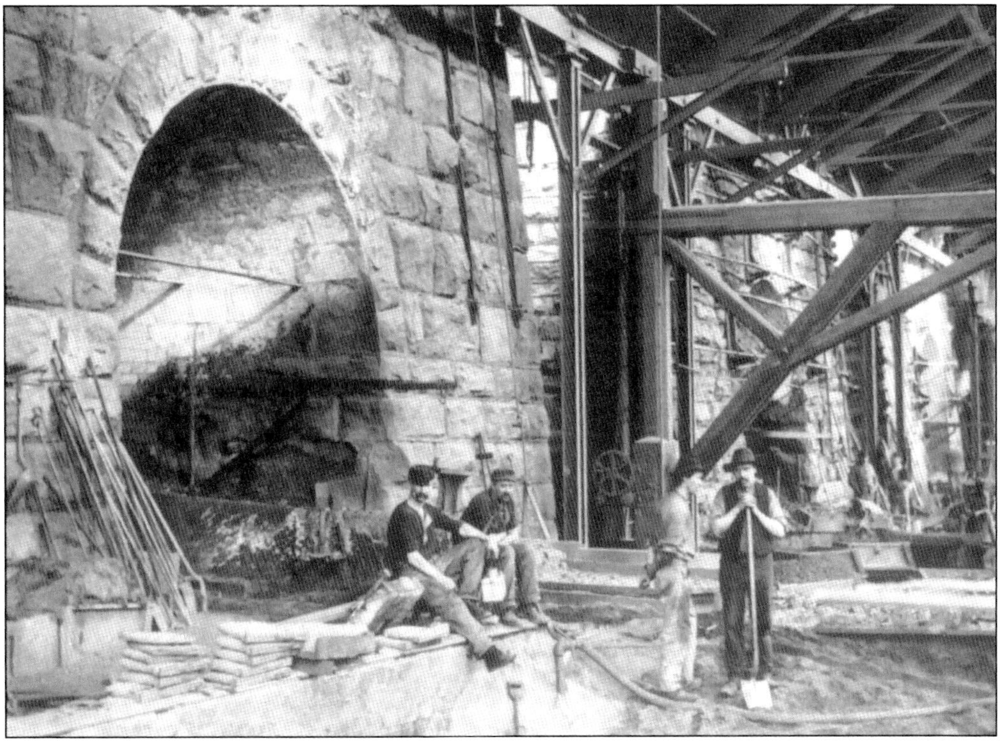

The Lackawanna Iron and Coal Company's blast furnaces heavily relied on a large labor force and hot-burning anthracite coal. European immigrants, mostly from Ireland, flocked to Scranton to meet the voracious labor demands of Lackawanna Iron and Coal and area anthracite mines.

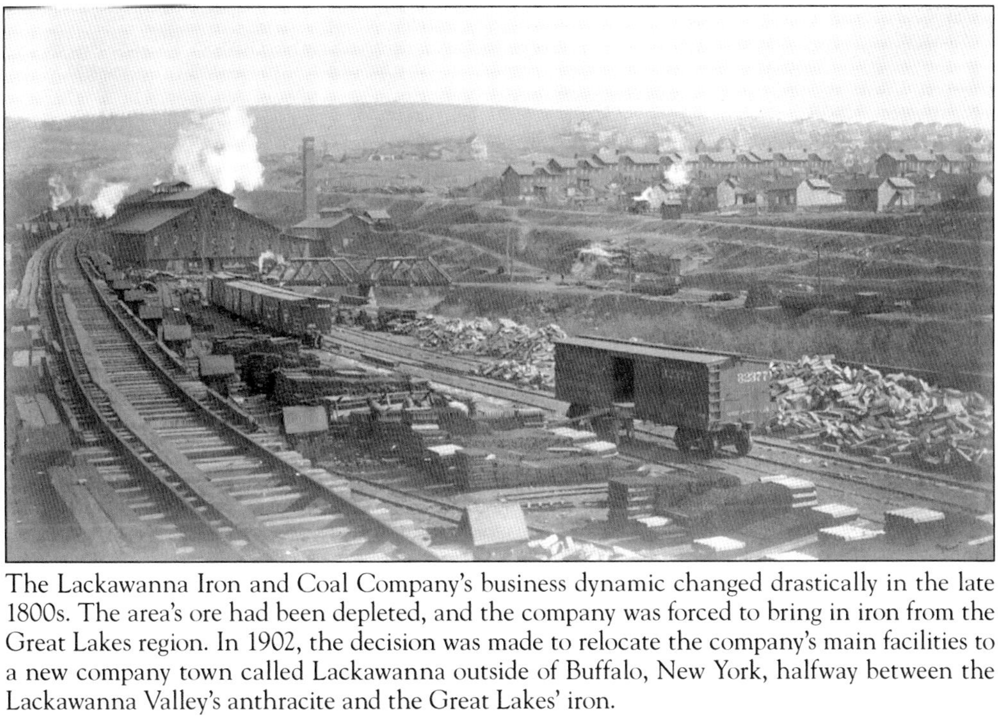

The Lackawanna Iron and Coal Company's business dynamic changed drastically in the late 1800s. The area's ore had been depleted, and the company was forced to bring in iron from the Great Lakes region. In 1902, the decision was made to relocate the company's main facilities to a new company town called Lackawanna outside of Buffalo, New York, halfway between the Lackawanna Valley's anthracite and the Great Lakes' iron.

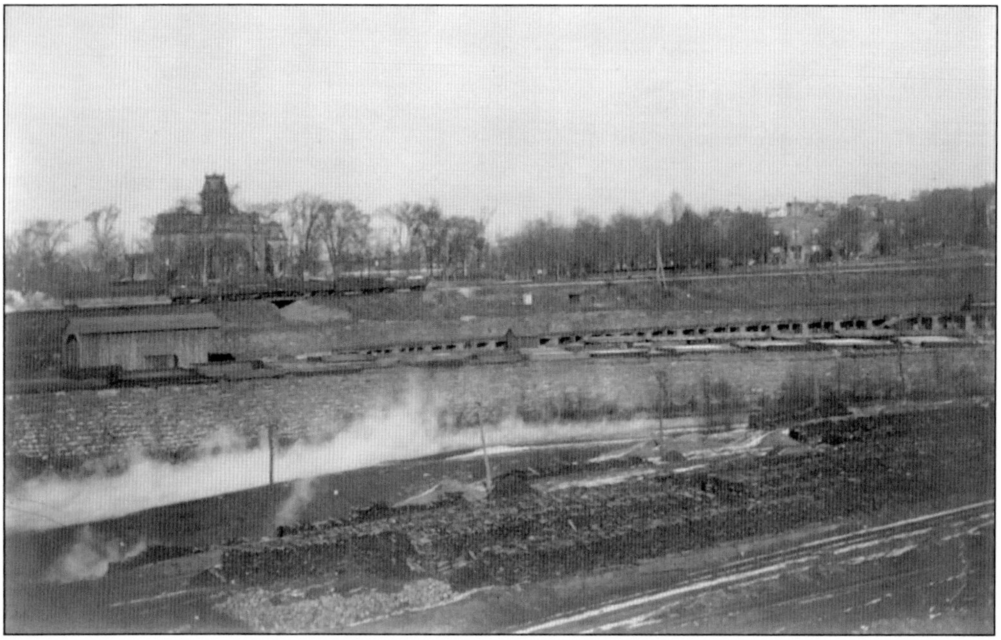

Visible here are parts of the Lackawanna Iron and Coal Company, the DL&W Railroad, and the Scranton and Archbald estates. The Scranton and Archbald families were highly involved in many of the efforts to construct the DL&W Railroad, which extended from Hoboken, New Jersey, to Buffalo, New York.

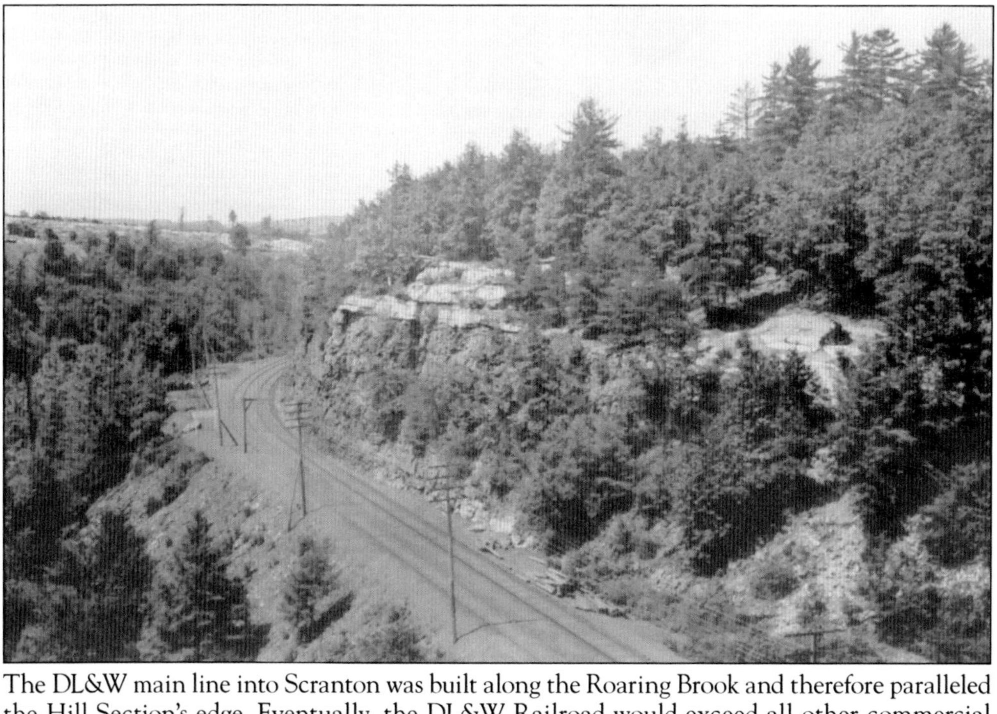

The DL&W main line into Scranton was built along the Roaring Brook and therefore paralleled the Hill Section's edge. Eventually, the DL&W Railroad would exceed all other commercial enterprises, including Lackawanna Iron and Coal, in importance and become the area's largest coal operator and employer.

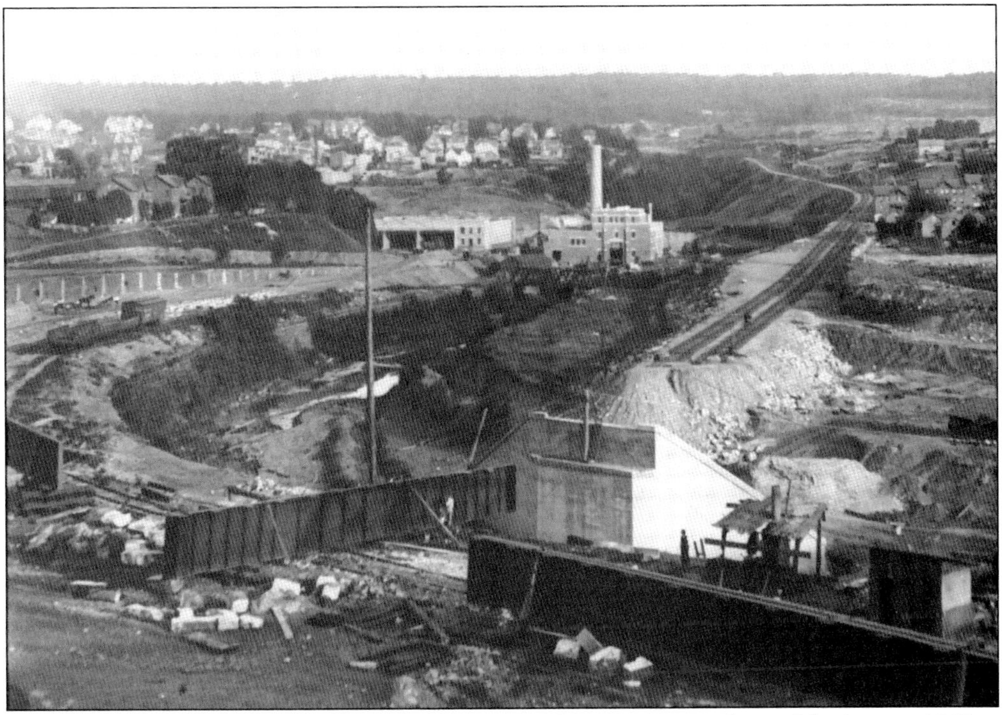

After the Lackawanna Iron and Coal Company closed its Scranton industrial facilities in 1902, it sold them to the Lackawanna & Wyoming Valley Railroad, or Laurel Line, an interurban electric railway that operated between the Lackawanna and Wyoming Valleys. The railroad company demolished most of the old blast furnaces and built its own new facilities.

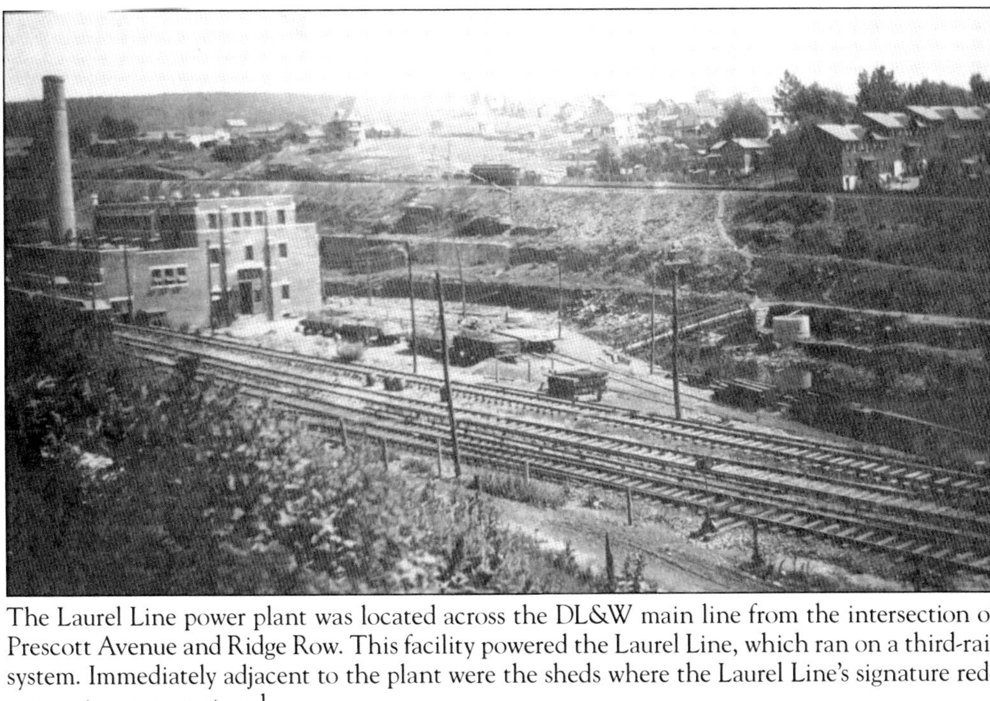

The Laurel Line power plant was located across the DL&W main line from the intersection of Prescott Avenue and Ridge Row. This facility powered the Laurel Line, which ran on a third-rail system. Immediately adjacent to the plant were the sheds where the Laurel Line's signature red-orange trams were stored.

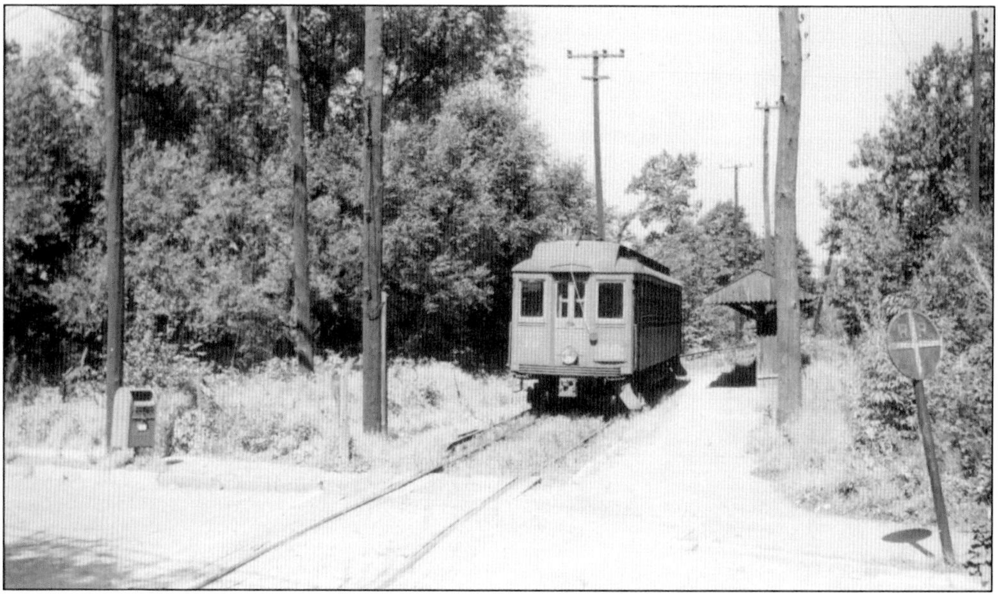

The Nay Aug Park station of the Laurel Line's Dunmore branch was located across the Roaring Brook from the main portion of the park along Elmhurst Boulevard, near the DL&W main line. The Laurel Line closed in 1952, and very little of this station remains.

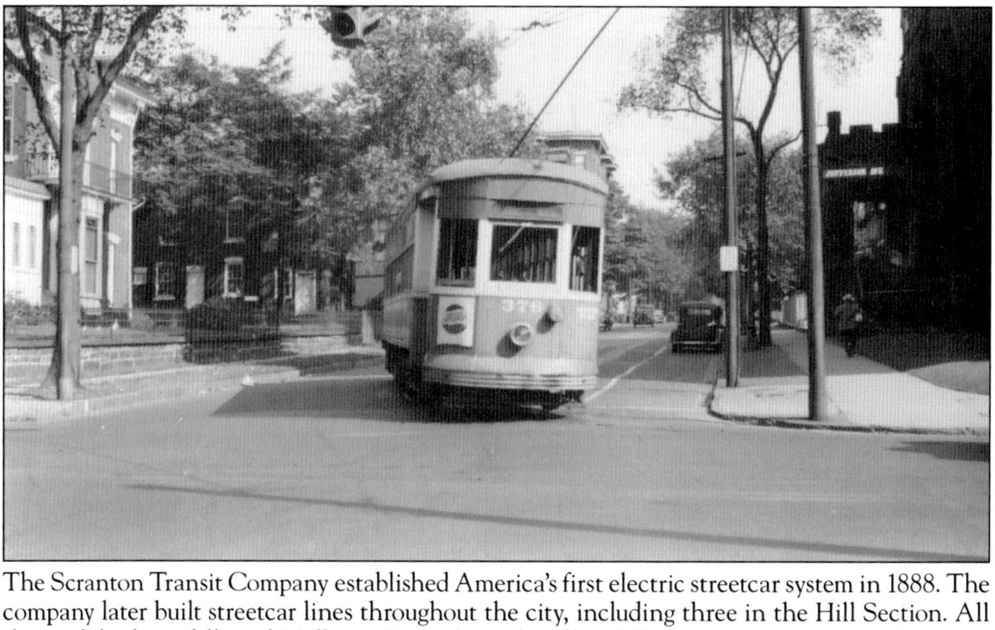

The Scranton Transit Company established America's first electric streetcar system in 1888. The company later built streetcar lines throughout the city, including three in the Hill Section. All three of the lines followed Mulberry Street but split off at different points. The Petersburg line split off at Prescott Avenue, the Nay Aug line split off at Arthur Avenue, and the Laurel Hill line split off at Adams Avenue.

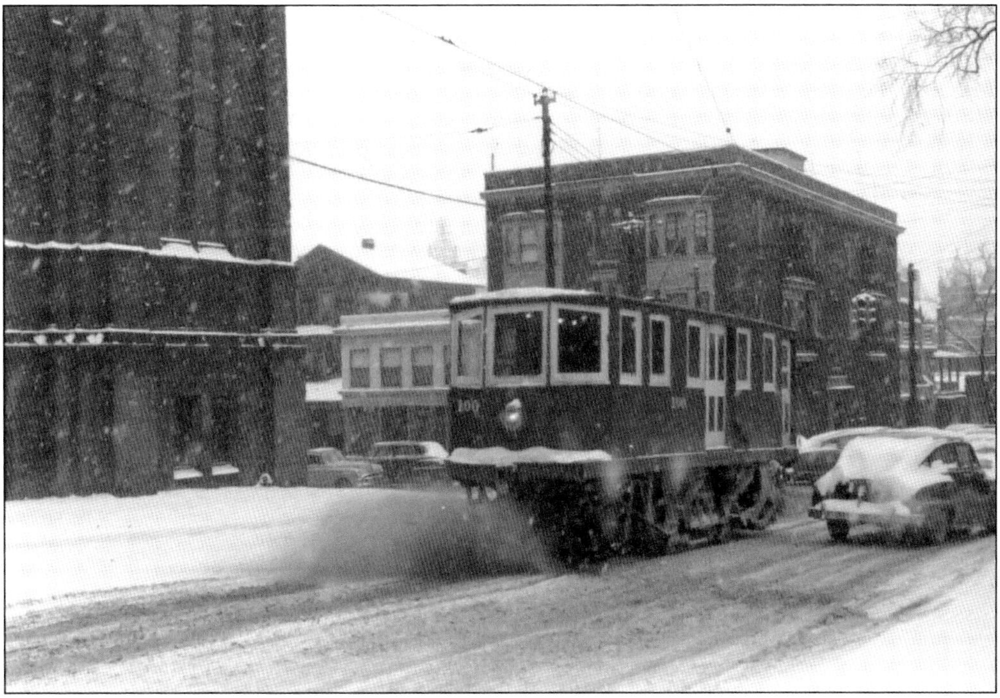

Here, a Scranton Transit Company maintenance tram is removing snow from the streetcar lines on Mulberry Street, near the corner of Jefferson Avenue, during the 1930s. The Scranton Transit Company went to great lengths to make sure that northeastern Pennsylvania's notorious winter weather did not stop trolley service on the most important Hill Section artery.

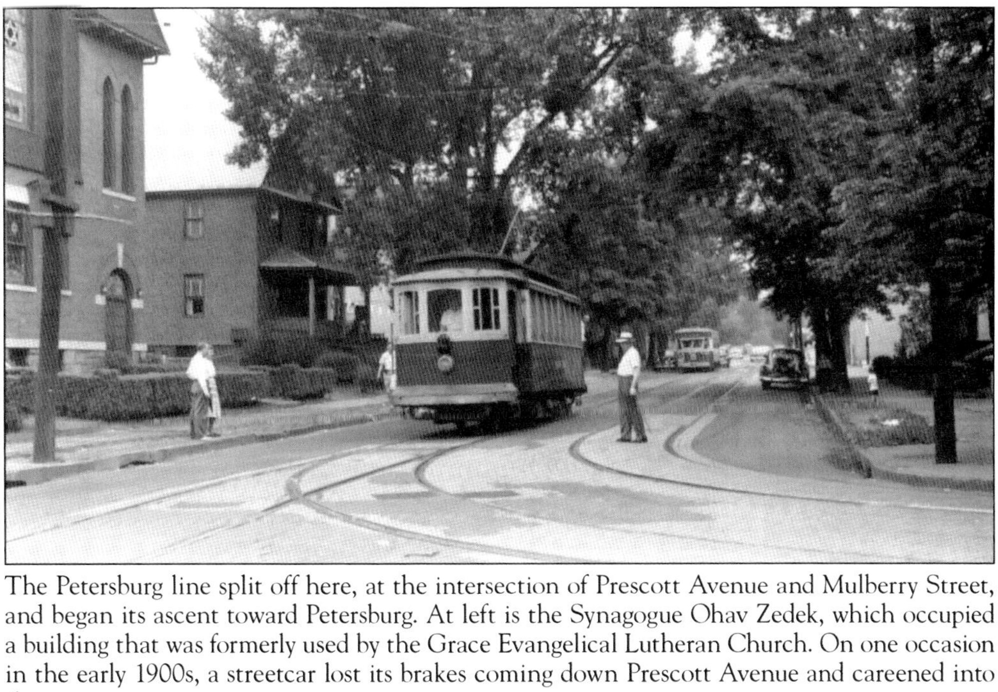

The Petersburg line split off here, at the intersection of Prescott Avenue and Mulberry Street, and began its ascent toward Petersburg. At left is the Synagogue Ohav Zedek, which occupied a building that was formerly used by the Grace Evangelical Lutheran Church. On one occasion in the early 1900s, a streetcar lost its brakes coming down Prescott Avenue and careened into the synagogue.

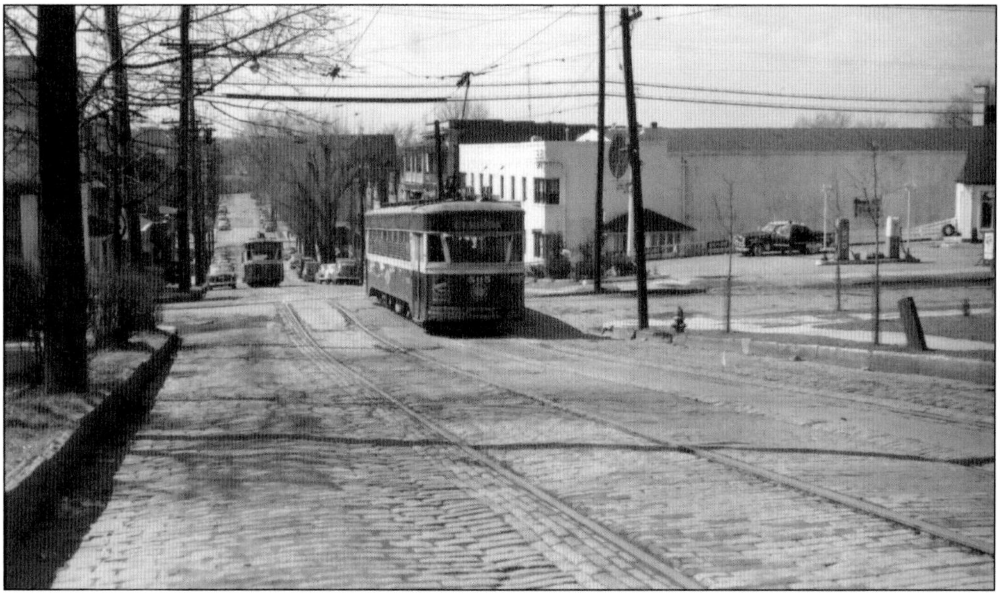

Pictured here is a streetcar traveling along the Petersburg line in the 400 block of Prescott Avenue in the mid-20th century. Visible at right of the trolley is Ebersole's Gulf Gas Station and Garage, as well as the Prescott Theater. Ebersole's Gas Station still operates, and the Prescott Theater still stands, repurposed as the Prescott Bingo Club.

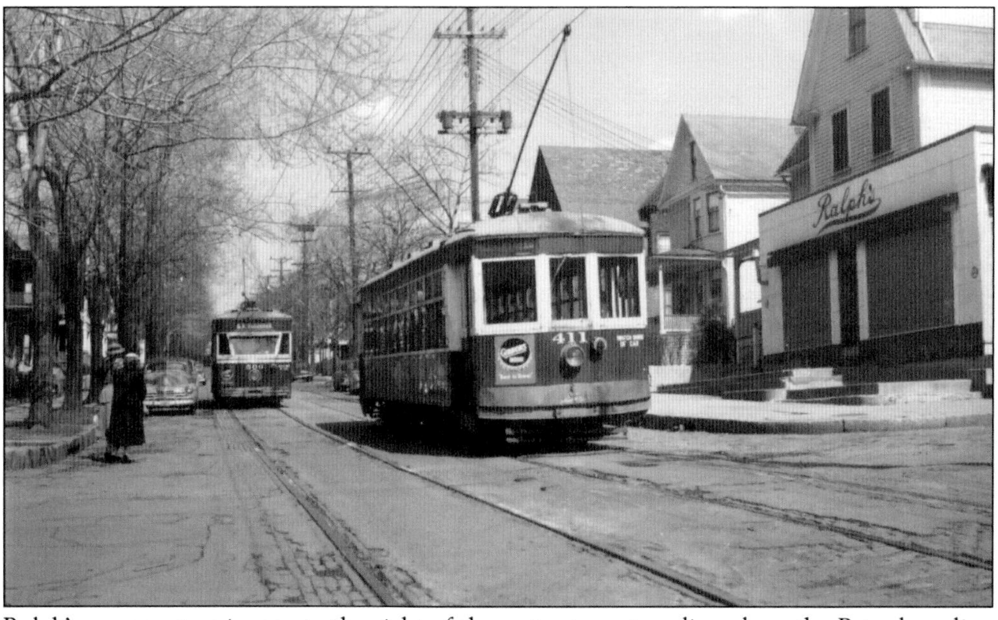

Ralph's grocery store is seen to the right of these streetcars traveling along the Petersburg line in the 600 block of Prescott Avenue. Ralph's later moved from this location at the corner of Prescott Avenue and Olive Street to a new, larger store at the corner of Prescott Avenue and Pine Street.

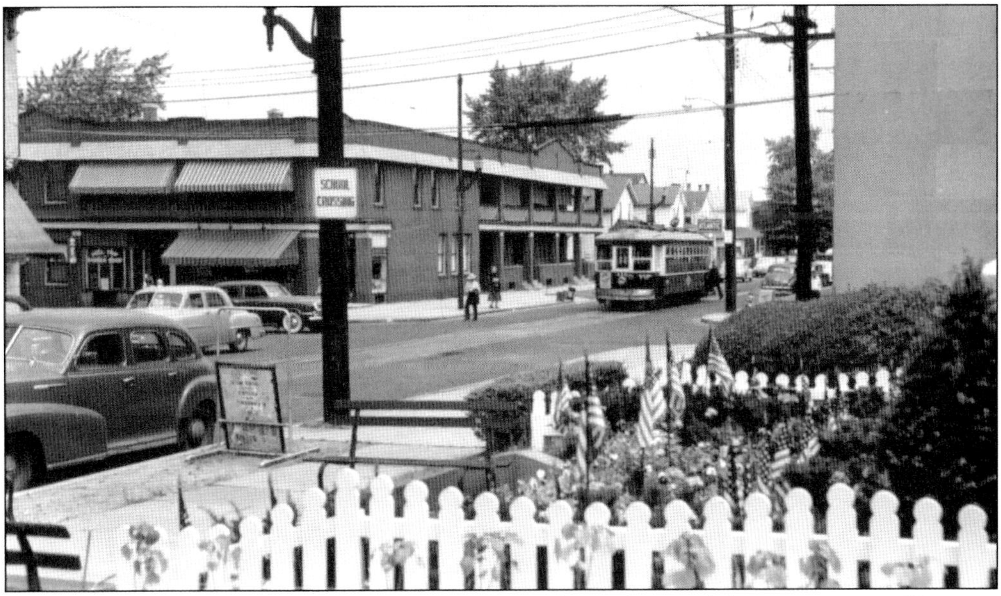

This streetcar is passing through Petersburg Corners, located around the intersection of Prescott Avenue and Ash Street. The East Scranton State Bank, which is now a branch of Peoples Security Bank, is visible on the right. On the left are the buildings that at one time housed historic Petersburg businesses like the Knoephel Family's Drug Store.

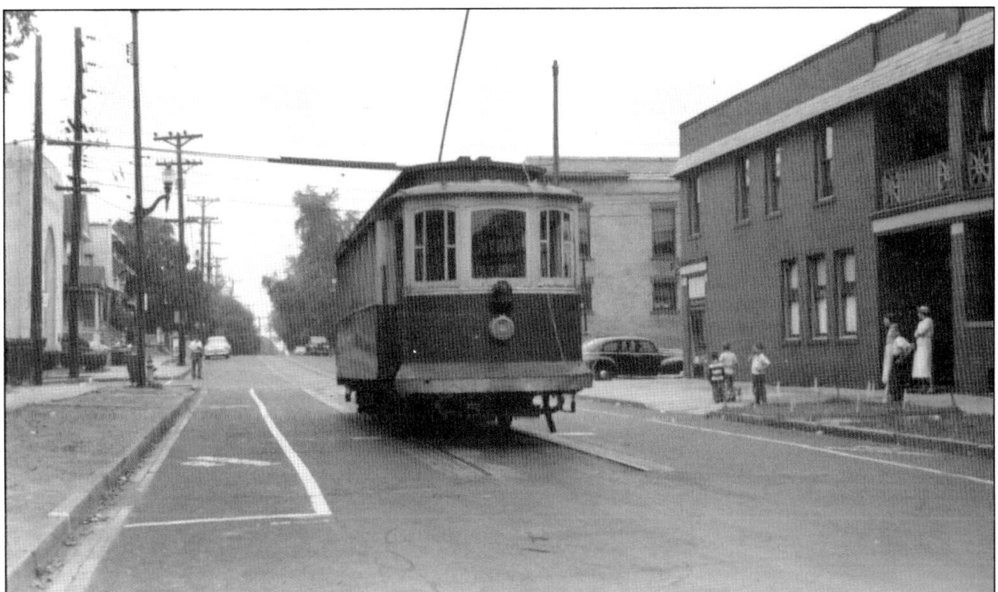

This streetcar is arriving at the end of the Petersburg line, near the present location of the Naturally Yours store. At right is what used to be the Schulties Floral building, now the location of Bar Hill. Also on the right, just past the intersection, is the former site of the Schultz Brothers General Store, where Mansour's Market is located today.

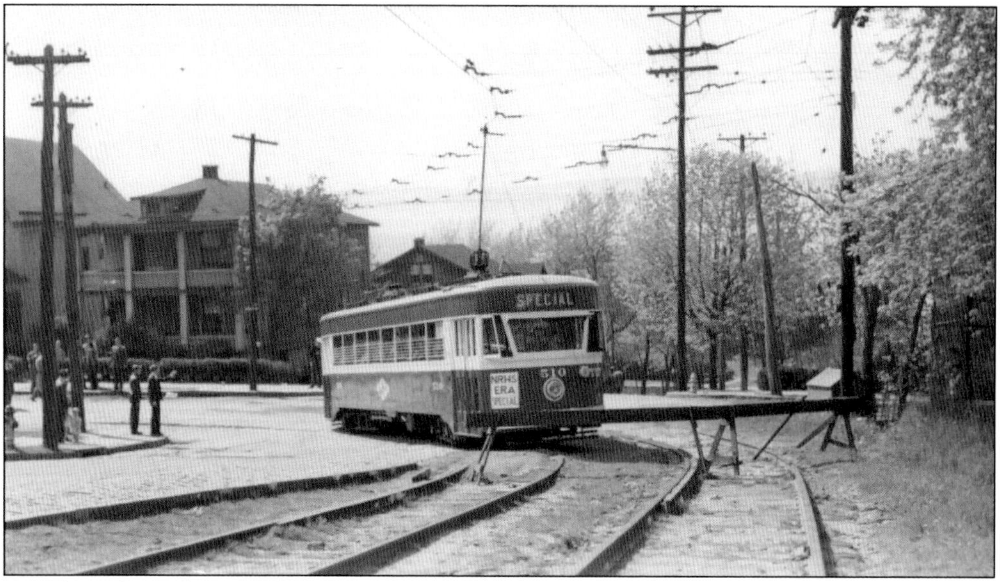

Traveling along the Laurel Hill line, this streetcar pauses at the corner of Quincy Avenue and Poplar Street. The Laurel Hill line followed Madison Avenue across the lower Hill Section before cutting up to Quincy Avenue at Pine Street. At Poplar Street, the double-track line cut diagonally across undeveloped land to where it met Blakely Street, which it followed into the Laurel Hill section of Dunmore.

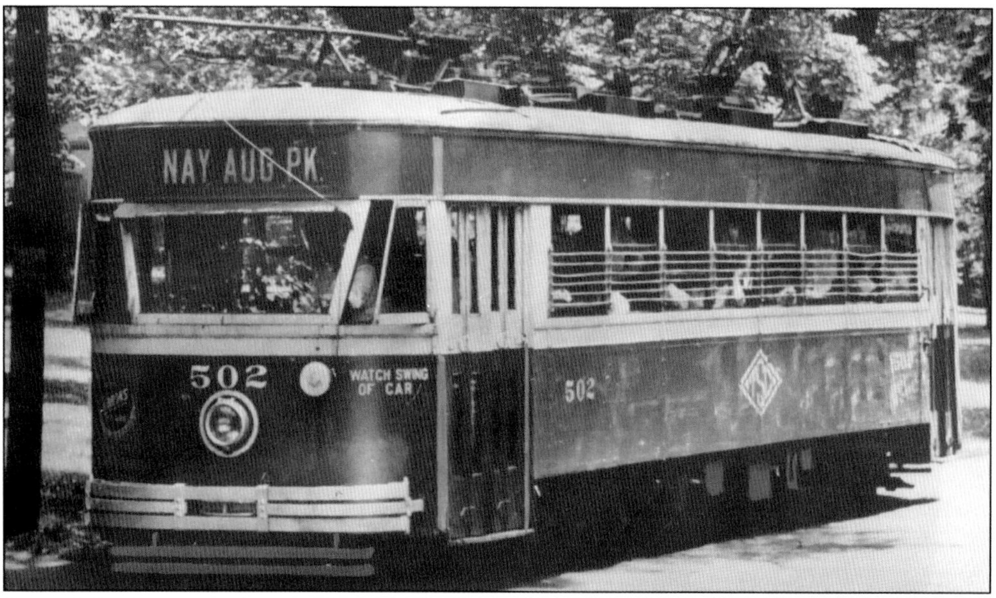

One of the Scranton Transit Company's blue streetcars is pictured on the Nay Aug line. In the postwar years, shifting economics slowly forced the closure of all the company's lines. The Petersburg and Nay Aug lines were among the last to close in the early 1950s.

This image captures an aerial view of parts of Little England and Bunker Hill. Visible in the center is the DL&W main line and the Petersburg Silk Mill. In 1898, the Petersburg Silk Mill was founded near the corner of James Avenue and Myrtle Street in Bunker Hill, and the factory employed over 300 people. The company has since closed, but its structure has been repurposed as offices and loft apartments.

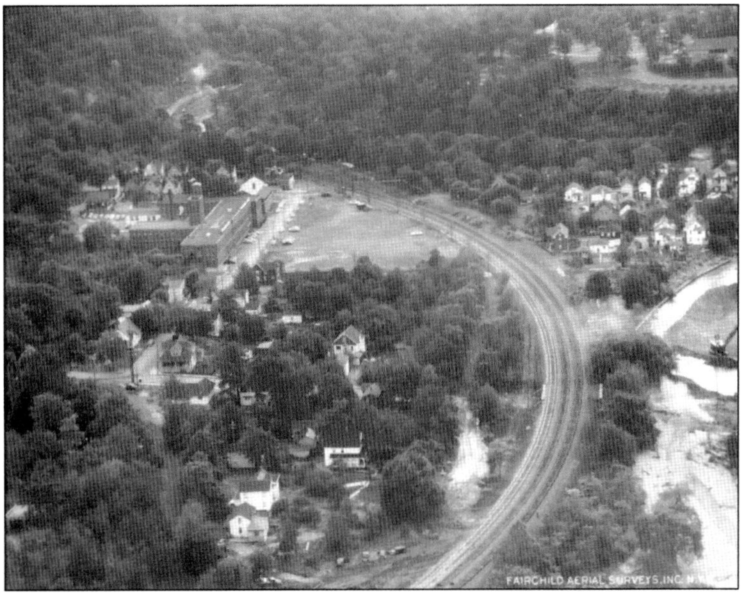

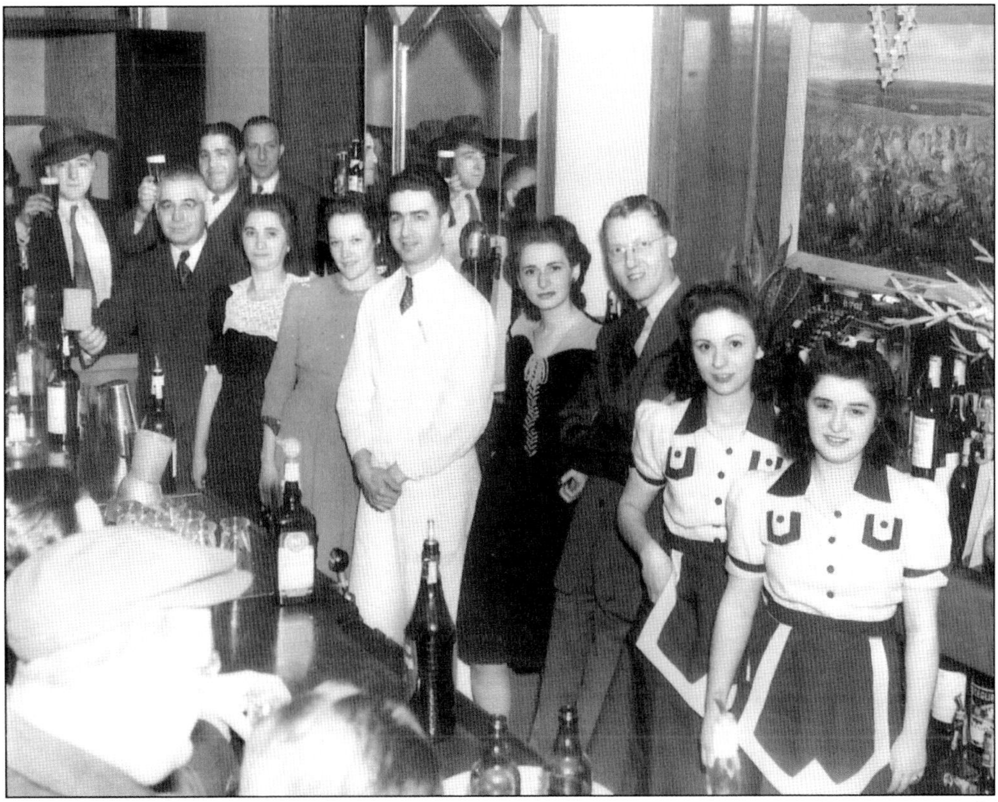

Pictured here are members of the Savino family at their family restaurant on Ash Street in Little England. At one time, Little England and Bunker Hill had one of the most vibrant Italian communities in the area. Guy and Emily Savino (second and third from left in the first row) owned and operated Savino's Restaurant for many years and raised their eight children in the apartment above it. Russell's Restaurant now occupies Savino's former location. (Courtesy of Emily Savino Perry.)

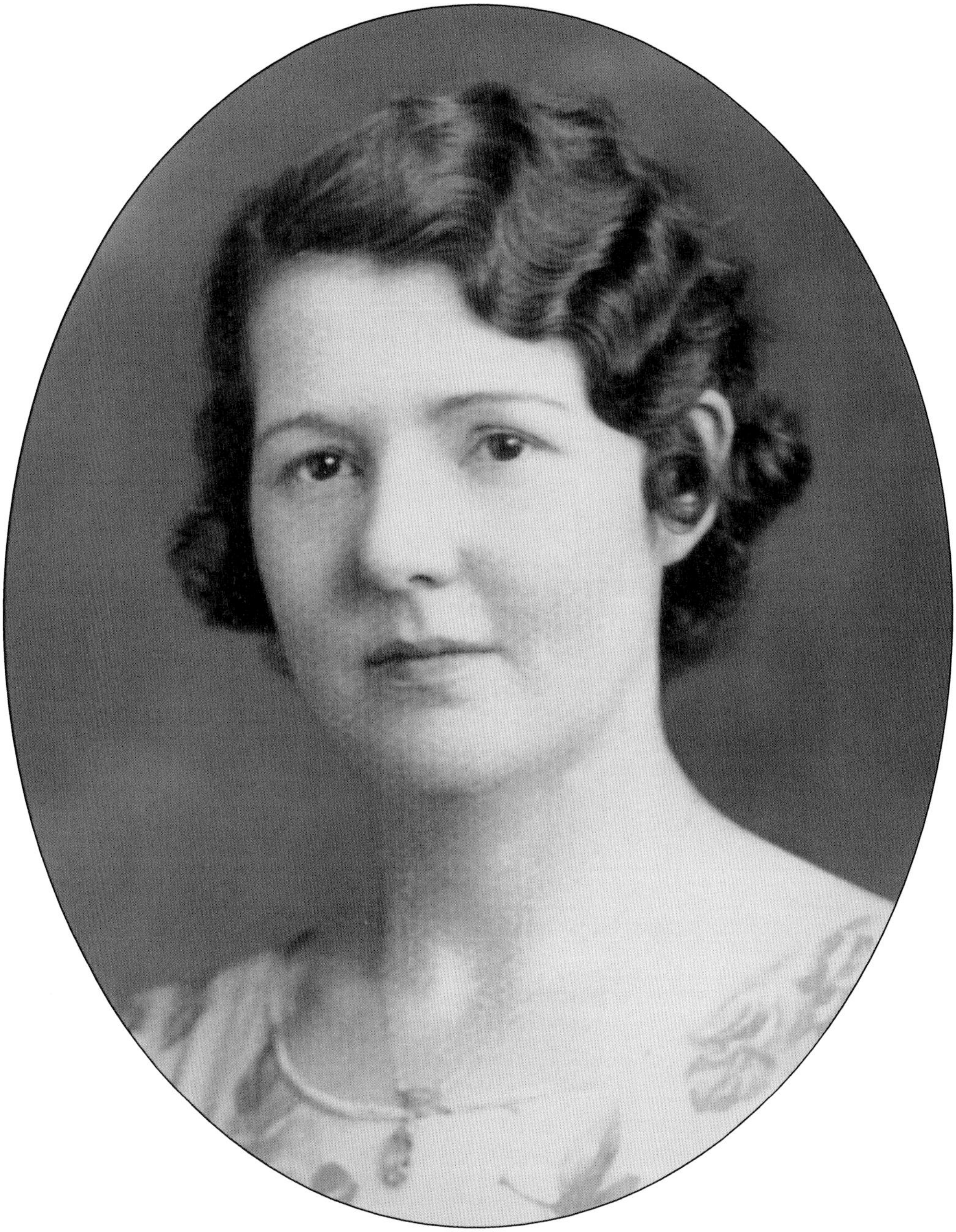

The story of Gertrude Hawk is one of a true American entrepreneur. Gertrude Jones Hawk was born to Gomer and Ellen Jones in Dunmore, Pennsylvania, in 1903. Gomer died when Gertrude was very young, and Ellen suffered from a severe heart ailment. As a result, Gertrude was forced to earn a living at the age of 12. She worked in a candy store, where she was taught the art of chocolate making. In 1922, she married Elmer G. Hawk, and the couple settled on Mark Avenue in Bunker Hill, where they raised their two sons. In 1936, during the height of the Great Depression, Gertrude Hawk used her chocolate-making skills to once again help support her family, and she eventually developed a profitable cottage industry. Gertrude's son Elmer R. Hawk greatly expanded the business, which has always remained committed to its community. (Courtesy of Gertrude Hawk Chocolates.)

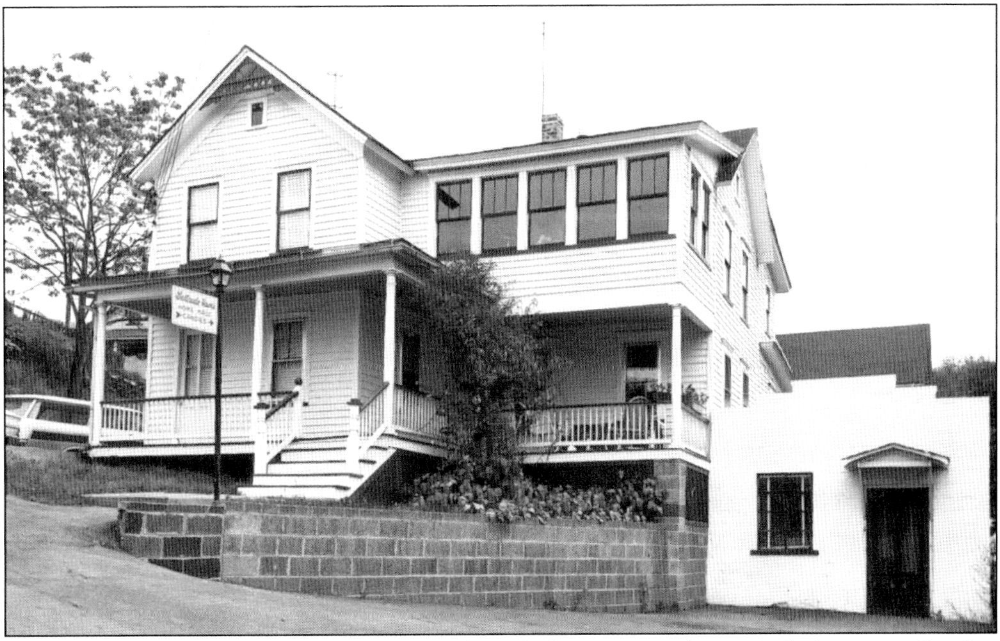

Shown here is the original home of Gertrude and Elmer G. Hawk on Mark Avenue in Bunker Hill. It was at this home in 1936 that Gertrude starting making and selling her famous chocolates. After Elmer R. Hawk returned from World War II, he used his military compensation to invest $3,500 in his mother's fledgling candy business. (Courtesy of Gertrude Hawk Chocolates.)

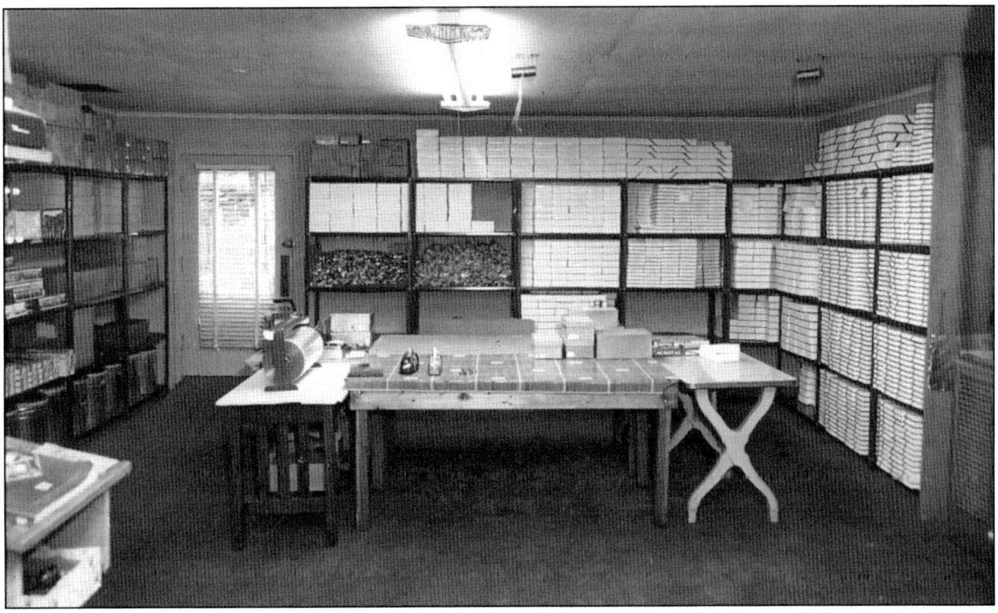

Over the years, Elmer R. Hawk expanded his mother's business far beyond Bunker Hill. But the company never forgot its humble beginnings and has always maintained a long tradition of providing chocolates for local fundraising efforts, which began with an alliance between Gertrude Hawk and the Petersburg Presbyterian Church. Gertrude Hawk Chocolates is still a family-owned business, and its headquarters are located in Dunmore, Pennsylvania. (Courtesy of Gertrude Hawk Chocolates.)

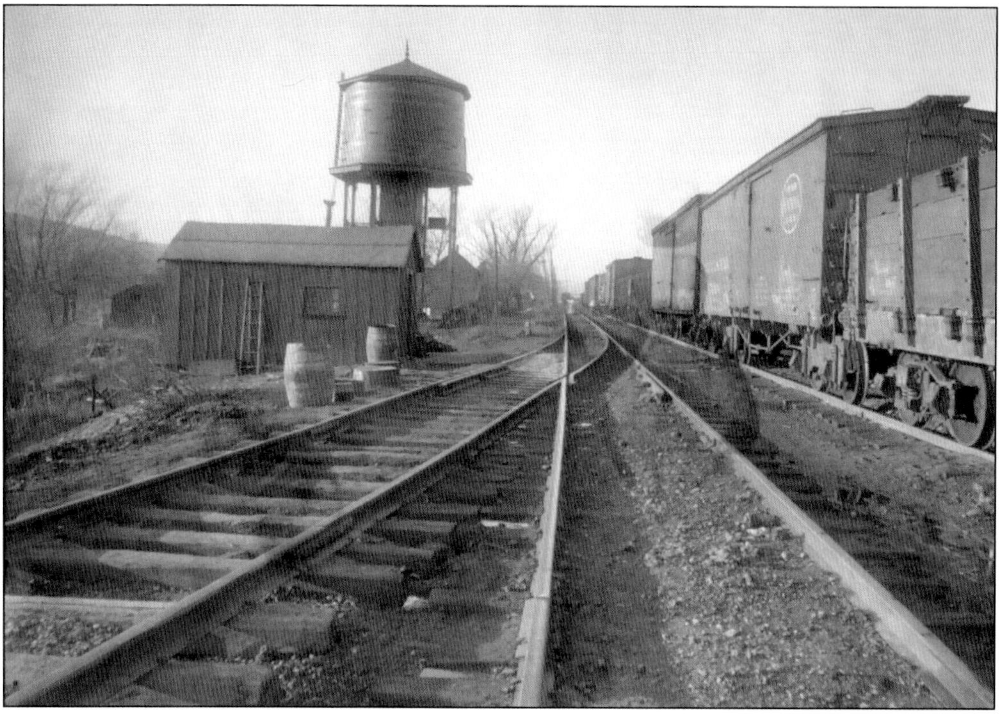

Pictured here is the junction of the Erie Railroad's Wyoming Division and Scranton spur near Matthew Avenue in Bunker Hill. The Wyoming Division paralleled the DL&W Railroad in several spots, including through Bunker Hill, where its spur split off into Scranton's downtown. This spur circled the Hill Section, weaving its way through Dunmore and Green Ridge, then along the edge of the lower Hill Section.

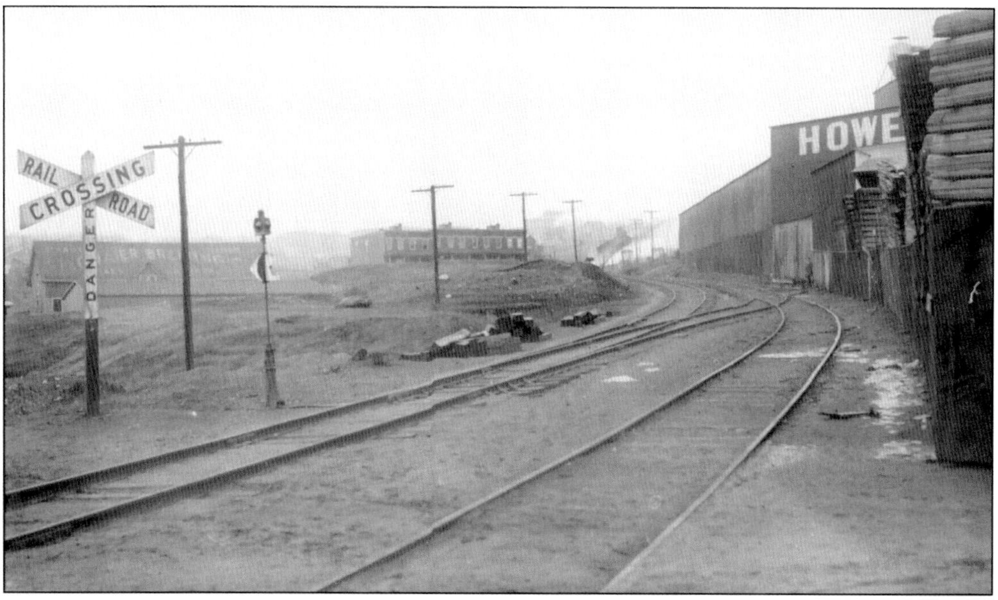

In this image of the Erie Railroad crossing at the intersection of Adams Avenue and Ash Street, the facilities of Hower & Stender Lumber and the Helious Manufacturing Company are visible on the right, and on the left are those of a Stegmaier Brewery.

The Stegmaier Brewery Company of Wilkes-Barre, Pennsylvania, was founded in 1857 by Charles Stegmaier but was later acquired by the Smulowitz family. Stegmaier brewed a wide variety of products at several locations. At one time, Stegmaier manufactured its popular Gibbon's Beer at its Ash Street facility in the Hill Section.

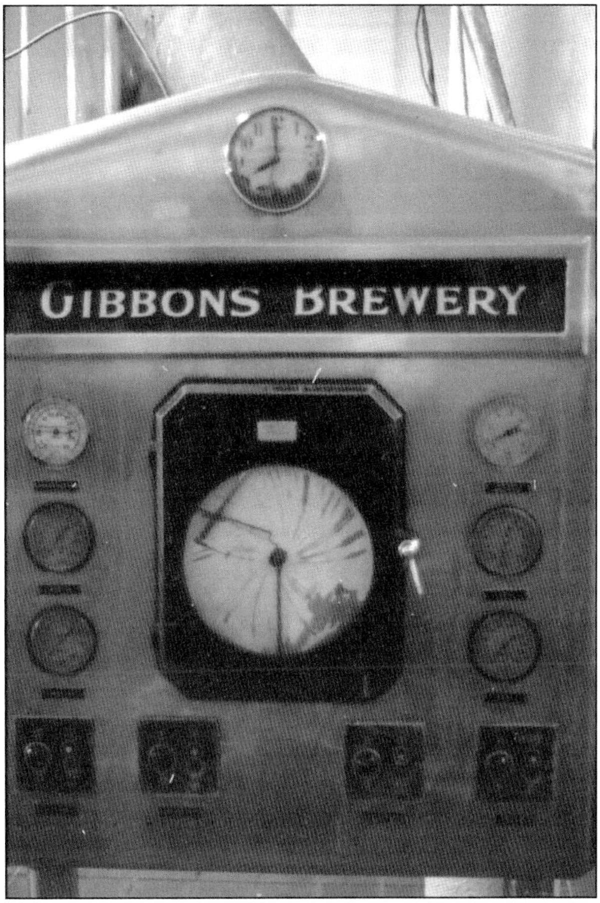

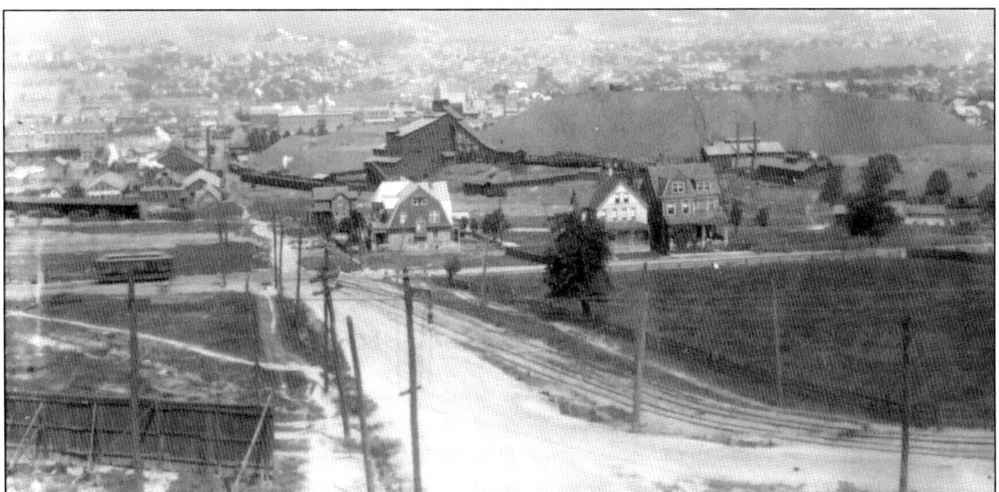

This image taken near the intersection of Clay Avenue and Poplar Street shows the Johnson Coal Breaker. The Hill Section was the only neighborhood in Scranton that did not have large-scale mining operations, but this breaker off Washington Avenue in Green Ridge was located right on its edge. Visible on the left is a streetcar on the Laurel Hill line.

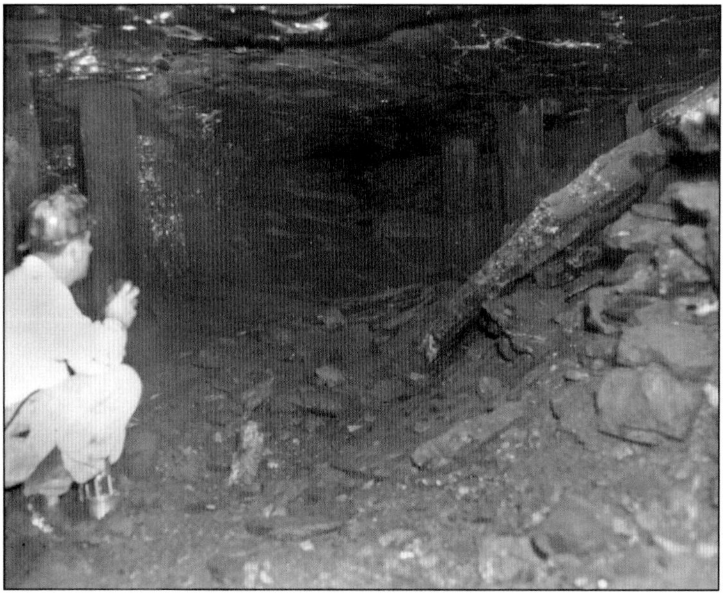

This coal mine lies beneath the current location of the University of Scranton's St. Thomas Hall. Unlike the rest of Scranton, very few coal mines existed in the Hill Section, mainly because the neighborhood's influential residents did not wish to undermine the foundations of their stately mansions. Nonetheless, a few mines did exist, including the one seen here. (Courtesy of the University of Scranton.)

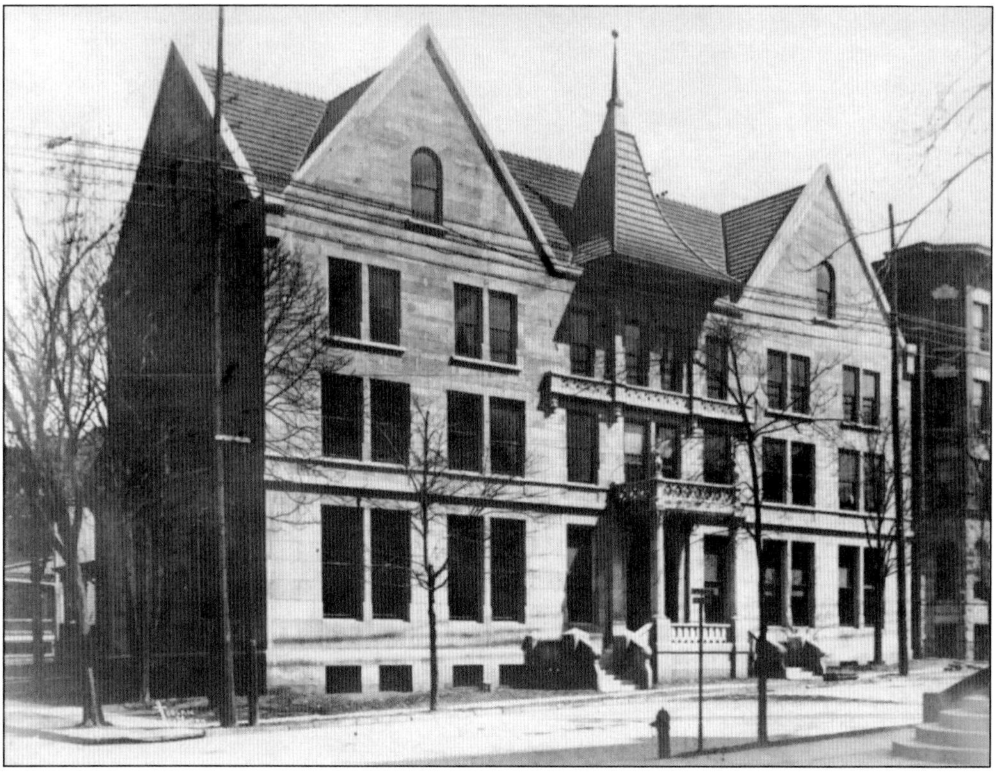

The Bowman Building, which housed the offices of the Pennsylvania Casualty and Coal Lands Securities Company, was originally located at the corner of Jefferson Avenue and Linden Street. In order to make way for a new structure in the 1920s, the entire building was moved in one piece to a new location at the corner of Madison Avenue and Linden Street. It was demolished in the 1970s, and a parking lot for Elm Park Methodist Church now occupies the site. (Courtesy of Jack Hiddlestone.)

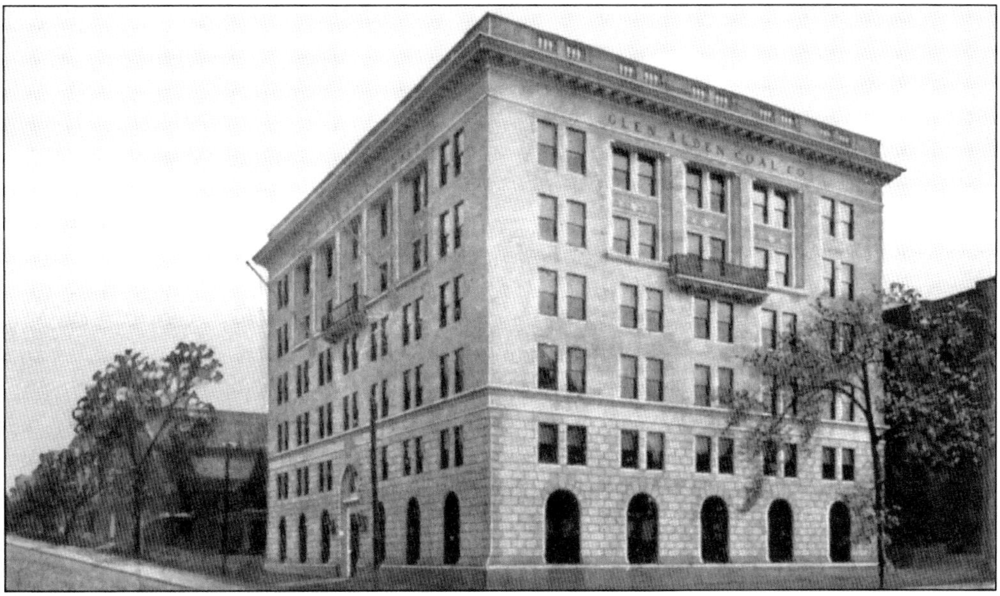

The Glen Alden Coal Company, which was formed as the result of an antitrust case that forced the DL&W Railroad to spin off its coal mining operations, erected this building at the corner of Jefferson Avenue and Linden Street in 1920. After the Glen Alden Coal Company was purchased by the Moffat Coal Company in the 1940s, the University of Scranton acquired the structure and renamed it O'Hara Hall. (Courtesy of Jack Hiddlestone.)

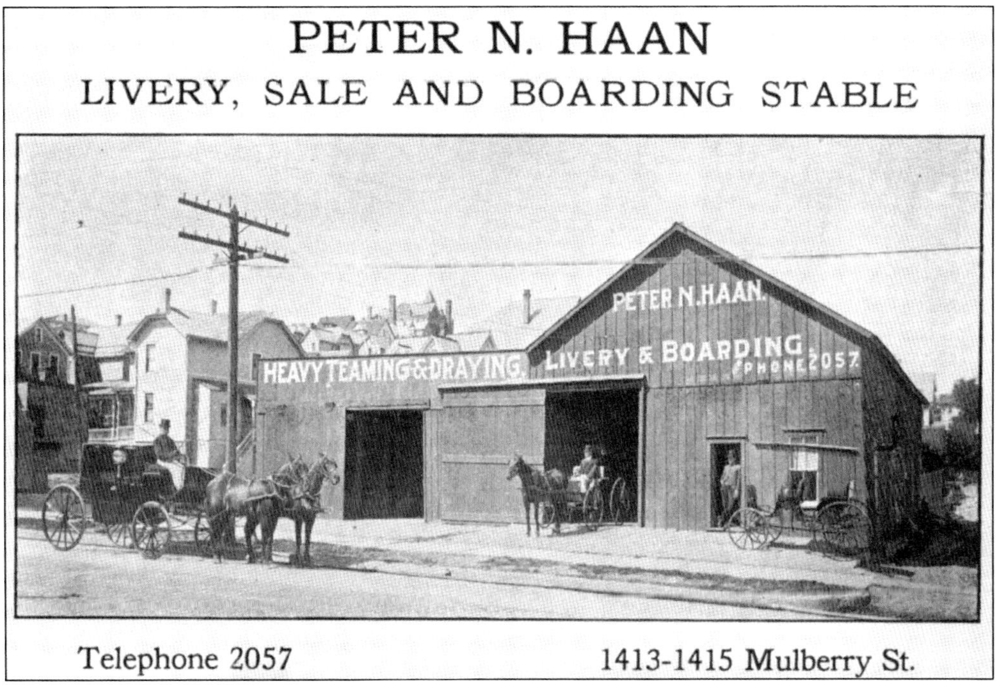

Peter N. Haan operated the draying, livery, and boarding stable business at 1413–1415 Mulberry Street. Before the advent of automobiles, services related to horses were very profitable. The building seen at the top of the hill was the Bayard Taylor School, which was located at the highest point in the city of Scranton. (Courtesy of Jack Hiddlestone.)

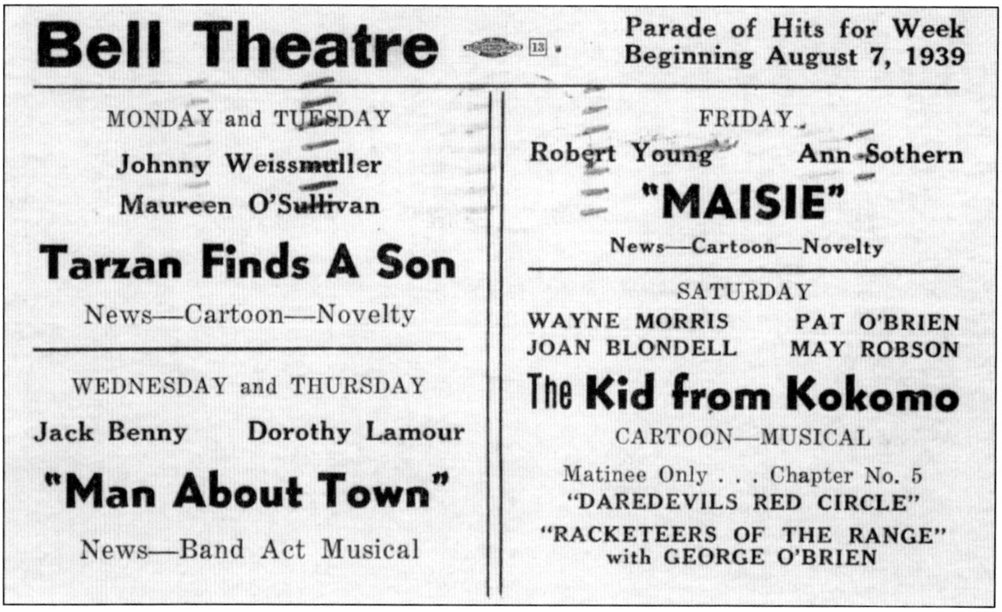

This is an advertisement for the Hill Section's Bell Theatre from the summer of 1939. The Bell Theatre at 817 Prescott Avenue operated from 1916 to 1955 and was a noted neighborhood attraction. The theater's Saturday matinees were particularly popular. The Bell Theatre has since been demolished and replaced by an apartment building. (Courtesy of Jack Hiddlestone.)

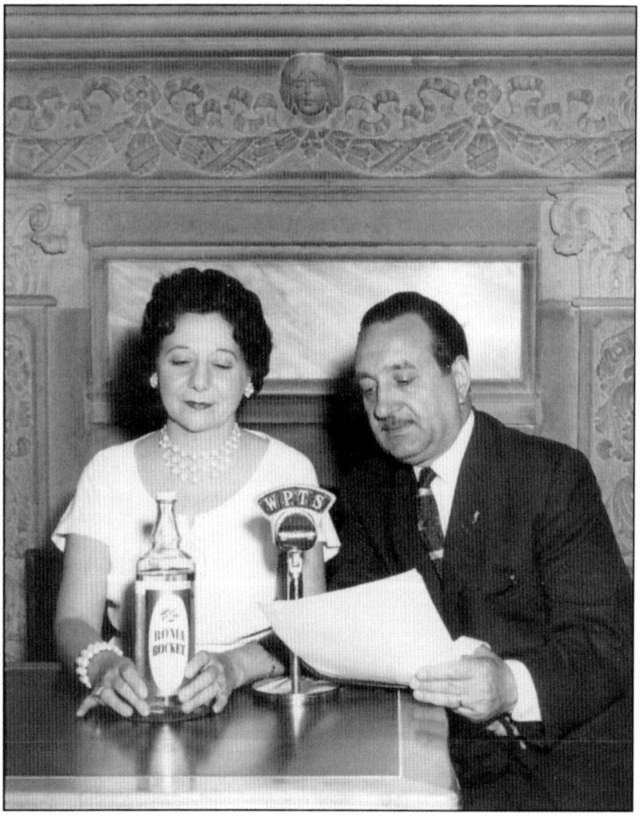

Rose and Angelo Fiorani, owners of the Italian language radio station WPTS, are pictured here broadcasting from their home at 1000 Clay Avenue. During the early 1950s, the Fiorani family conducted most of the broadcasts of their immensely popular and successful ethnic radio station from their historic Hill Section residence.

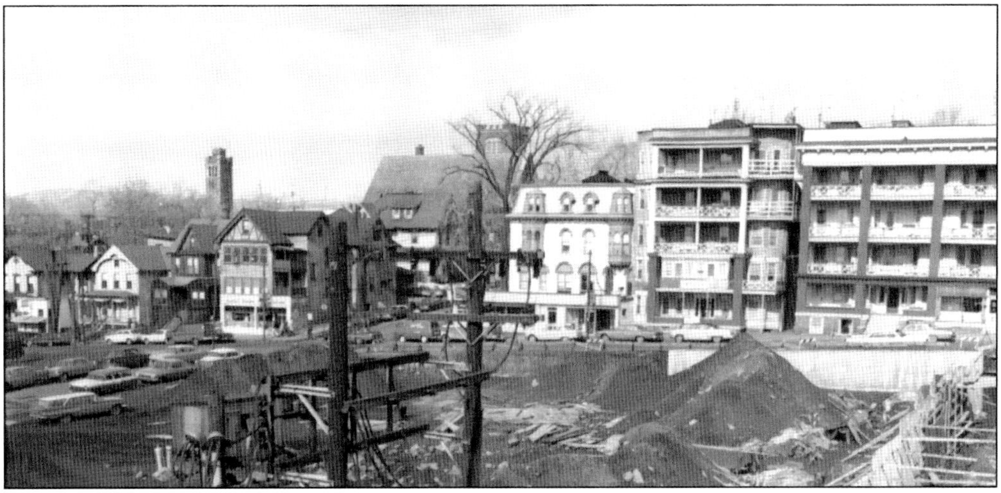

Shown here are the 900 and 1000 blocks of Mulberry Street. On the left is Granteed's Pizza at the corner of Monroe Avenue and Mulberry Street, and on the far right are the Storier Apartments. Although the University of Scranton has demolished and replaced both structures, Granteed's remains open in a new location at 817 Mulberry Street. (Courtesy of the University of Scranton.)

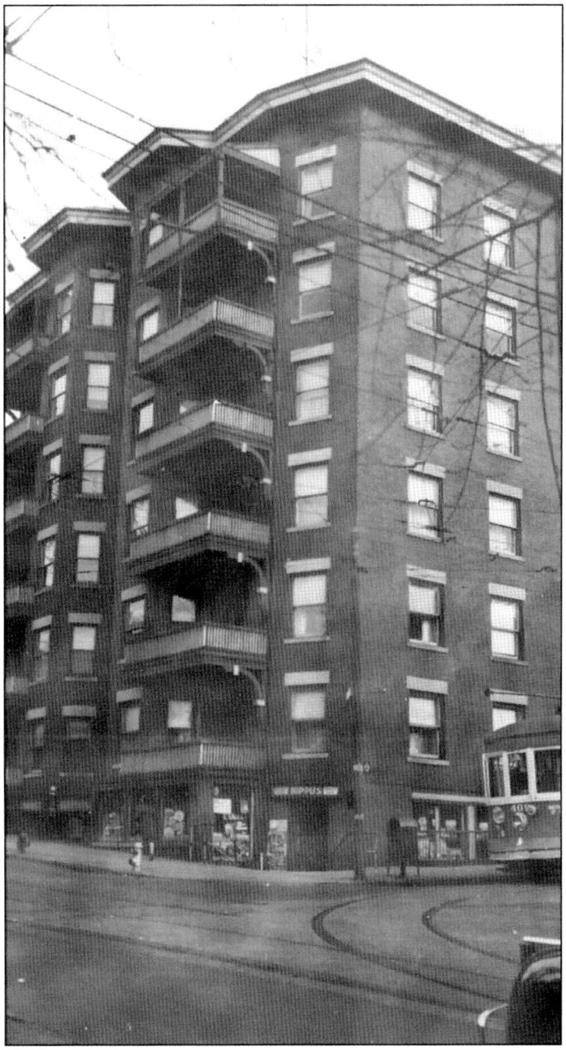

For many years, Scott's Market, a small grocery store, operated on the ground floor of the Carter Apartments. The Hill Section residents heavily relied upon similar businesses, such as Johnny's Market at the corner of Pine and Quincy Streets and Ralph's Market on Prescott Avenue.

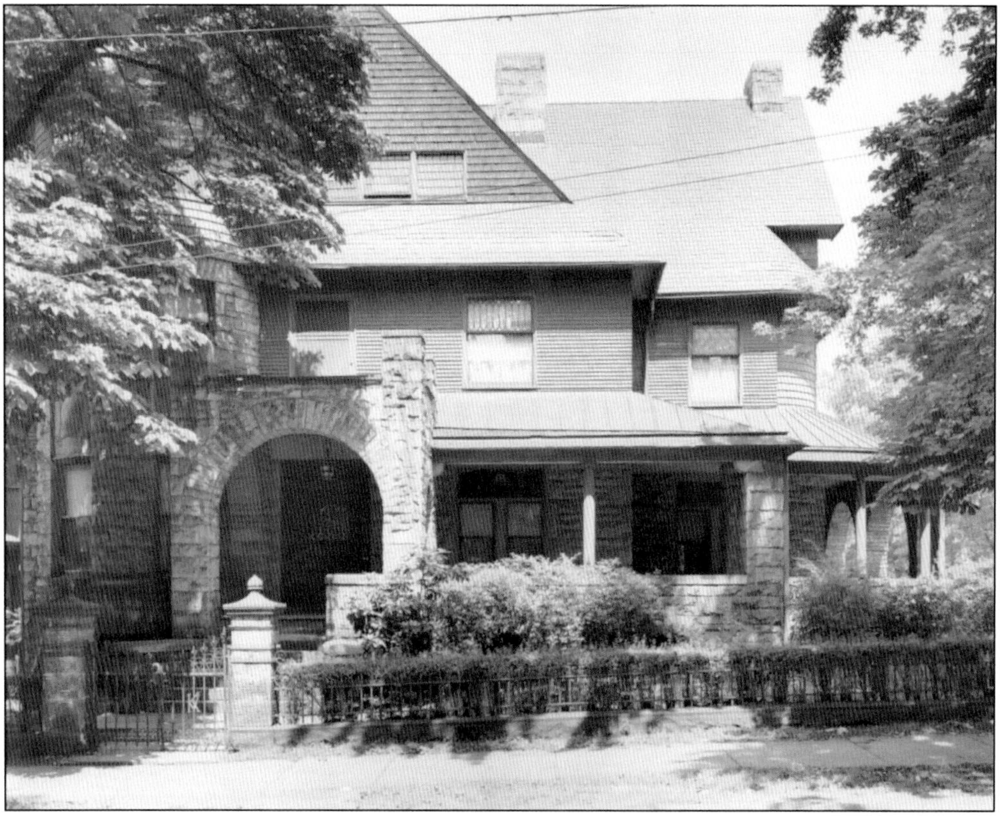

The Chipak Funeral Home was founded in 1909 when Samuel Chipak opened a funeral parlor in Scranton's South Side flats to serve the neighborhood's Eastern European immigrants. In 1948, Samuel Chipak and his son John Chipak decided to purchase the Victor Koch home at the corner of Madison Avenue and Mulberry Street, and after the flood of 1955 destroyed their original location, the family moved its business to the Hill Section. (Courtesy of the Chipak Funeral Home.)

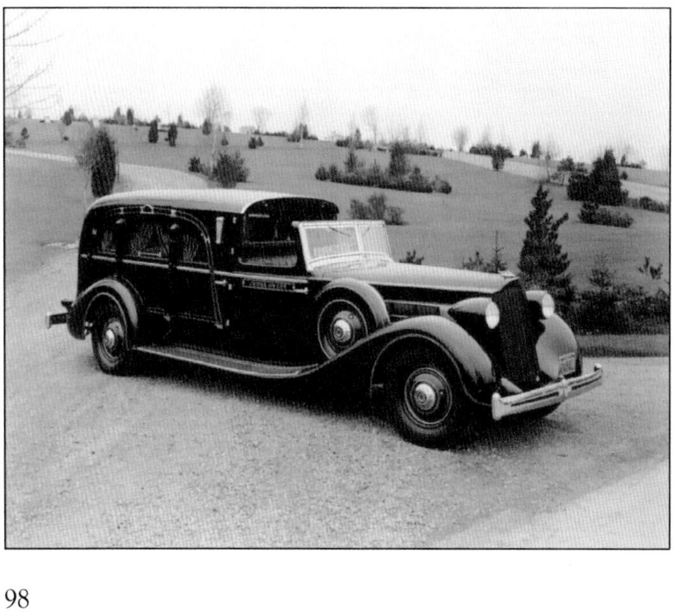

The Chipak Funeral Home's antique Packard hearse is pictured here in the 1950s. Today, Chipak's Funeral Home is still a thriving family-run business based out of their historic Hill Section location. (Courtesy of the Chipak Funeral Home.)

Five

Medical and Educational Institutions

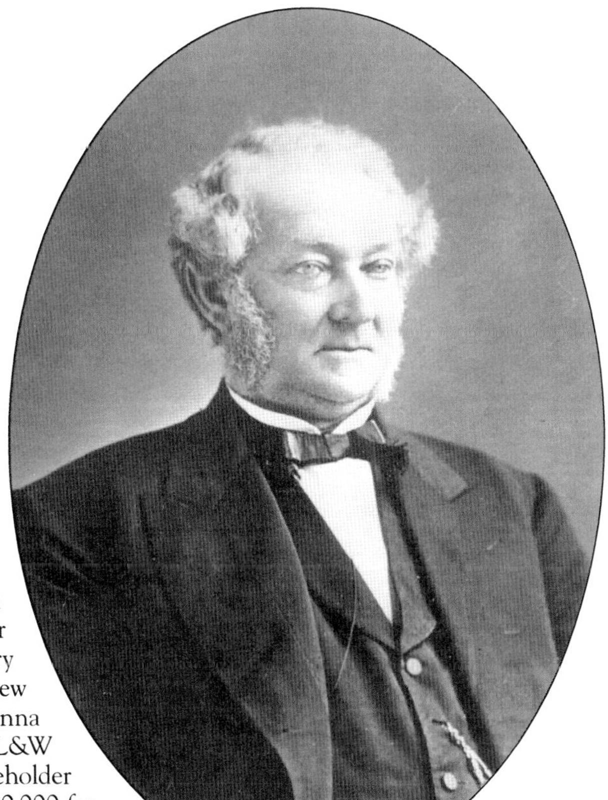

Moses Taylor was born in New York City in 1806. He was an entrepreneur who made a fortune in the sugar industry and as president of the City Bank of New York. He later invested in the Lackawanna Iron and Coal Company and the DL&W Railroad, becoming the largest shareholder in both. In 1882, Taylor donated $250,000 for a hospital that would provide free health care to his Scranton employees.

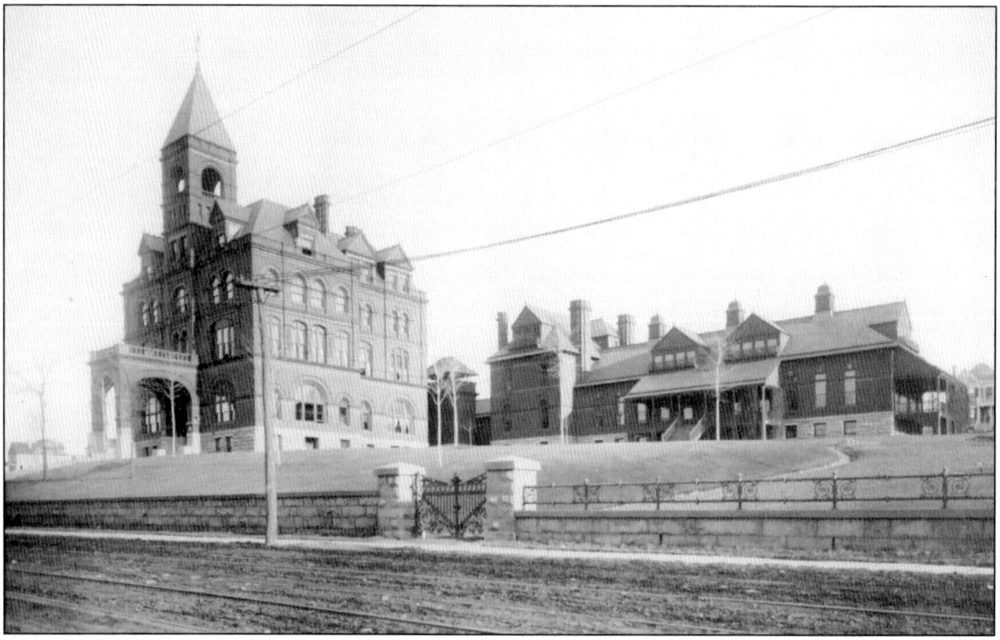

The original facilities of Moses Taylor Hospital occupied the entire block bounded by Quincy and Clay Avenues and Pine and Gibson Streets. When Moses Taylor endowed his namesake hospital, he took precautions to ensure that mining operations could never occur under its property. The wall visible in this image was a well-known meeting place for Hill Section children.

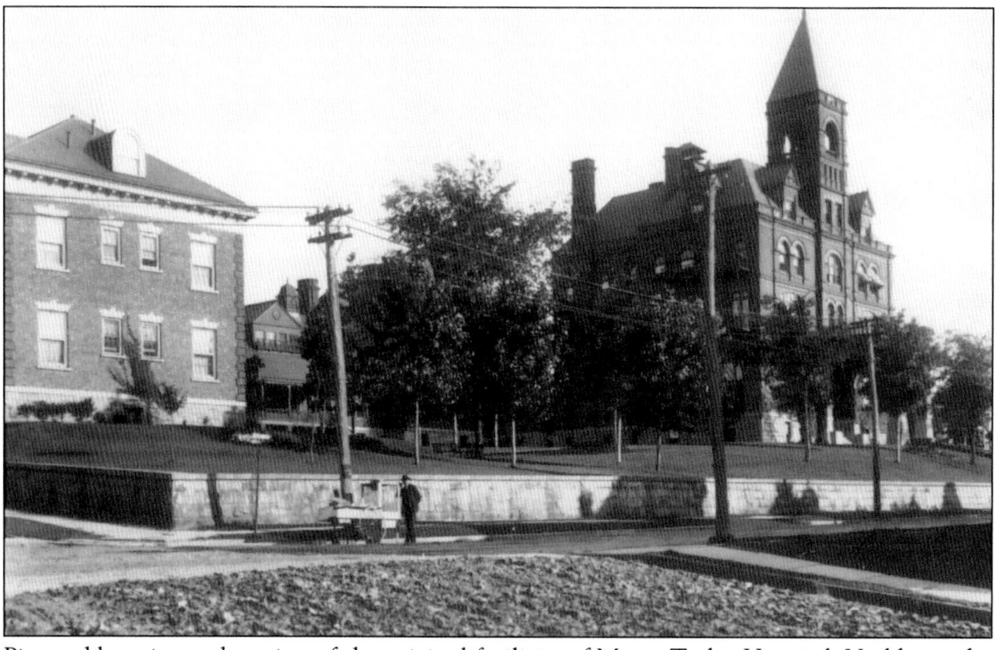

Pictured here is another view of the original facilities of Moses Taylor Hospital. Visible on the far left side of the image is the hospital's nursing school. The Moses Taylor Hospital Training School for Nurses operated from 1892 to 1954. The school trained numerous nurses over the years through hands-on experience at Moses Taylor Hospital and affiliated hospitals like the Manhattan Maternity Hospital.

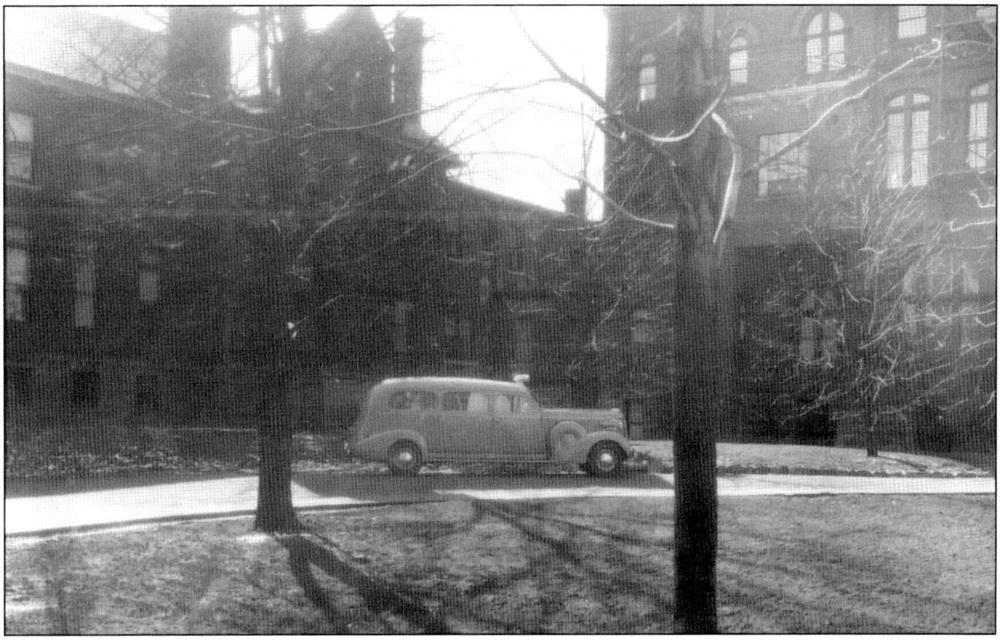

Pictured here is one of Moses Taylor Hospital's ambulances. In the days before motorized vehicles, horse-drawn ambulances were used to transport sick or injured patients to the hospital. The horses that pulled these ambulances had to be very strong in order to climb the Hill Section's steep grades.

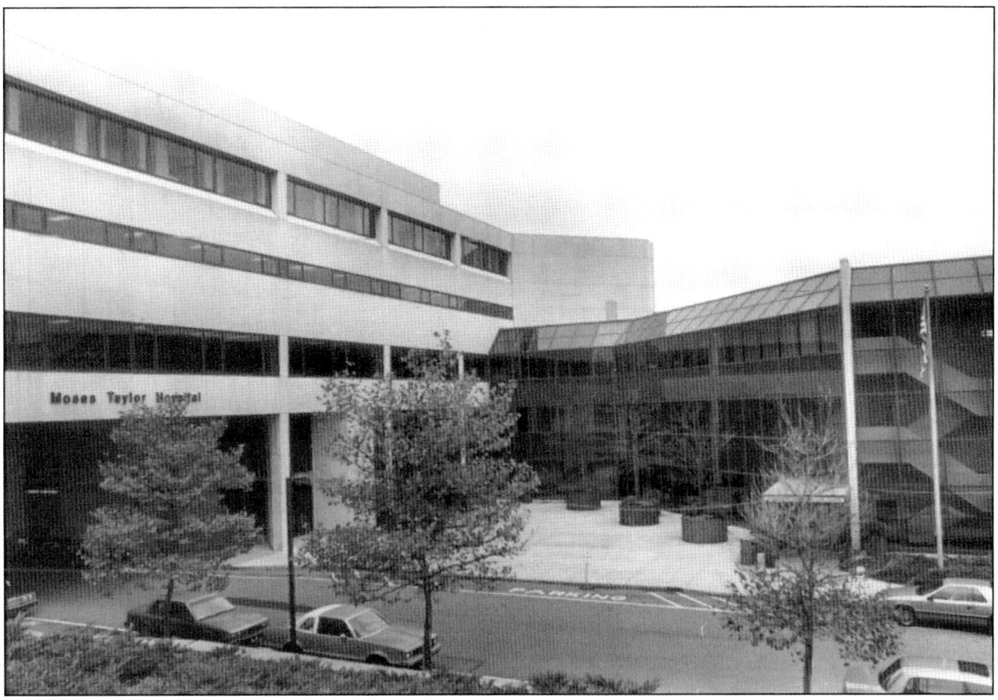

By the late 1970s, Moses Taylor Hospital had shifted away from a private charity hospital to a public health hospital, and new facilities were built across Quincy Avenue, which effectively doubled the hospital's size. In the early 2000s, Commonwealth Health acquired the hospital.

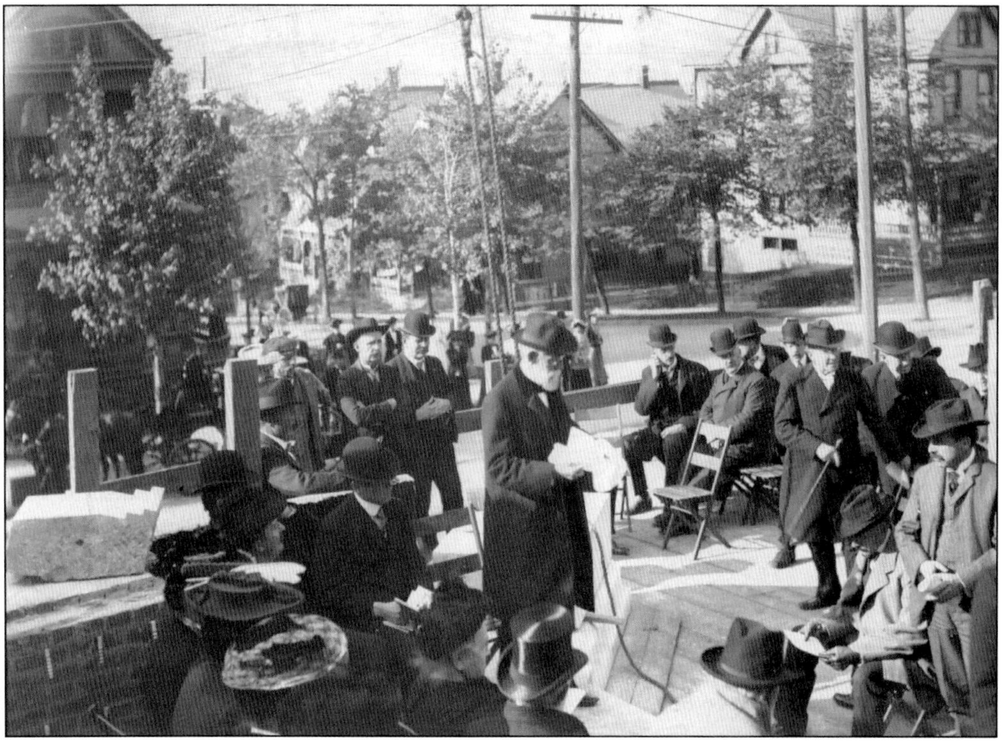

On May 24, 1905, the ground-breaking ceremony for the new Hahnemann Hospital took place in the 300 block of Colfax Avenue, near Nay Aug Park. The hospital was founded in 1899 by a group of local philanthropists who wanted to establish a homeopathic hospital based on the practices of Dr. Samuel Hahnemann in Scranton.

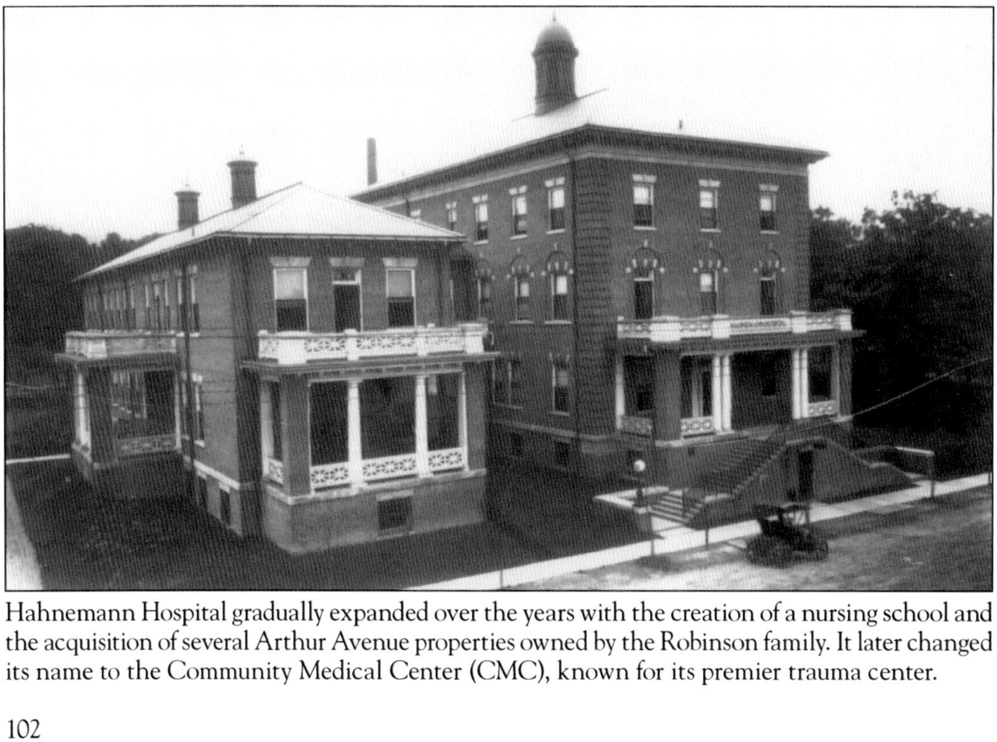

Hahnemann Hospital gradually expanded over the years with the creation of a nursing school and the acquisition of several Arthur Avenue properties owned by the Robinson family. It later changed its name to the Community Medical Center (CMC), known for its premier trauma center.

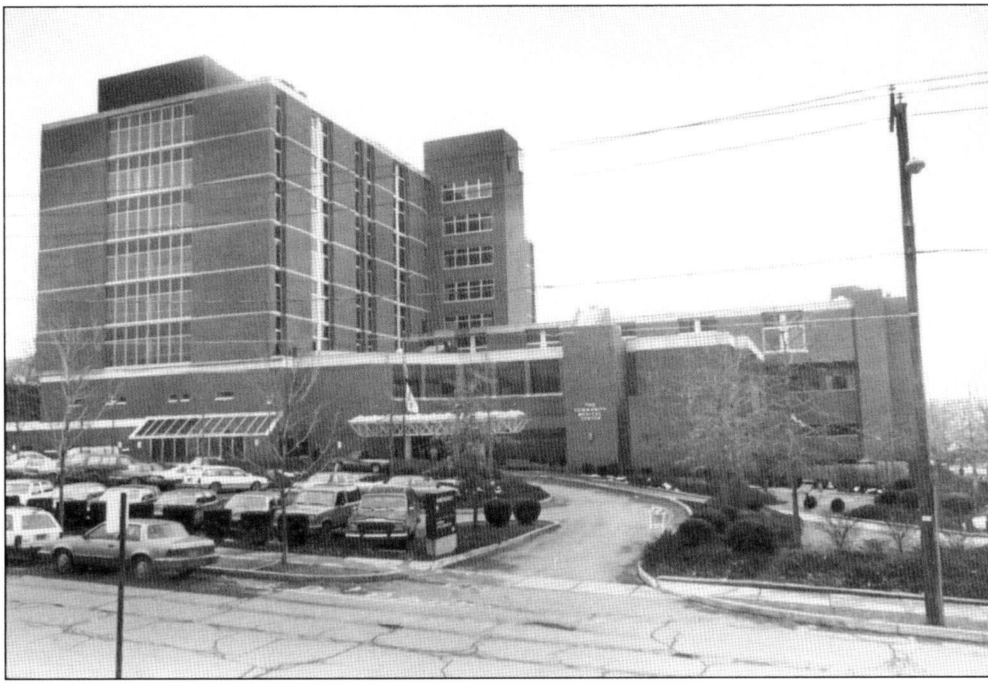

The CMC greatly expanded in the late 1980s, with the construction of a new complex on the block bounded by Colfax and Arthur Avenues and Linden and Mulberry Streets. In the early 2000s, Geisinger Health System acquired the hospital, renaming it Geisinger CMC. Currently, the hospital is once again undergoing an expansion.

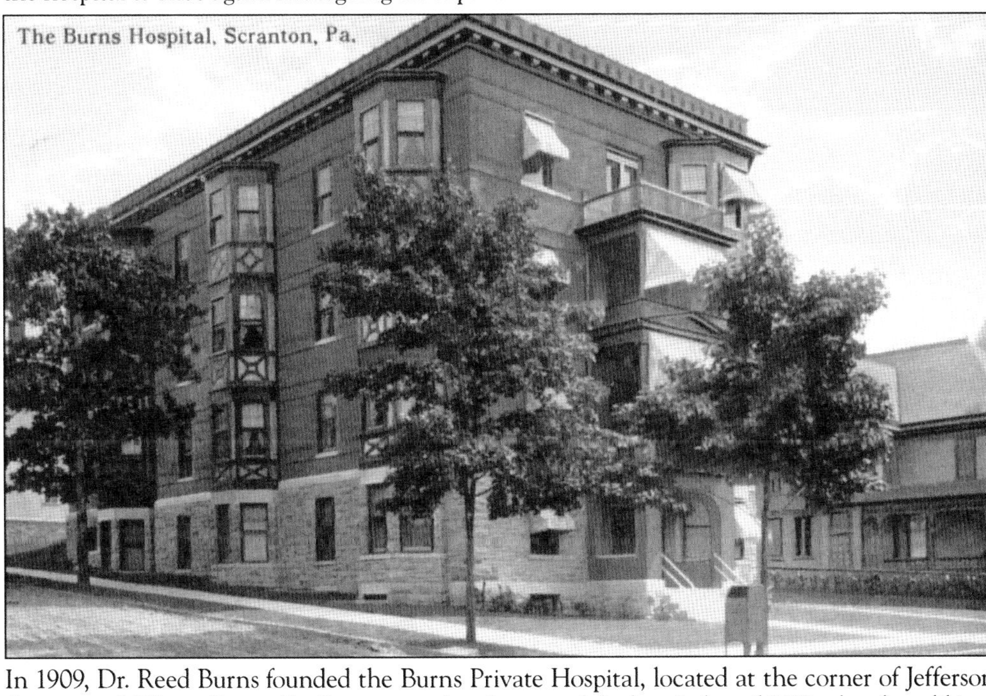

In 1909, Dr. Reed Burns founded the Burns Private Hospital, located at the corner of Jefferson Avenue and Gibson Street. Dr. Burns owned and operated the hospital until 1917, when he sold it to the Catholic Sisters of Mercy, who renamed it Mercy Hospital. (Courtesy of Jack Hiddlestone.)

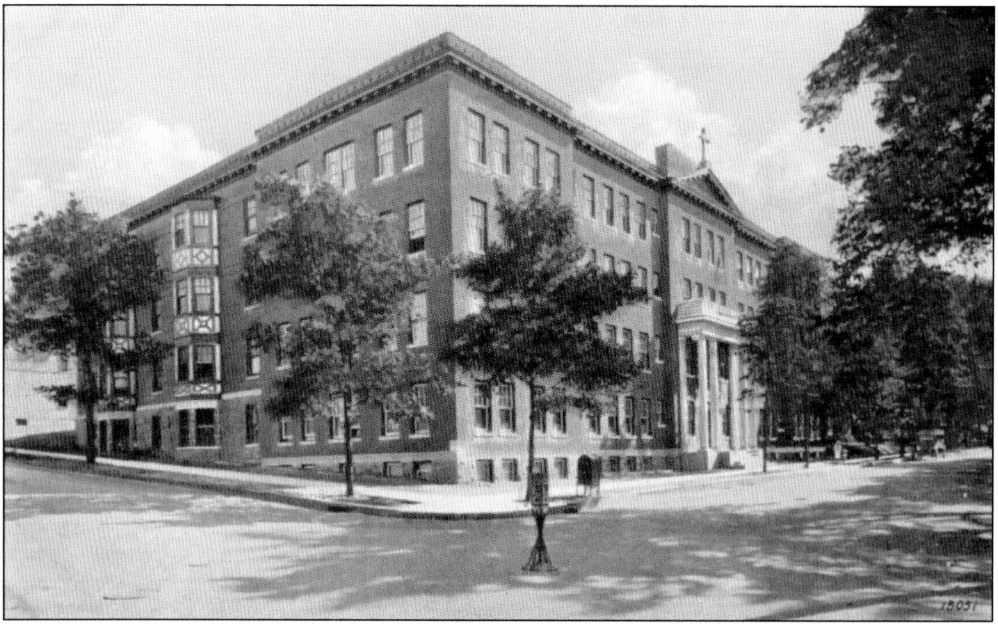

With the help of the Diocese of Scranton, the Sisters of Mercy greatly expanded the former Burns Private Hospital. At its height, Mercy Hospital was the largest medical employer in the Scranton area, with a well-known cardiovascular department and nursing school based in the nearby Woolworth mansion. (Courtesy of Jack Hiddlestone.)

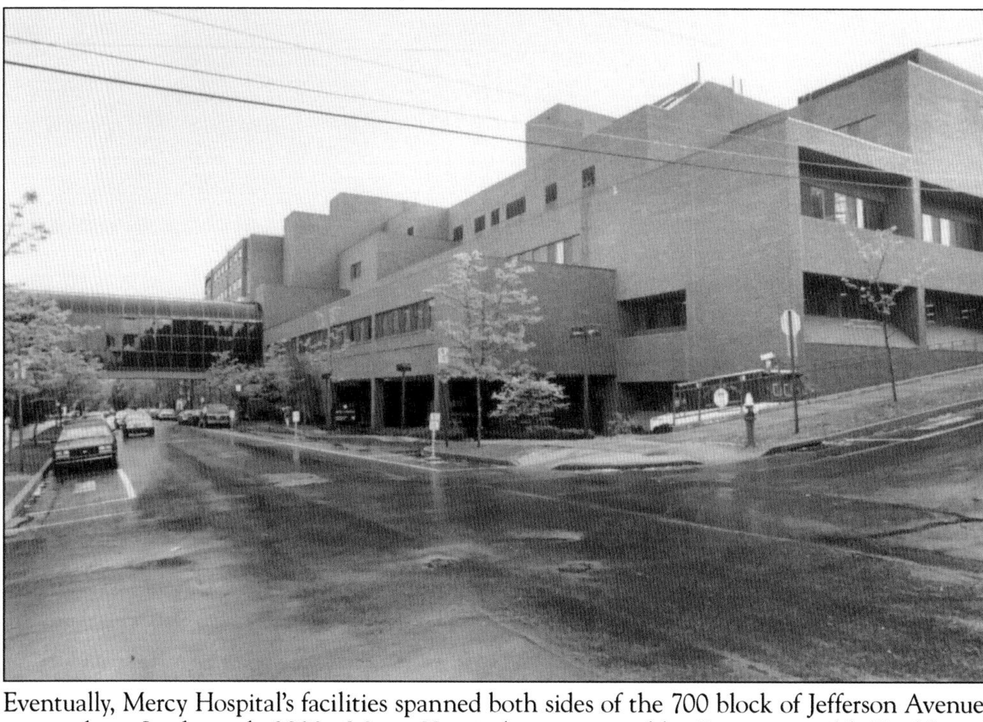

Eventually, Mercy Hospital's facilities spanned both sides of the 700 block of Jefferson Avenue, as seen here. In the early 2000s, Mercy Hospital was acquired by Commonwealth Health and renamed Scranton Regional Hospital. Plans are currently under way to develop and connect the hospital to nearby Moses Taylor Hospital.

The Commonwealth Medical College (TCMC) was incorporated in 2008 as the result of a grassroots campaign. In 2011, the medical college opened its highly sophisticated 185,000-square-foot medical science building at 525 Pine Street. TCMC has operations throughout northeastern Pennsylvania and is affiliated with all three of the Hill Section's hospitals.

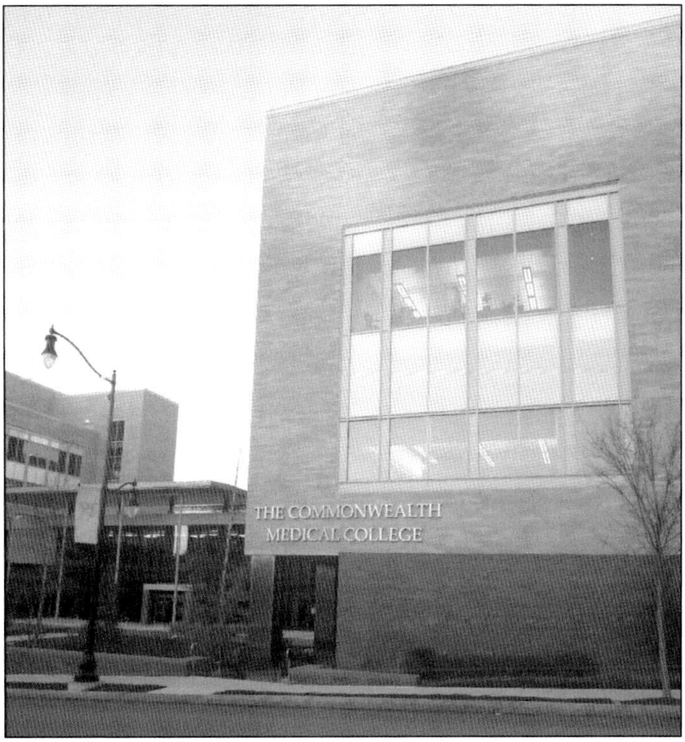

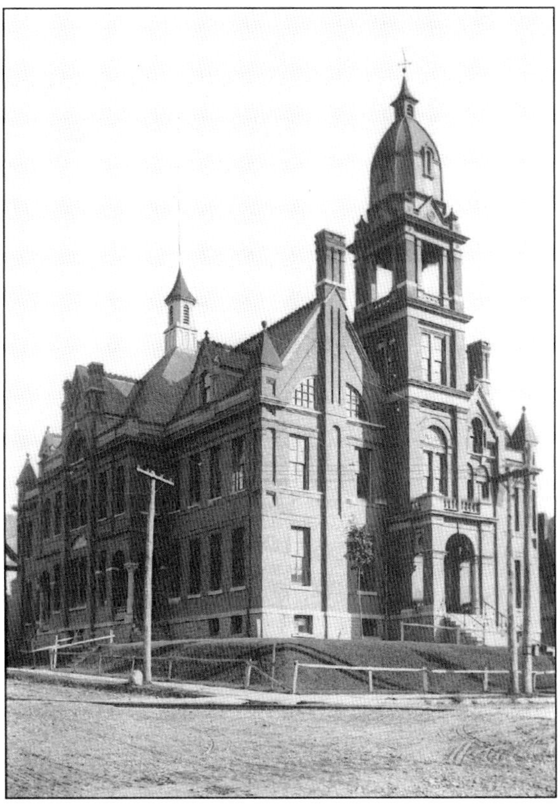

To educate the Hill Section's children, the Scranton School District built several public primary schools throughout the area. James Madison No. 36, pictured here, is located at the corner of Madison Avenue and Pine Street. Madison School was the largest in the Hill Section, and in the 1920s, it was forced to relocate to a new building to accommodate more students. The original school was later demolished and replaced with a WPA office.

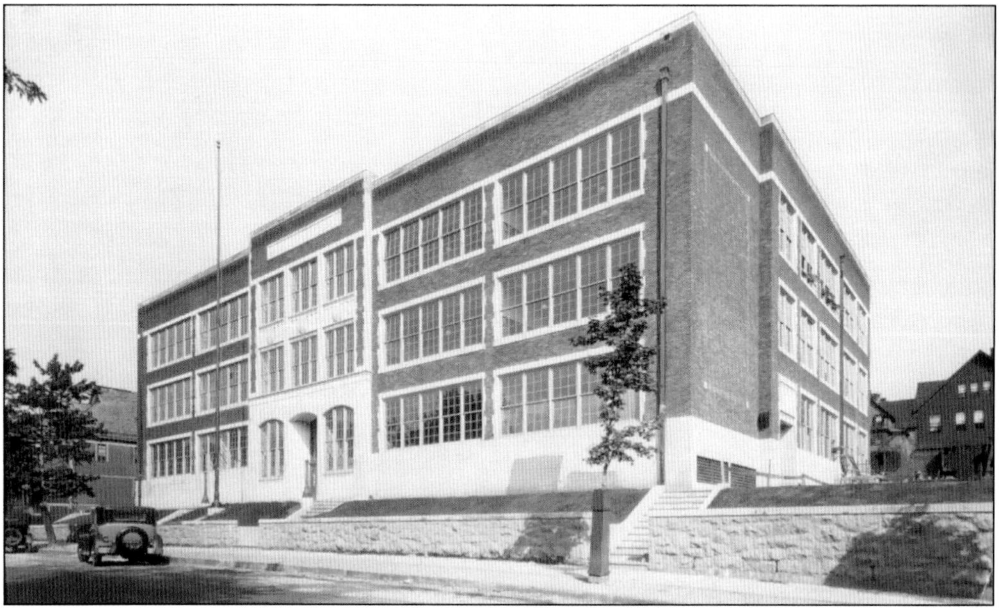

The new James Madison School, located at 528 Quincy Avenue, was built in 1928. The Gothic Revival structure housed an institution that provided quality education to thousands of Hill Section children over the years. In the 1970s, the school became East Scranton Junior High School, which closed in the early 2000s. The building, listed in the National Register of Historic Places, is currently being redeveloped.

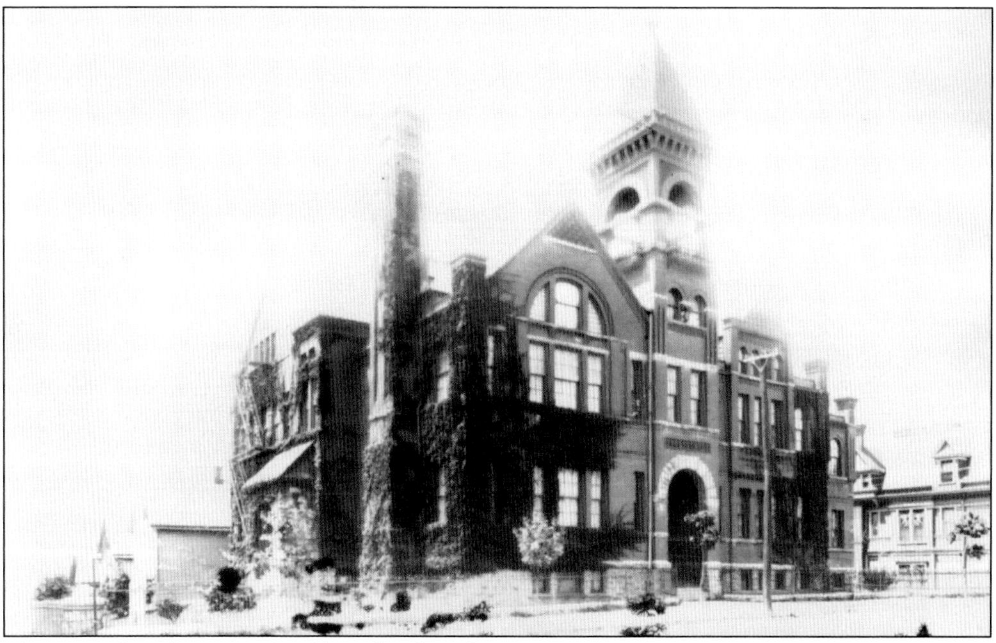

The Bayard Taylor No. 35 public school at the corner of Taylor Avenue and Olive Street was located at the highest point in the Hill Section. In 1941, the Diocese of Scranton purchased the school for use as the Immaculate Conception Chapel School. The parochial institution educated many of the Hill Section's Catholic residents prior to its closure in the 1970s. The building was later demolished and replaced with luxury townhomes.

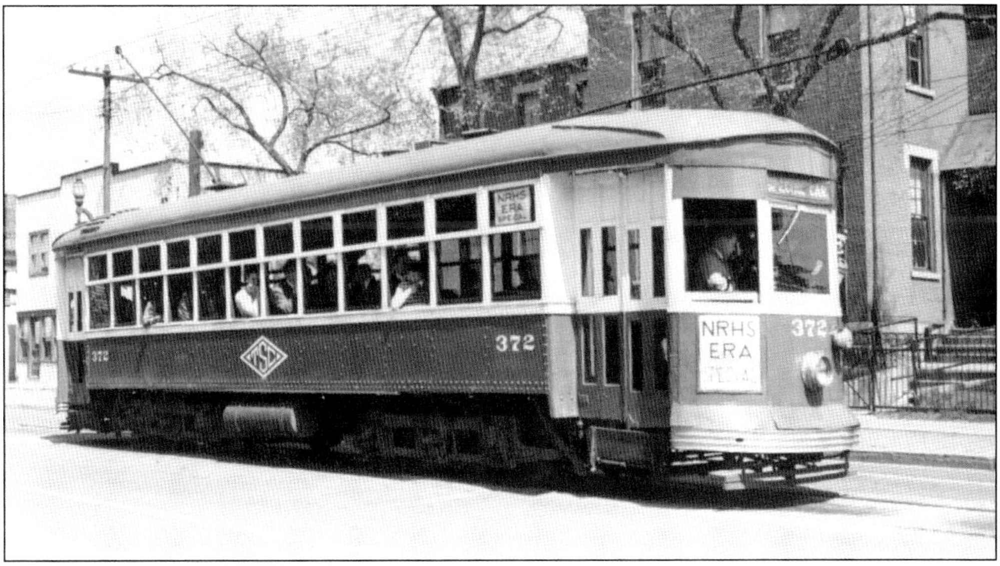

This streetcar is passing the Peter Gabriel Muhlenberg School at Petersburg Corners. The public school was built at the corner of Prescott Avenue and Ash Street in the late 1800s. For most of its existence, the Muhlenberg School acted as an annex for the nearby Prescott School. The school was demolished many years ago, but its former cornerstone has been incorporated into the modern retail structure that occupies its former site.

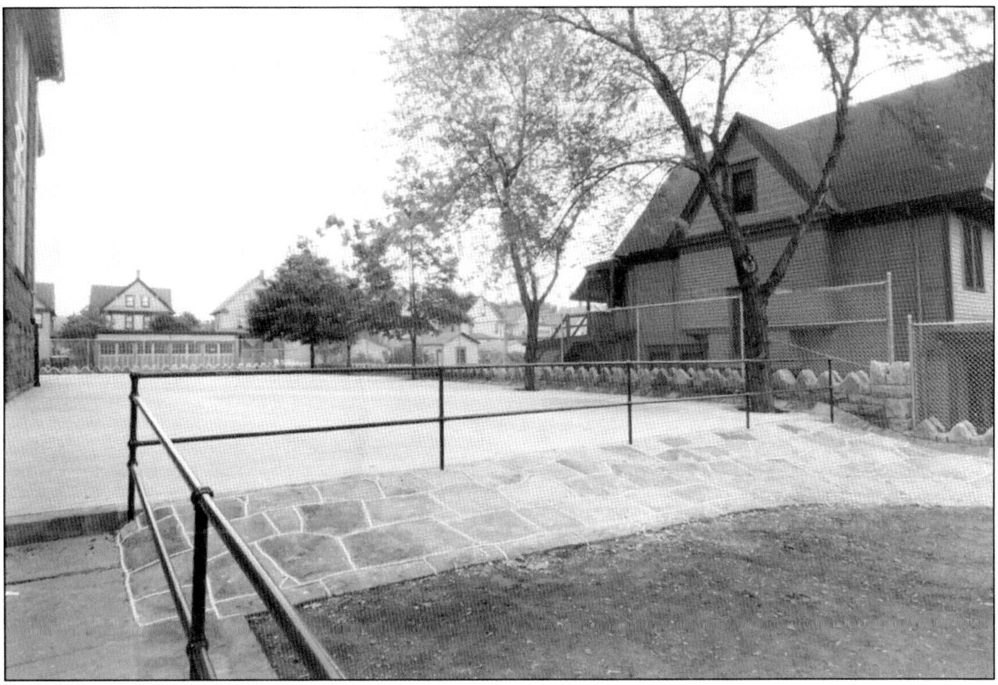

Shown here is the playground of the new William Prescott School. The original Prescott School, of which there are no accessible images, was located at the corner of Prescott Avenue and Myrtle Street. In the postwar years, the original school was replaced by a more modern structure that is still in use today. In 2007, the Prescott School was recognized by the US Department of Education's prestigious National Blue Ribbon Schools Program.

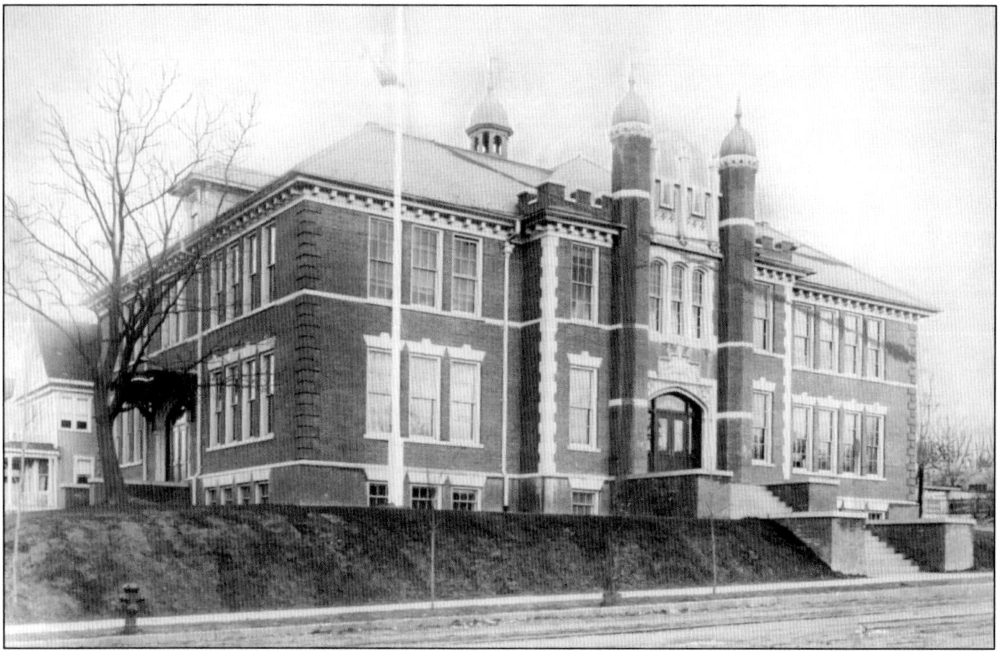

The John Audubon School was located at the corner of Colfax Avenue and Mulberry Street and served many Hill Section children throughout its existence. In the early 2000s, the Audubon School was closed, and Geisinger CMC Hospital acquired its former building.

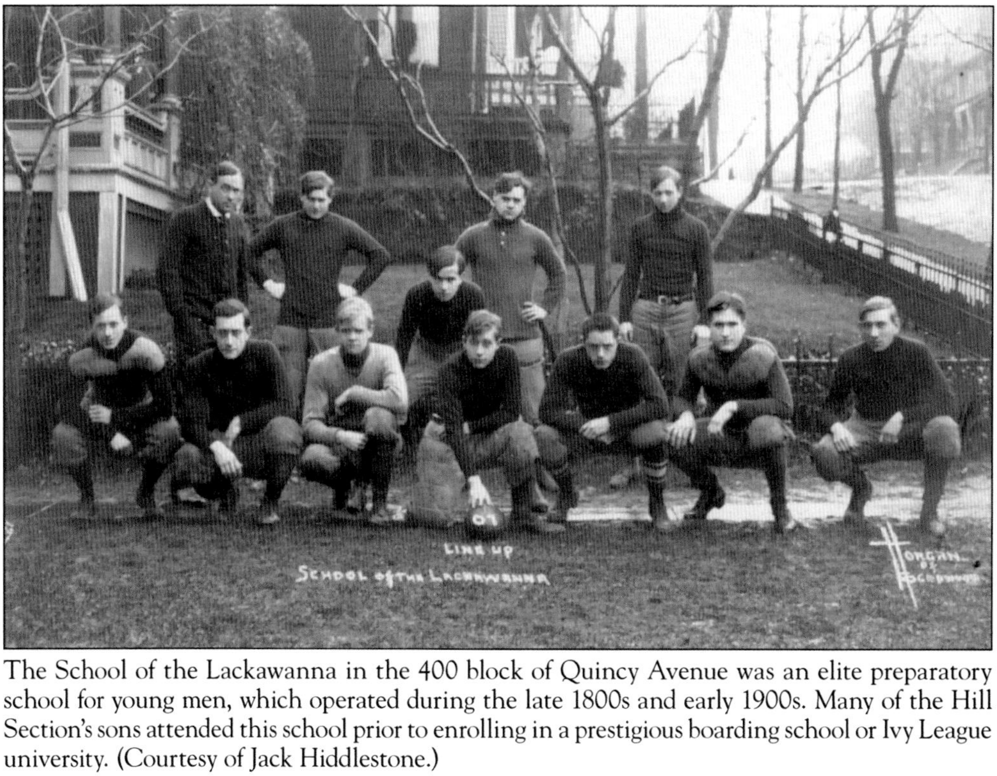

The School of the Lackawanna in the 400 block of Quincy Avenue was an elite preparatory school for young men, which operated during the late 1800s and early 1900s. Many of the Hill Section's sons attended this school prior to enrolling in a prestigious boarding school or Ivy League university. (Courtesy of Jack Hiddlestone.)

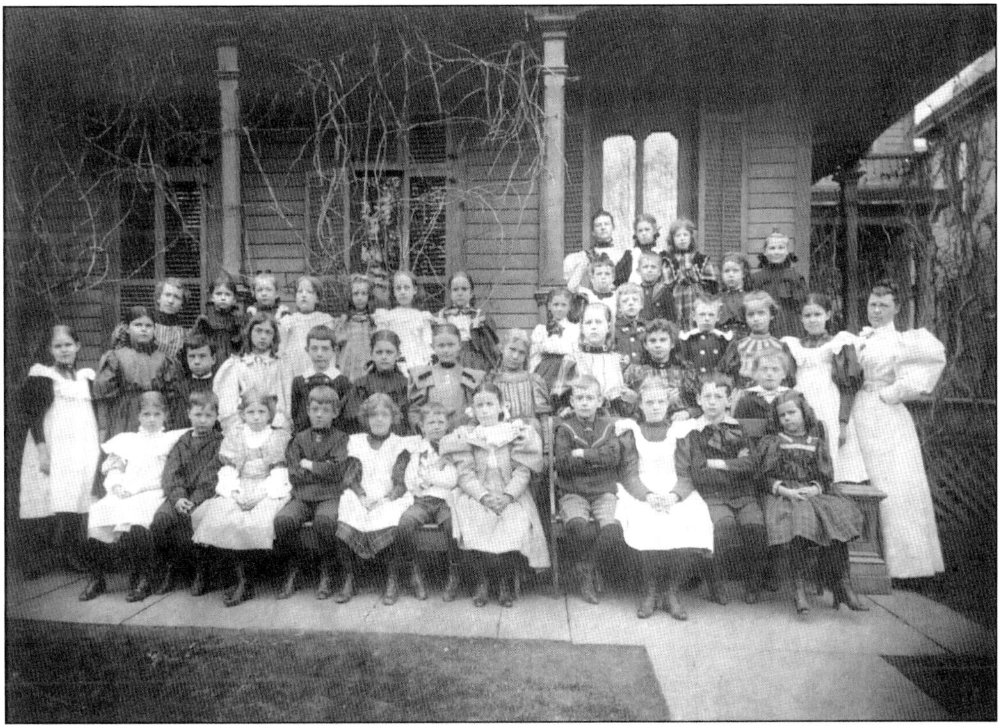

Students at Merrill's School are pictured here in the early 1900s. Augusta Merrill operated this private school for young girls at 612 Jefferson Avenue. The school closed not long after this photograph was taken, and W.W. Katherine Scranton later acquired the property and donated it to the Century Club. In 1912, the Century Club constructed its building on the school's former site.

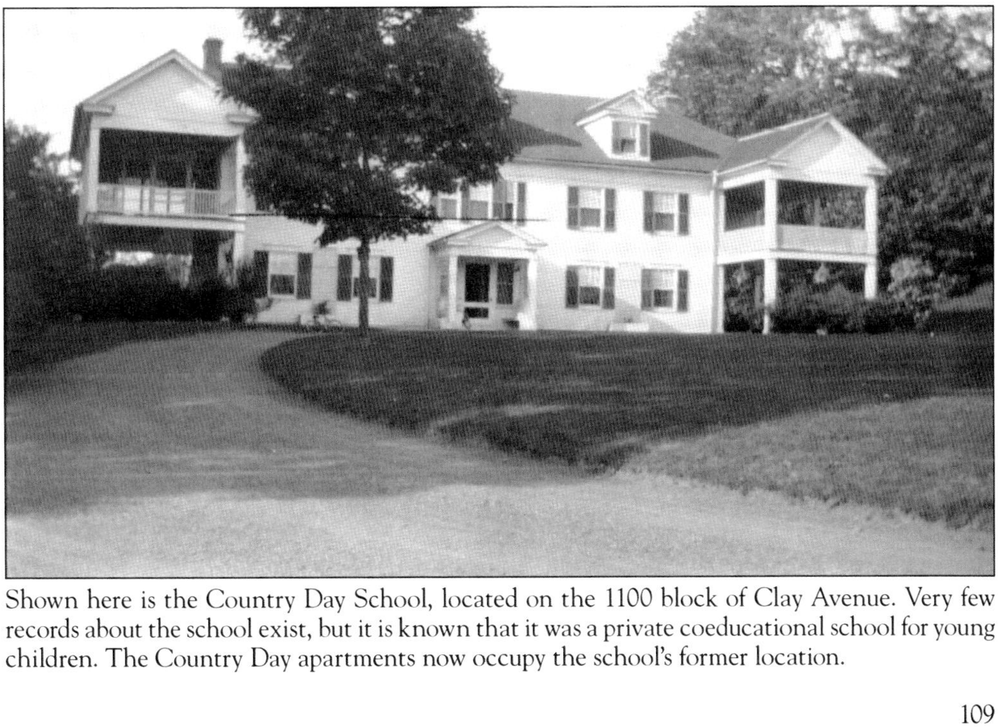

Shown here is the Country Day School, located on the 1100 block of Clay Avenue. Very few records about the school exist, but it is known that it was a private coeducational school for young children. The Country Day apartments now occupy the school's former location.

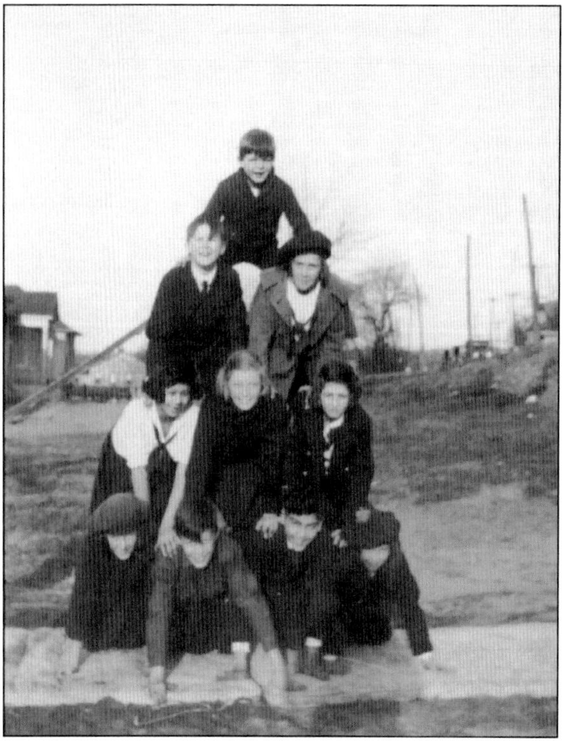

Students of Country Day School form a human pyramid on school grounds in the early 1900s. It is interesting to see such an informal and whimsical scene from an era known for its seriousness and formality.

The Scranton estate is pictured here at the time of its donation to the Diocese of Scranton. In 1941, Worthington Scranton donated his family's estate on Ridge Row to the Diocese of Scranton for St. Thomas College, located on Wyoming Avenue in Scranton's downtown. At the time, it was an all-men's institution run by the Christian Brothers religious order. (Courtesy of the University of Scranton.)

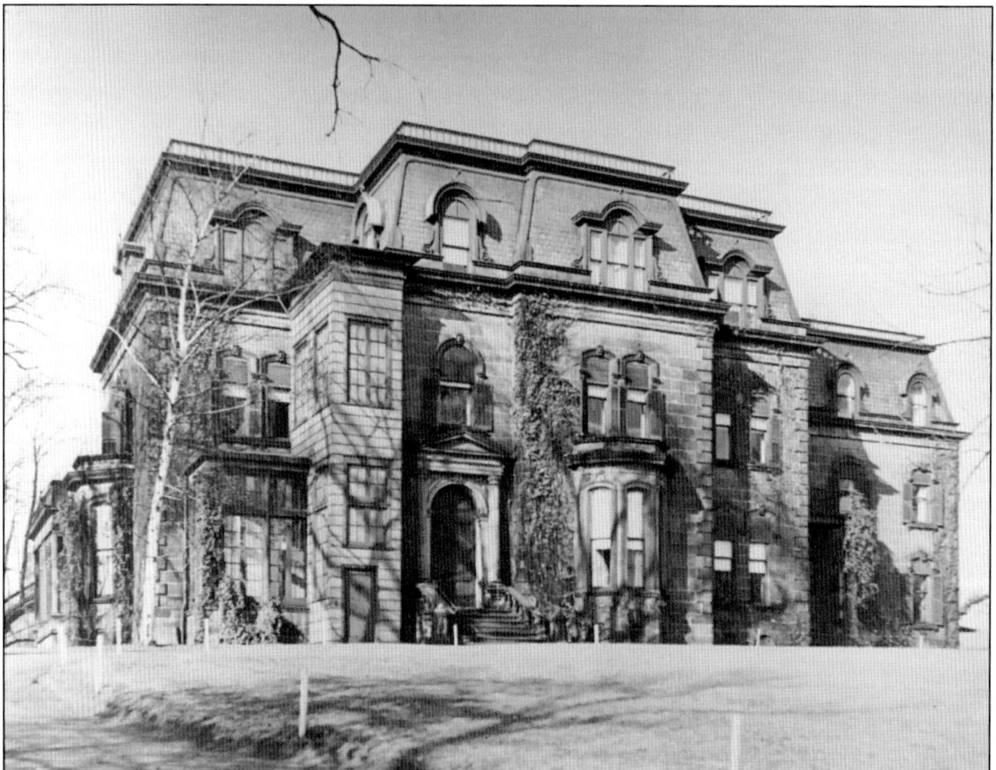

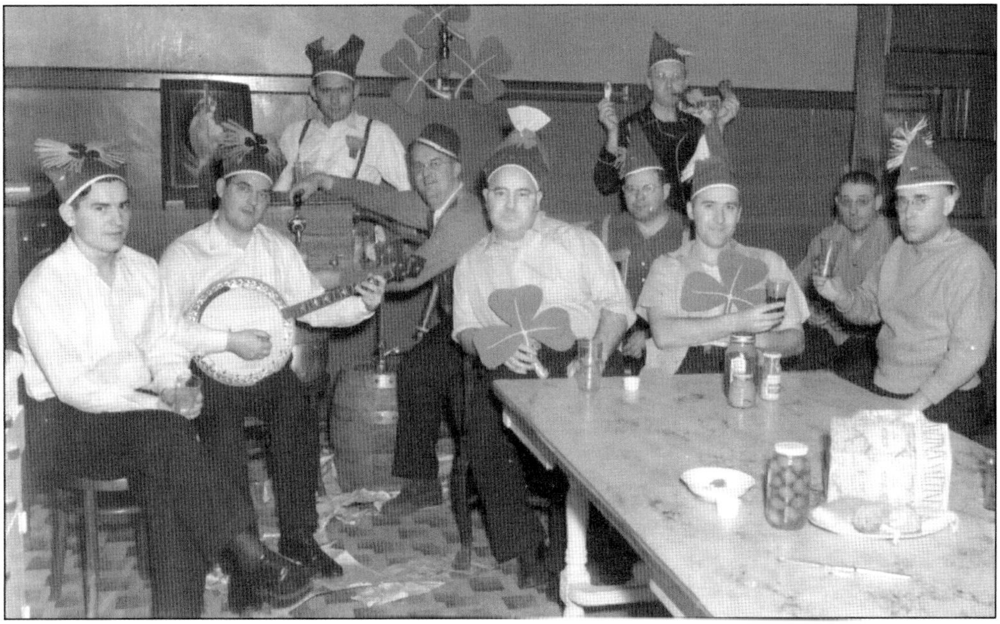

The Christian Brothers priests operated St. Thomas College for the Diocese of Scranton from its founding in 1888 until 1942. They are pictured here celebrating St. Patrick's Day, a major event for Scranton's large Irish American population, as well as the college. (Courtesy of the University of Scranton.)

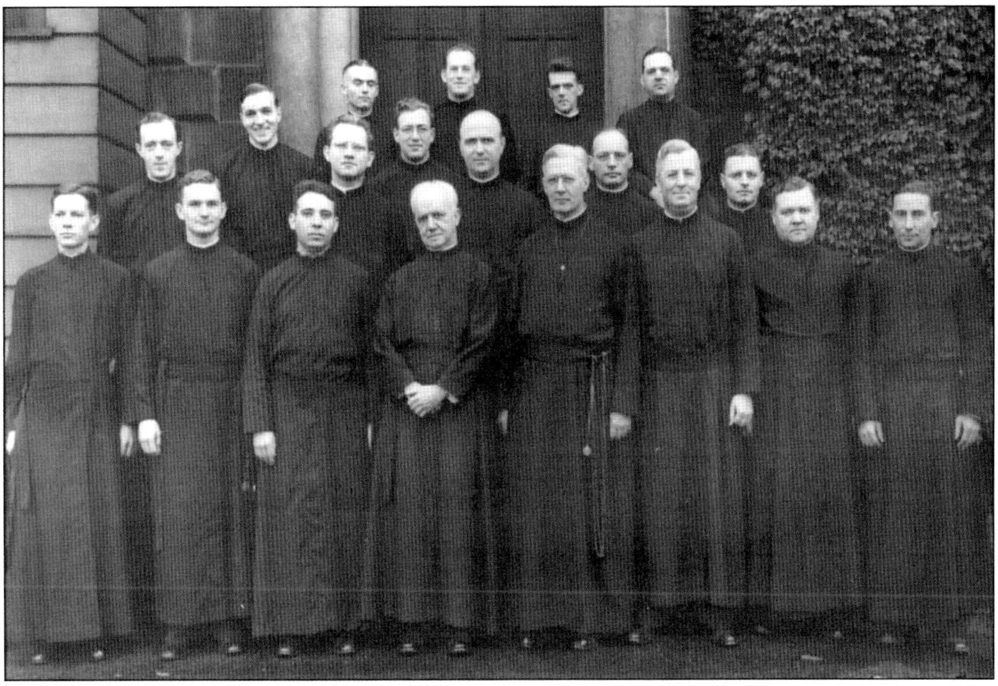

The original Jesuit priests of the University of Scranton are seen here at the Scranton estate. The Christian Brothers and the Diocese of Scranton turned over St. Thomas College to a group of Jesuit priests in 1942. The Jesuits renamed the institution the University of Scranton and began building a campus around the former Scranton estate. (Courtesy of the University of Scranton.)

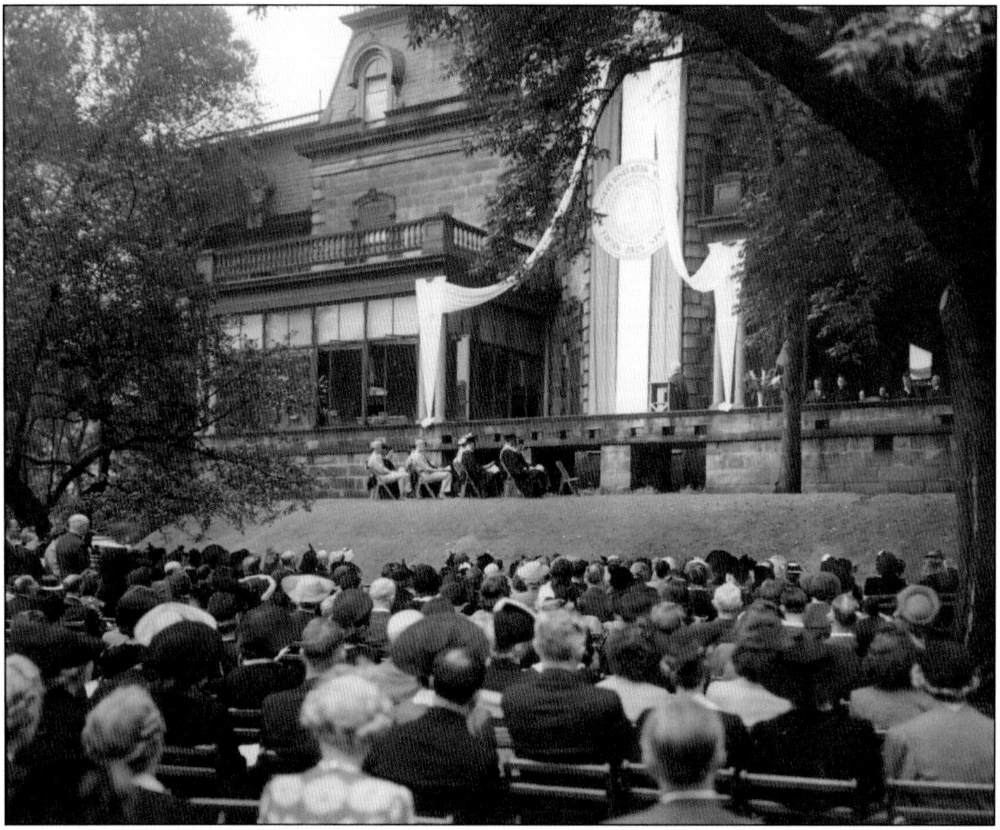

Shown here is a University of Scranton commencement ceremony at the Scranton estate in 1943. Since the university was an all-male institution and most young men were away fighting in World War II, enrollment was low throughout the early 1940s. It is interesting to note that almost all of the graduates are dressed in military uniforms. (Courtesy of the University of Scranton.)

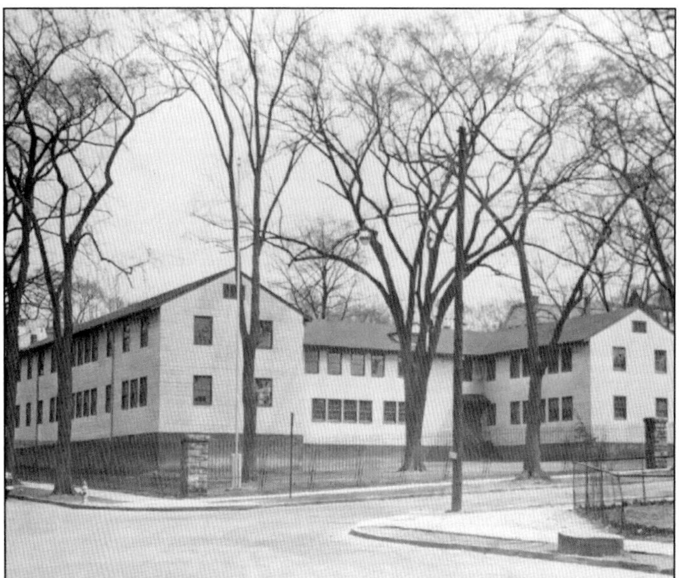

With the end of World War II and the institution of the GI Bill, the University of Scranton's enrollment skyrocketed. In order to meet the demands of these new students, the university hastily acquired and constructed three prefabricated surplus military barracks around the intersection of Monroe Avenue and Linden Street. One of the barracks, seen here along Linden Street, was called A Building and housed liberal arts classrooms. (Courtesy of the University of Scranton.)

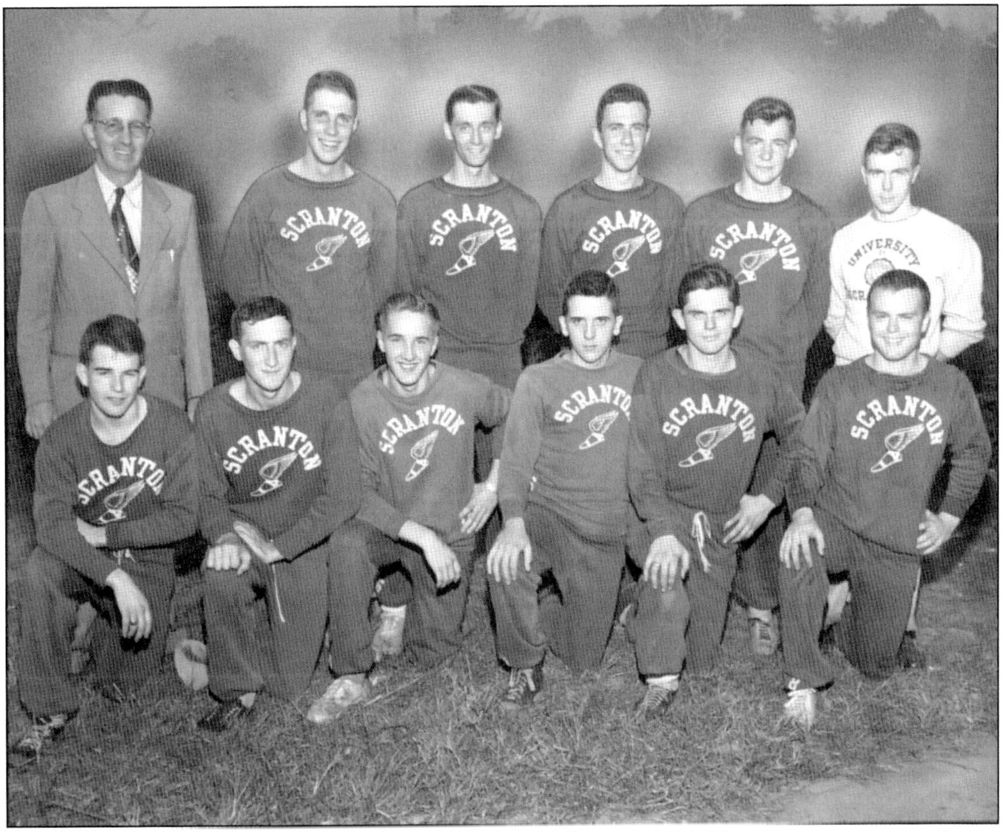

The University of Scranton's cross-country team poses here in 1951. The university was a vibrant institution throughout the 1950s, with many commuter students from the Hill Section. During this time period, the university also acquired many Hill Section properties from private owners and the Scranton Redevelopment Authority. (Courtesy of the University of Scranton.)

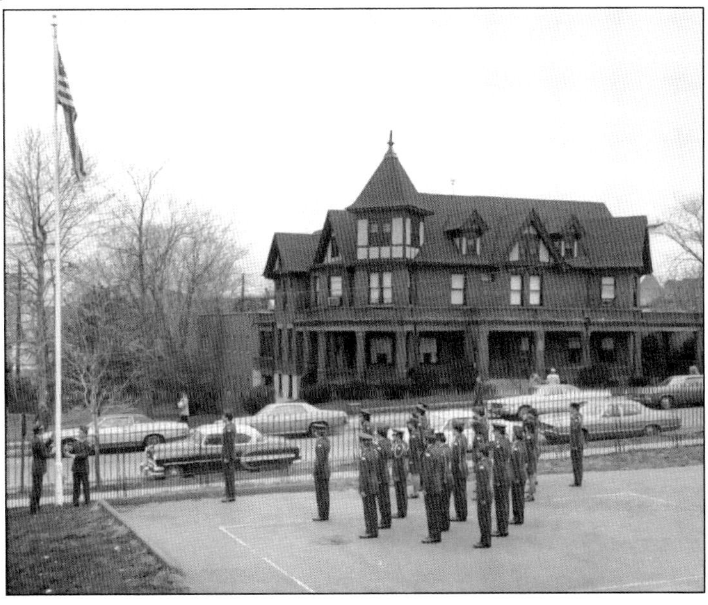

Here, ROTC students are performing drills on Galvin Terrace, which replaced the A Building. The Lackawanna Juvenile Detention Center, formerly the Crawford mansion, is visible across the street. The Harry and Jeanette Weinberg Memorial Library was later constructed on the Galvin Terrace's site. (Courtesy of the University of Scranton.)

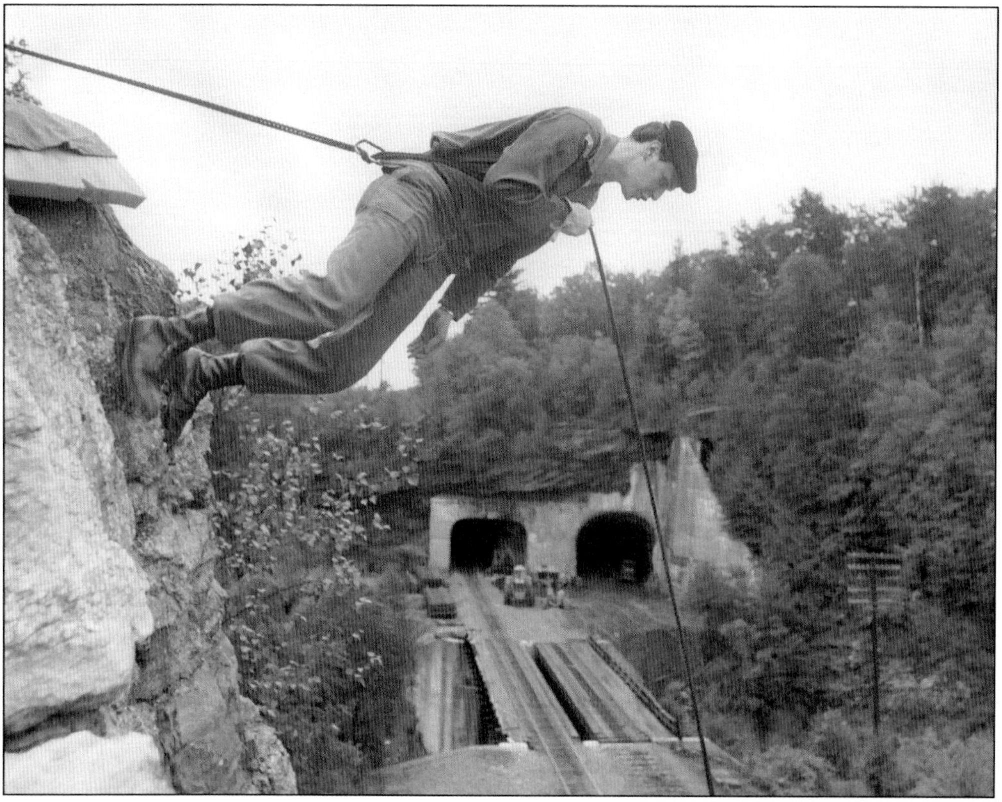

A University of Scranton ROTC student is seen here repelling off a cliff in the Nay Aug Park Gorge above the DL&W main line and tunnels in 1975. ROTC students were not the only individuals to use this spot for repelling. For many years, members of the 13th Regiment of the Pennsylvania National Guard also used this site, which was popular with train watchers as well. (Courtesy of the University of Scranton.)

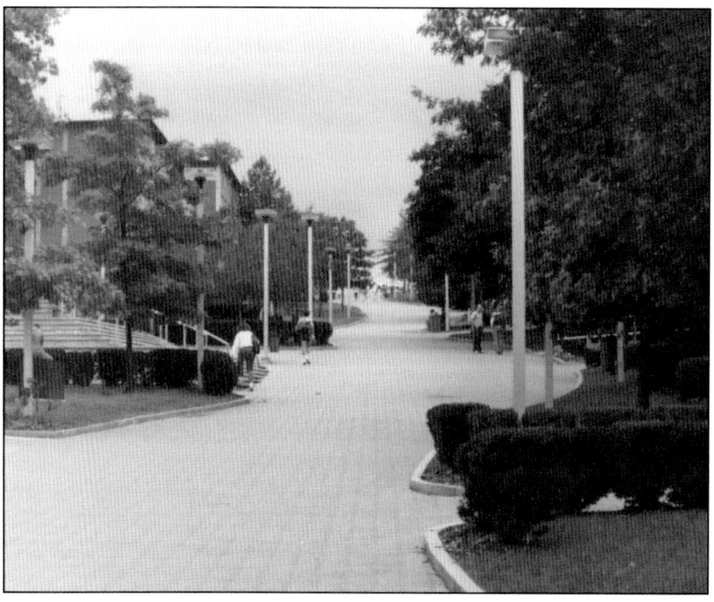

The University of Scranton has greatly altered the Hill Section. It has transformed entire segments into campus commons like the 900, 1000, and 1100 blocks of Linden Street seen here. Today, the University of Scranton has over 6,000 students and is a constant source of growth and innovation for the Scranton area. (Courtesy of the University of Scranton.)

Six

Nay Aug and Luna Parks

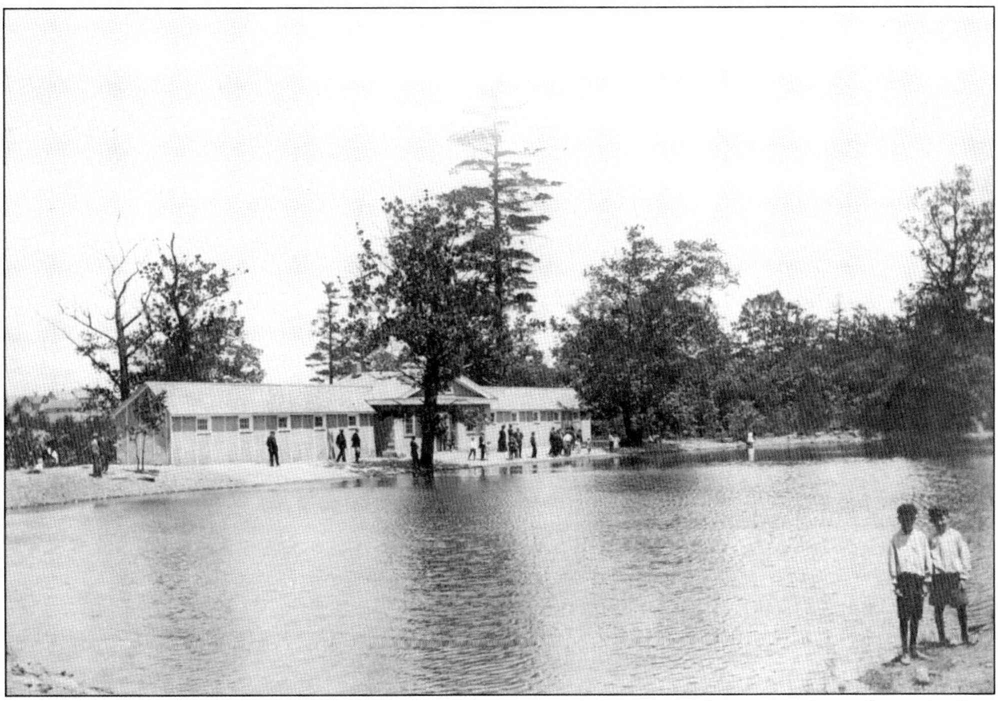

The 136 acres that comprise Nay Aug Park were acquired from several sources throughout the late 19th century. Landscape architect Fredrick Law Olmstead, designer of New York City's Central Park, was hired to plan Scranton's largest public park, which spans the entire length of the upper Hill Section. Eventually, numerous amenities, such as the Lake Lincoln swimming complex seen here, would be built in Nay Aug Park.

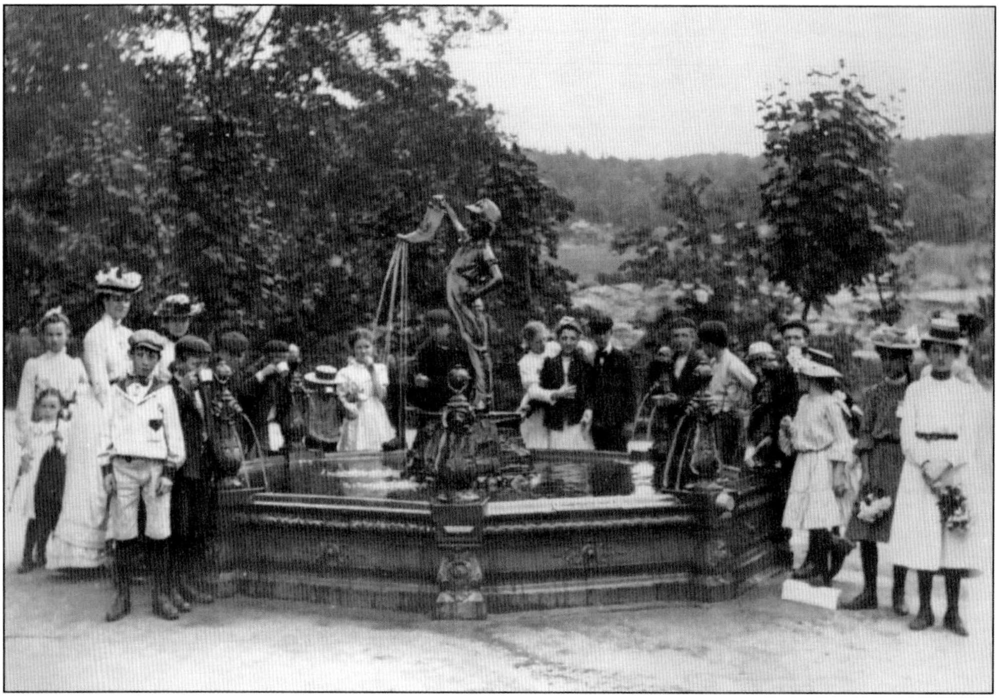

John Jermyn donated this fountain at Nay Aug Park in honor of Dr. Benjamin Throop. The ornate fountain was located in one of the most beautiful parts of Nay Aug Park, near several pavilions and a bandstand. A community greenhouse, donated by Globe Store owner and Hill Section resident John Cleland, is also close to this site. In subsequent years, the fountain was dismantled.

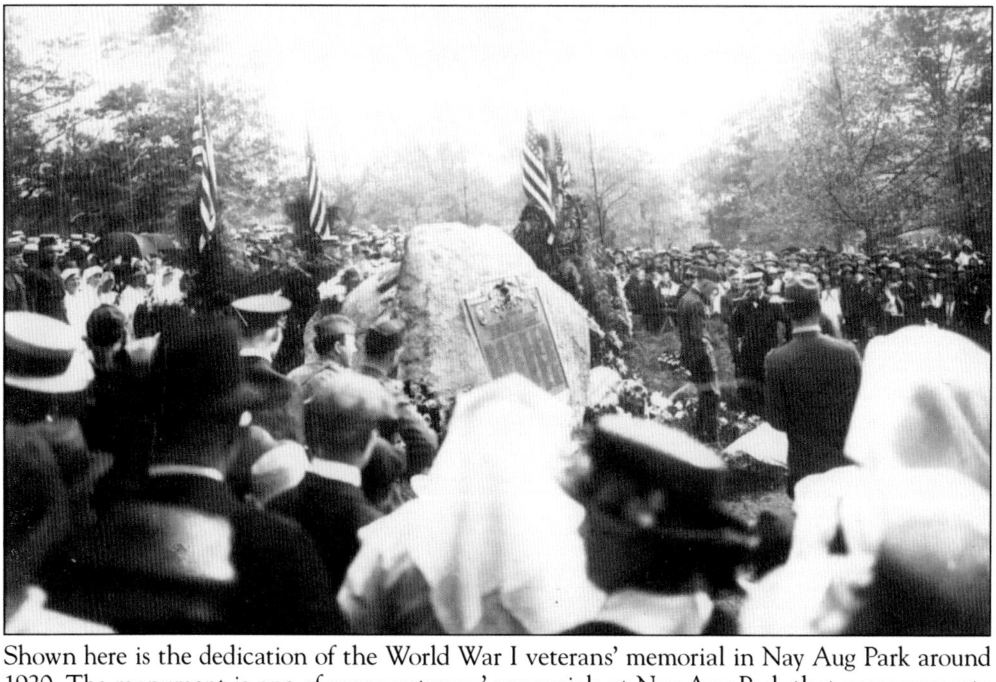

Shown here is the dedication of the World War I veterans' memorial in Nay Aug Park around 1920. The monument is one of many veterans' memorials at Nay Aug Park that commemorate local citizens who gave their youth and lives for their country.

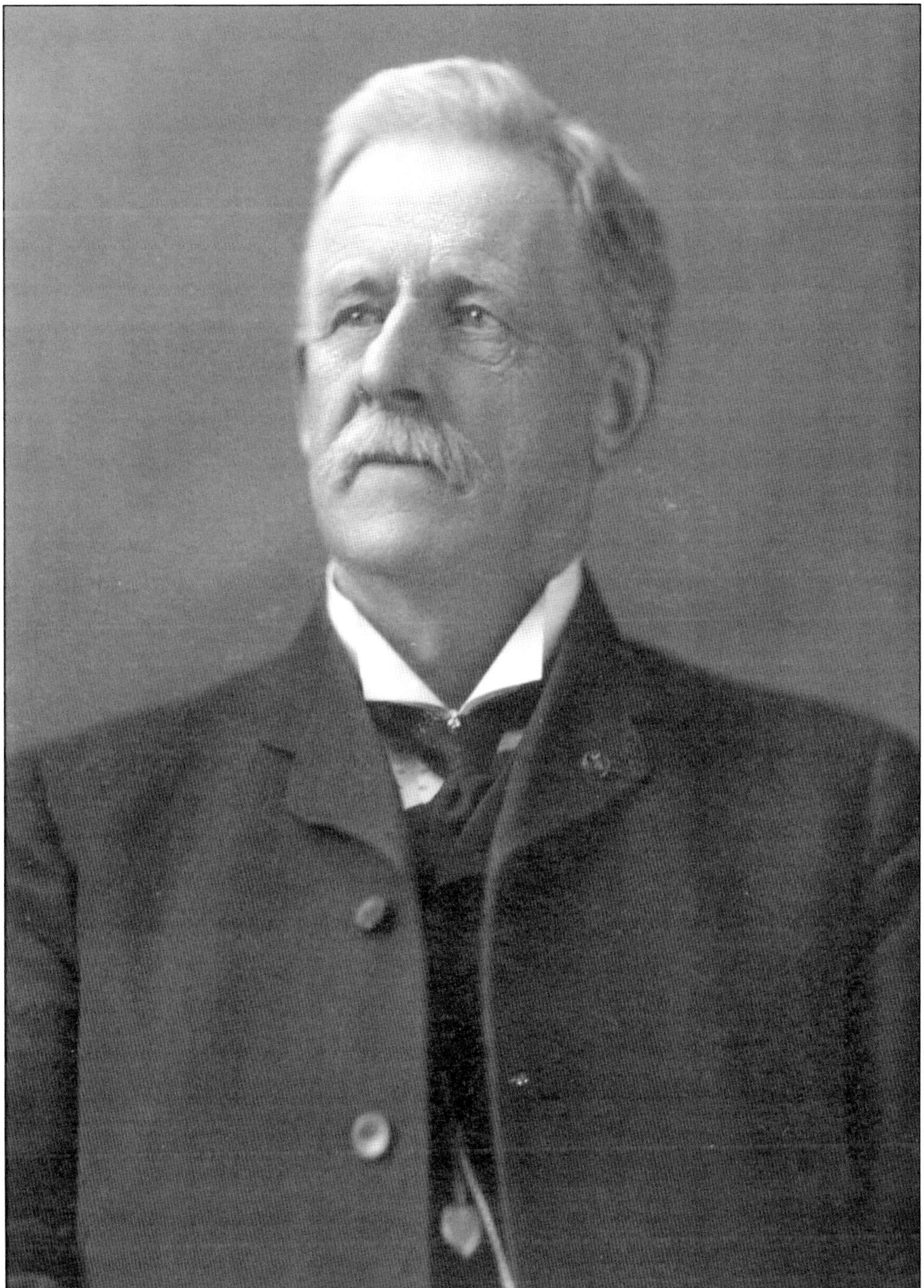

Dr. Isaiah Fawkes Everhart was a Scranton-area physician, ornithologist, taxidermist, and naturalist. Dr. Everhart amassed a substantial collection of preserved birds and other animals that eventually outgrew his home. As a result, he founded the Everhart Museum in Nay Aug Park in 1908 to house his collection. When Dr. Everhart died in 1911, the bulk of his fortune went to the museum.

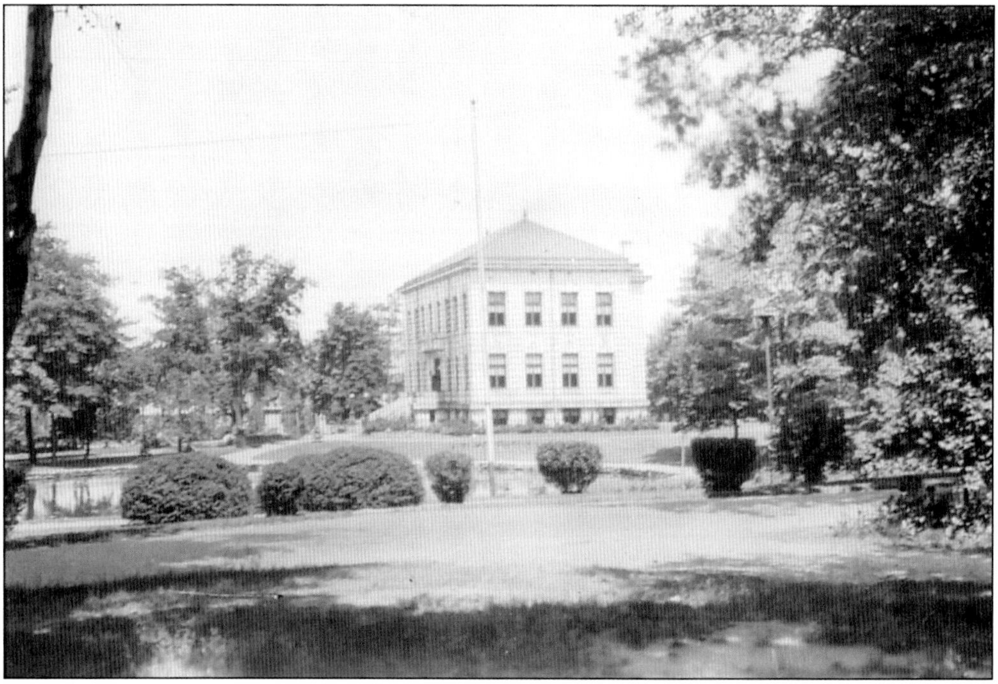

Pictured here is the original Everhart Museum in Nay Aug Park, near the end of Mulberry Street. Dr. Everhart initially planned to construct three separate buildings for natural history, science, and art; however, when the museum outgrew its original structure, different plans were made.

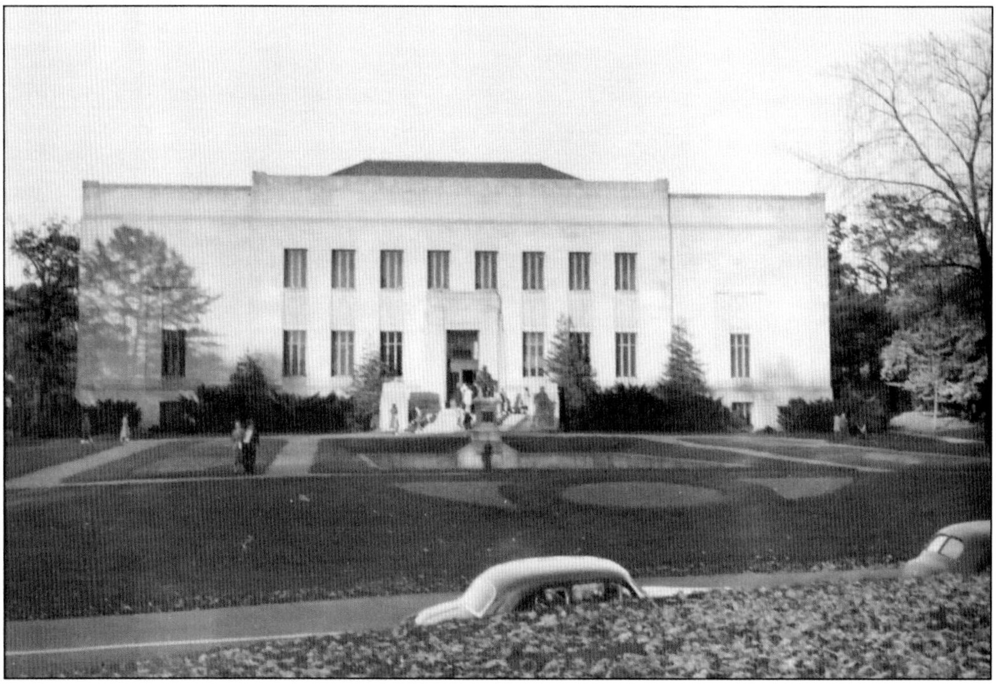

The current Everhart Museum was built in the late 1920s. This Art Deco building with engravings of famous scientists and artists was built around the original structure to incorporate its signature terra-cotta dome. The statue visible in front of the museum is that of Dr. Everhart.

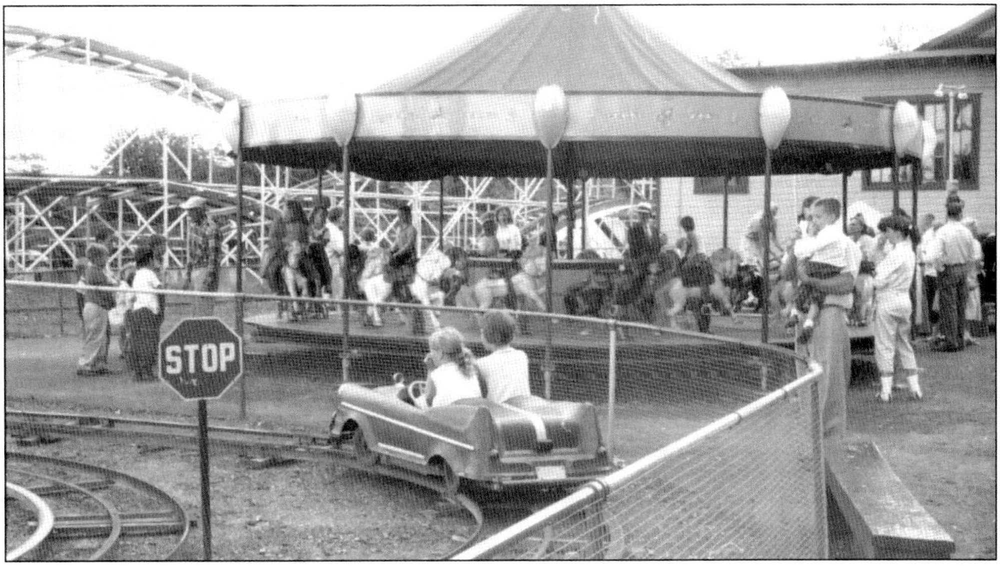

The Strohl family operated the Nay Aug Amusement Park for nearly 70 years. The amusement park was located by the Gibson Street entrance to Nay Aug Park, near the original Scranton Humane Society, firefighter training school, and a private helicopter storage facility. (Courtesy of the Lackawanna Valley Digital Archives.)

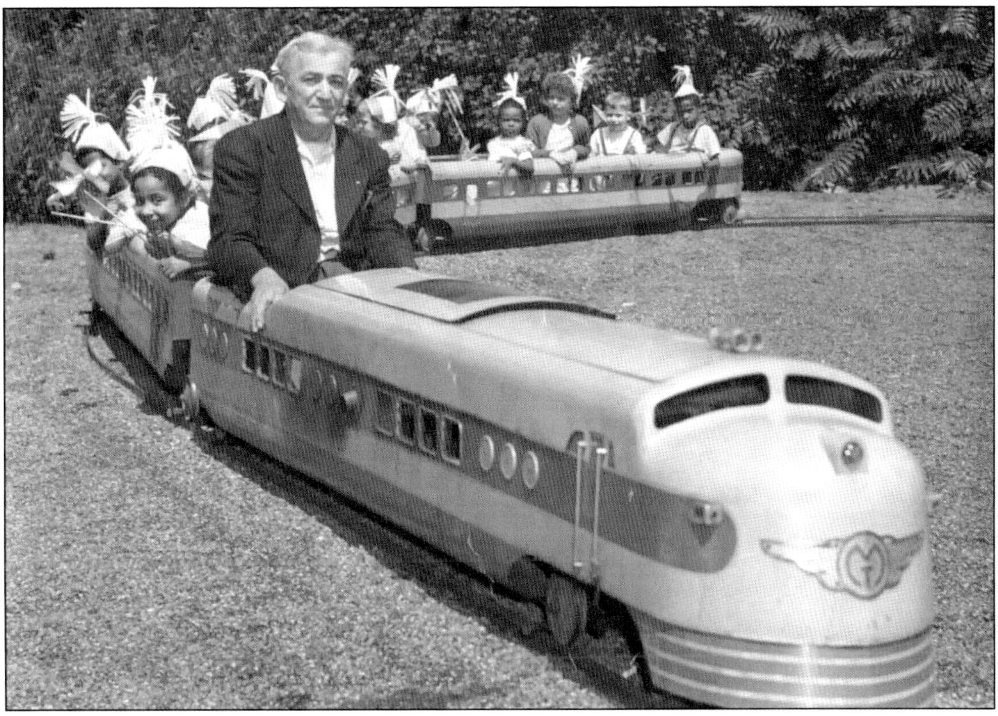
Shown here is an early version of the Nay Aug Amusement Park's famous miniature train. A later version of this train was modeled after the Erie Lackawanna's *Phoebe Snow*. Following the amusement park's closure in the 1970s, the train was sold to a private collector from outside the Scranton area. The train was later returned to Scranton in the early 2000s and is now on display at the Steamtown Historic Site. (Courtesy of the Lackawanna Valley Digital Archives.)

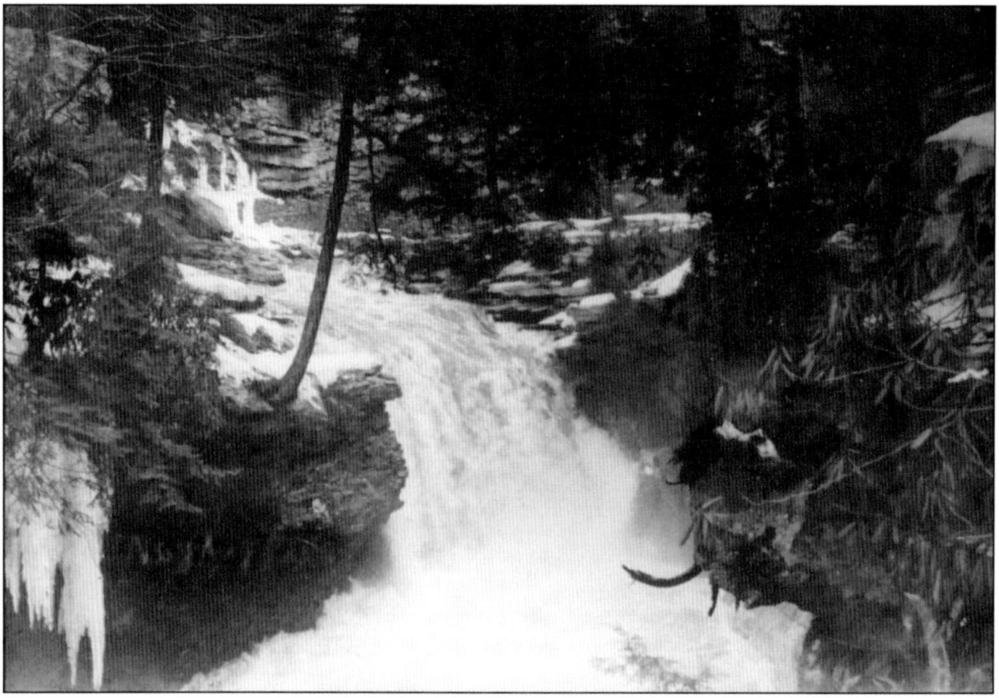

Nay Aug Falls is one of the most beautiful places in Scranton. These falls were created by the Roaring Brook in the heart of the rocky Nay Aug Gorge, which is a local natural wonder.

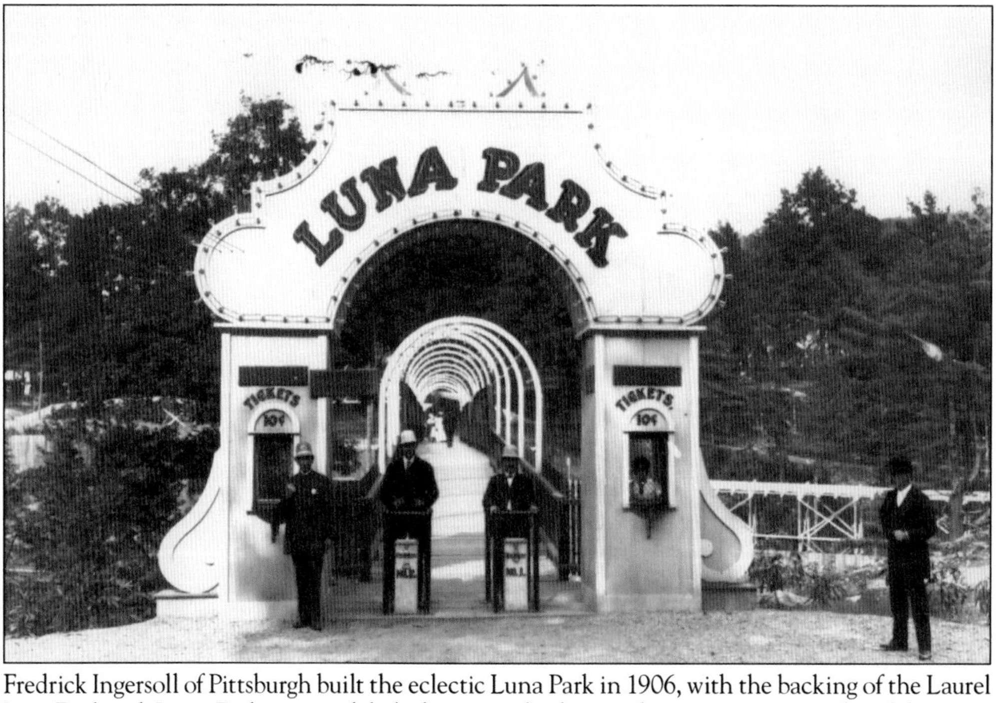

Fredrick Ingersoll of Pittsburgh built the eclectic Luna Park in 1906, with the backing of the Laurel Line Railroad. Luna Park was modeled after several other opulent amusement parks of the same name, including one on New York's Coney Island. Luna Park was constructed on 20 acres across the Roaring Brook from Nay Aug Park, connected by the ornate bridge seen here.

Luna Park was extravagant in its design. It boasted a plethora of rides and attractions like the ones seen here that bordered the shoot-the-chutes pond in the heart of the park. The tower at right was part of the Trip to Rockaway ride. The building in the middle housed the Edisonia, Temple of Mystery, and Scenitorium, and the structure on the end housed the carousel.

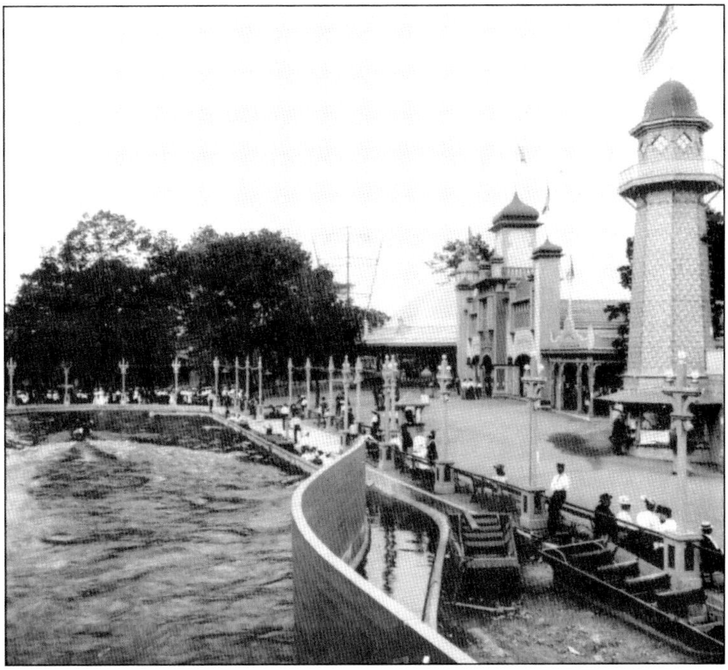

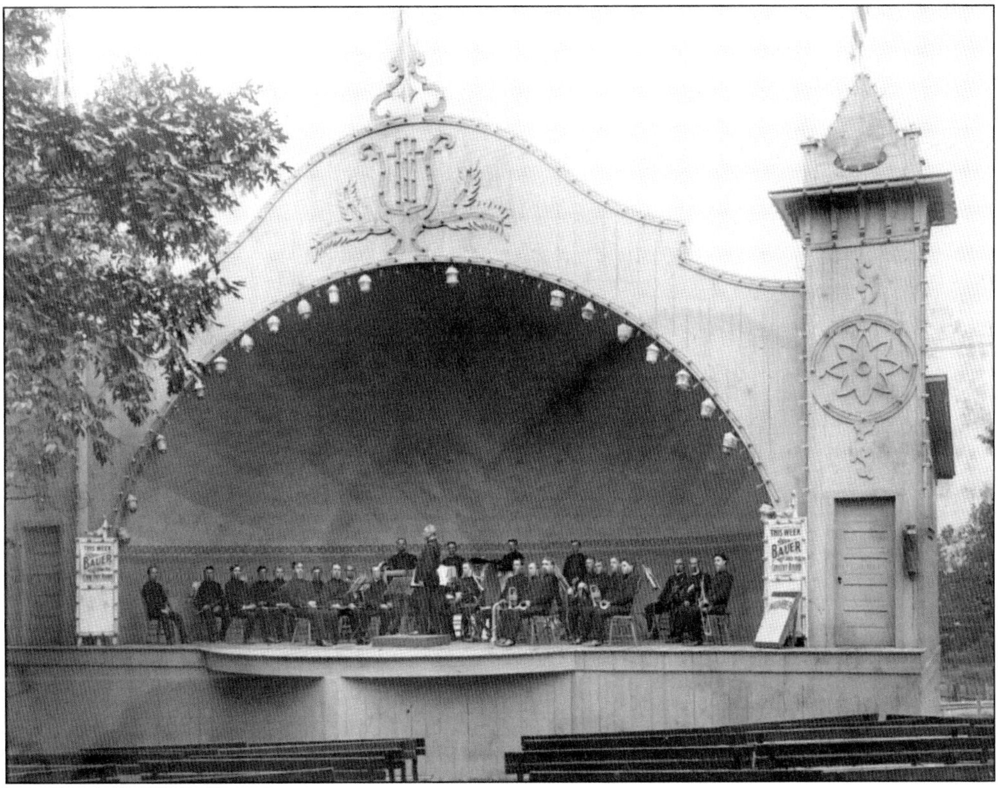

The band shell at Luna Park hosted many popular musical performances every season. The nearby circus platform also featured many notable circus acts, guaranteeing the park's importance as an entertainment center.

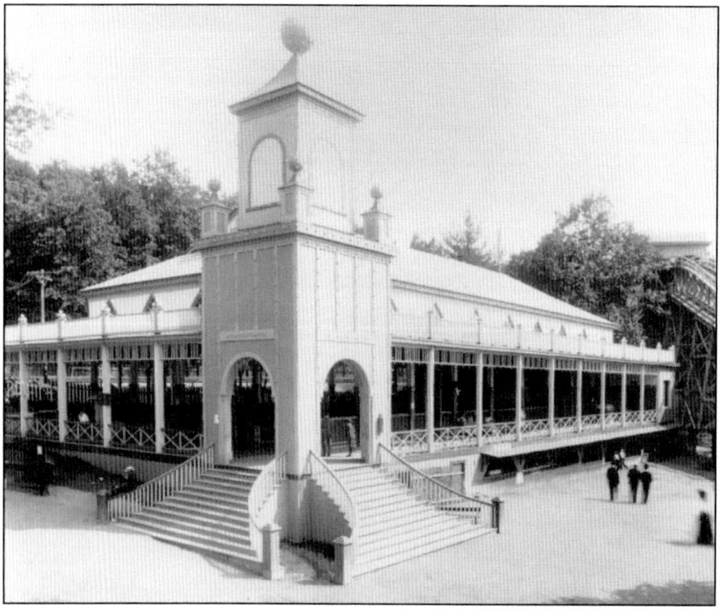

One of the largest attractions at Luna Park was its dance hall, which had a capacity of 3,000 picnickers and a dance floor that was 60 by 100 feet. At night, 3,000 incandescent lightbulbs illuminated the hall.

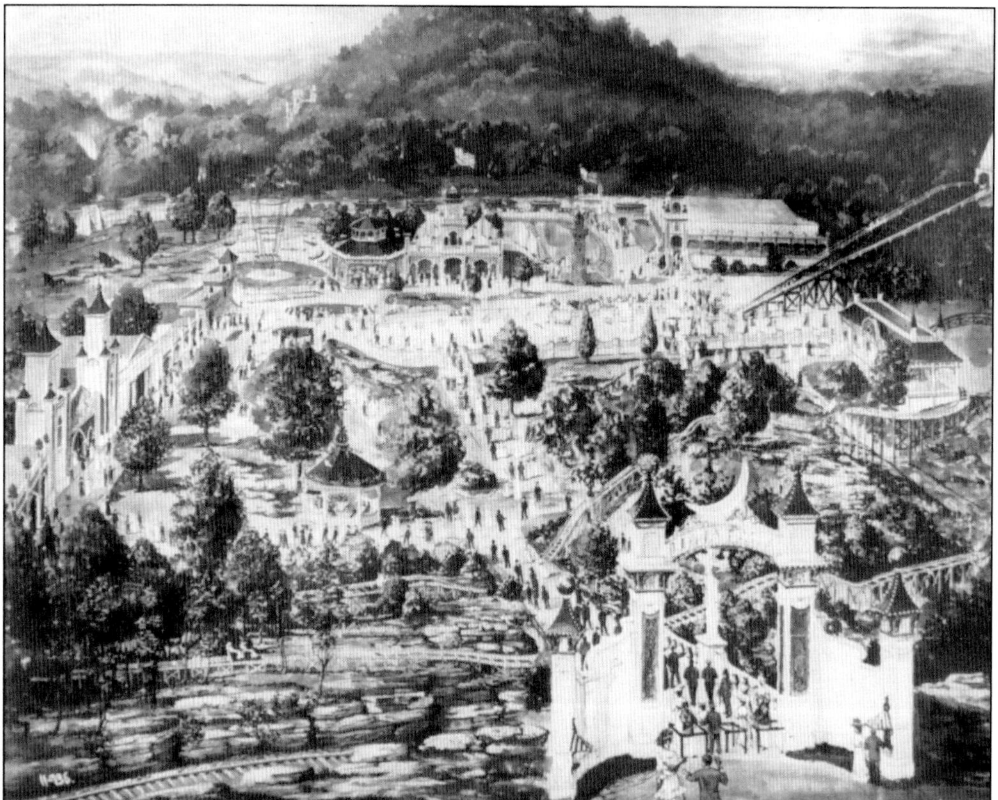

Luna Park was open for only 11 seasons. In 1916, the park suffered a tragic fire that destroyed all its wooden structures. The park's owners decided against rebuilding the park, and the ruins slowly became overgrown. Luna Park was forgotten until recently, when new interest was sparked in the amusement park's ruins.

Seven

OVERVIEW

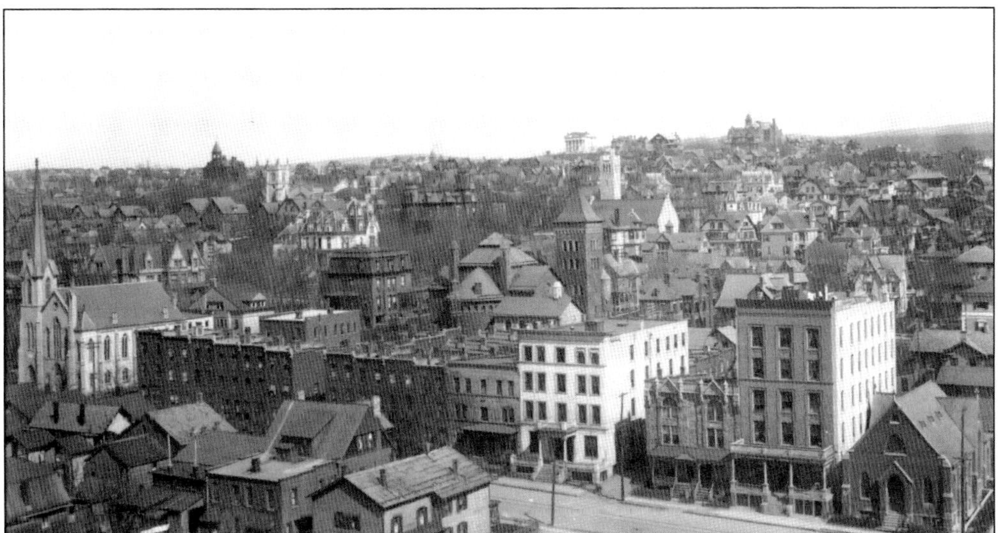

This panoramic view of the Hill Section was taken from the roof of Scranton's city hall around the turn of the century. Visible in this image are numerous Hill Section mansions, such as the highly recognizable hilltop home of George Jermyn; religious edifices like the First and Second Presbyterian Churches and the Madison Avenue Temple; and medical and educational institutions of the Moses Taylor Hospital and the Bayard Taylor School.

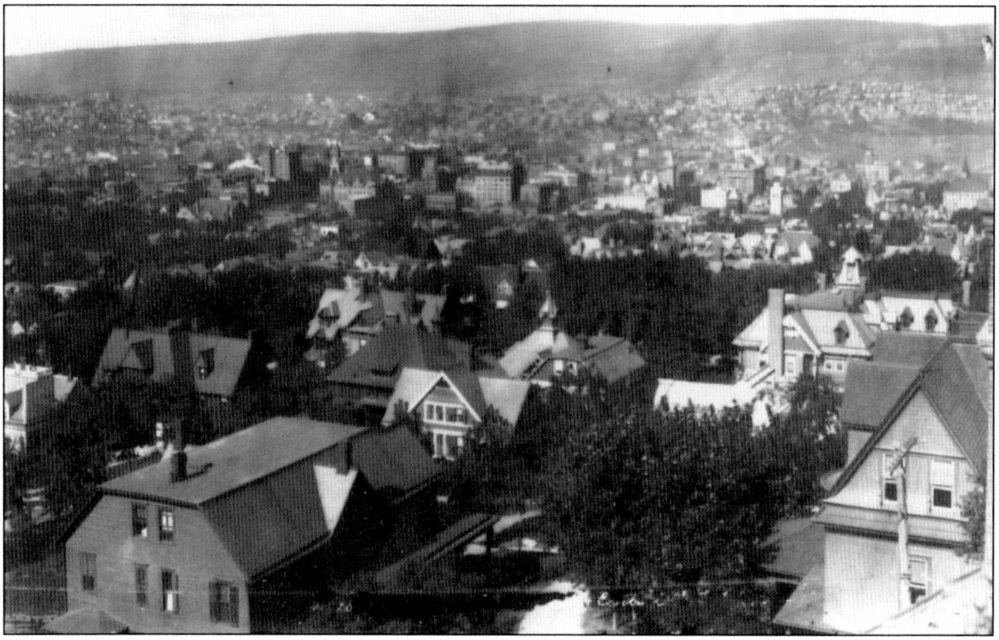

This image was taken from the top of the Bayard Taylor School (later, Chapel School), the highest point in the Hill Section, in the early 1900s. Visible in the image are the homes of the lower Hill Section, the skyline of Scranton's downtown, and the communities on the other side of the Lackawanna Valley.

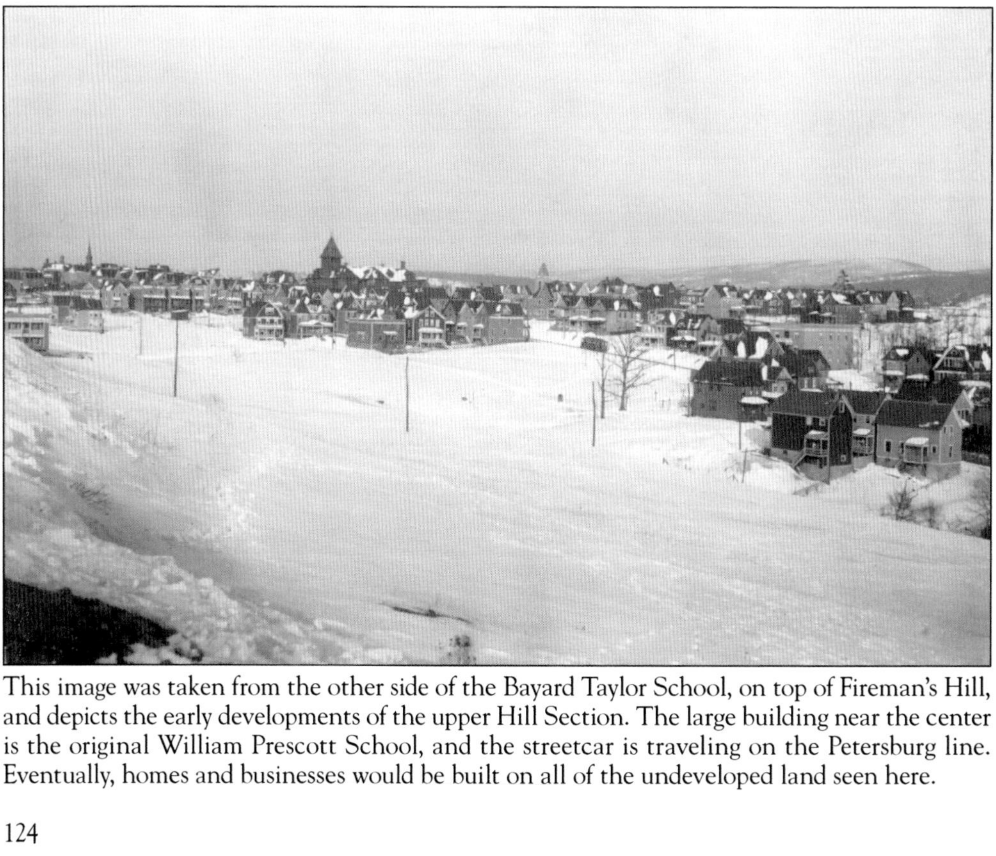

This image was taken from the other side of the Bayard Taylor School, on top of Fireman's Hill, and depicts the early developments of the upper Hill Section. The large building near the center is the original William Prescott School, and the streetcar is traveling on the Petersburg line. Eventually, homes and businesses would be built on all of the undeveloped land seen here.

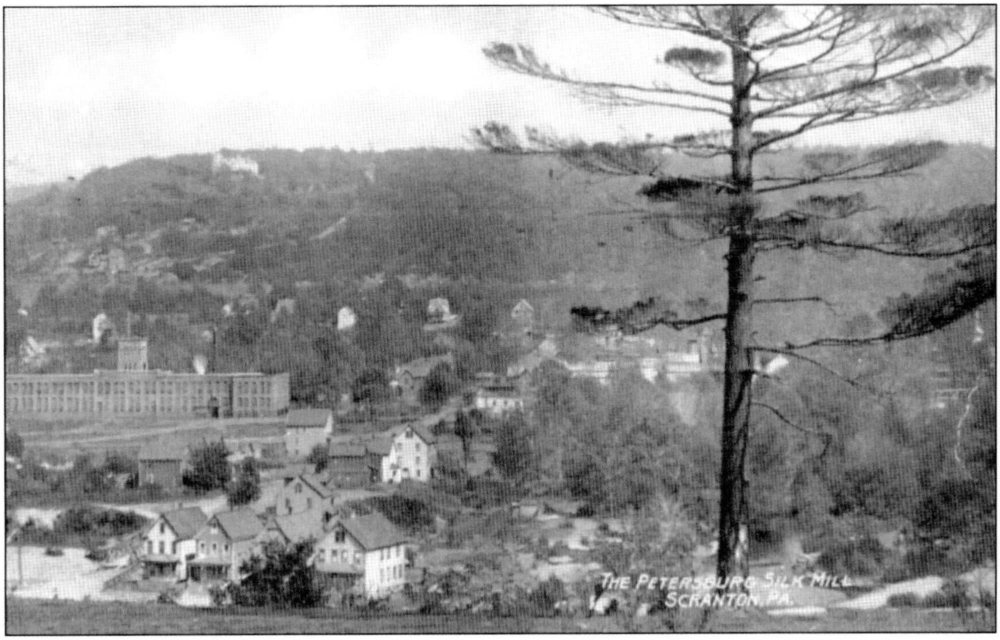

This is a rare glimpse of the other side of the Hill Section around the turn of the century. The homes in the foreground were part of the Little England community. The large structure on the other side of the Roaring Brook is that of the Petersburg Silk Mill. The large hill in the background is East Mountain, and the large home visible on it is the Watres estate, called Pen y Byrn. (Courtesy of Jack Hiddlestone.)

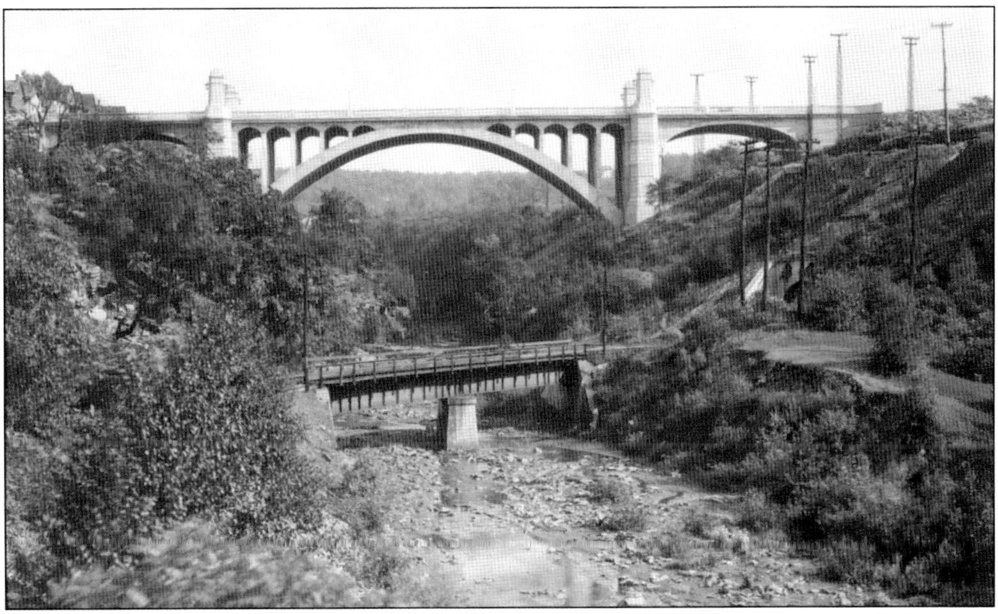

The Harrison Avenue Bridge, which connects the Hill Section to Scranton's South Side, was built in 1922. This reinforced concrete bridge spanned the DL&W main line, Roaring Brook, and Laurel Line. The lower bridge in the foreground was used by the Laurel Line's Crown Avenue Tunnel line, which ran under Scranton's South Side. Construction is currently under way to replace the Harrison Avenue Bridge.

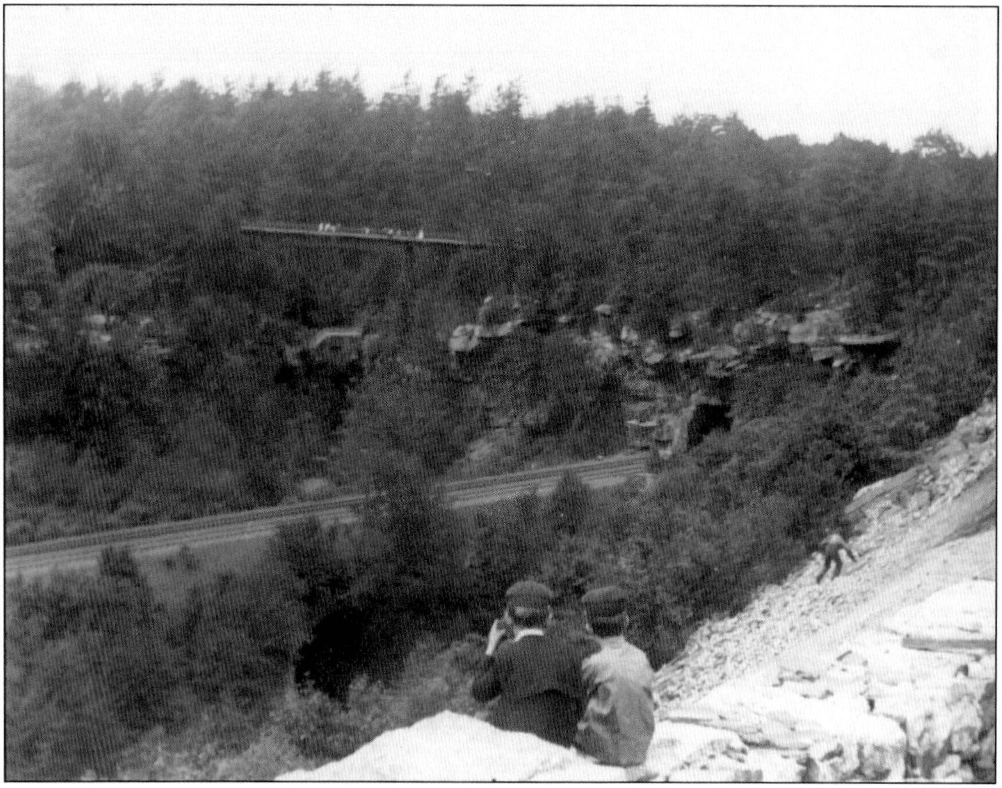

Shown here is Elmhurst Boulevard Bridge, which transversed the Nay Aug Gorge. Elmhurst Boulevard was an important road that bisected Nay Aug Park and connected Scranton to outlying communities like Elmhurst. In later years, traffic patterns changed, and the bridge was demolished after its wooden planking caught fire in the 1970s. Also visible beneath the Boulevard Bridge is a small footbridge that was used to transverse the gorge.

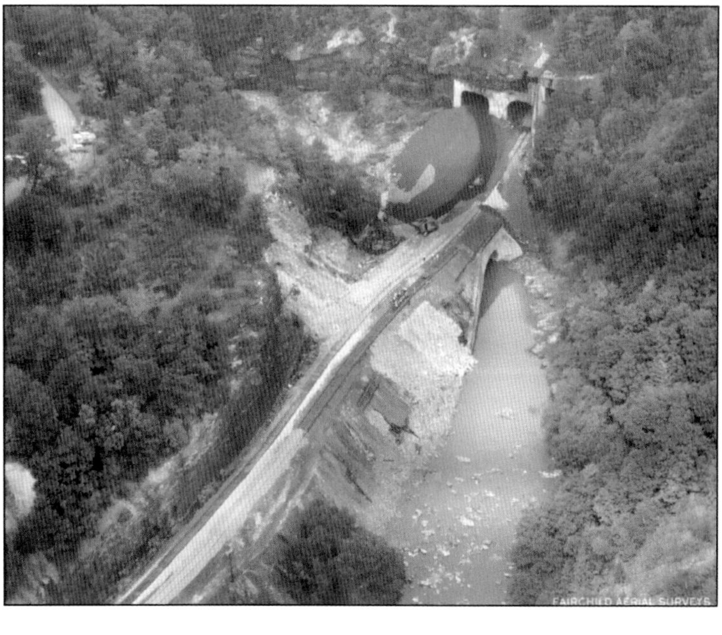

Shown here are the DL&W tunnels near Nay Aug Park after the flood of 1955. Debris formed in the upper part of the Nay Aug Gorge, submerging Little England and releasing floodwaters to flow through the tunnels. The damage from the flood of 1955 was one of the leading factors in the merger of the DL&W and Erie Railroads.

Shown here is another glimpse of the damage caused by the flood of 1955. The flood affected the Hill Section in many different ways and set it on its present course. Also visible in this image are Nay Aug Park's Cleland greenhouse and the homes around Nay Aug Park.

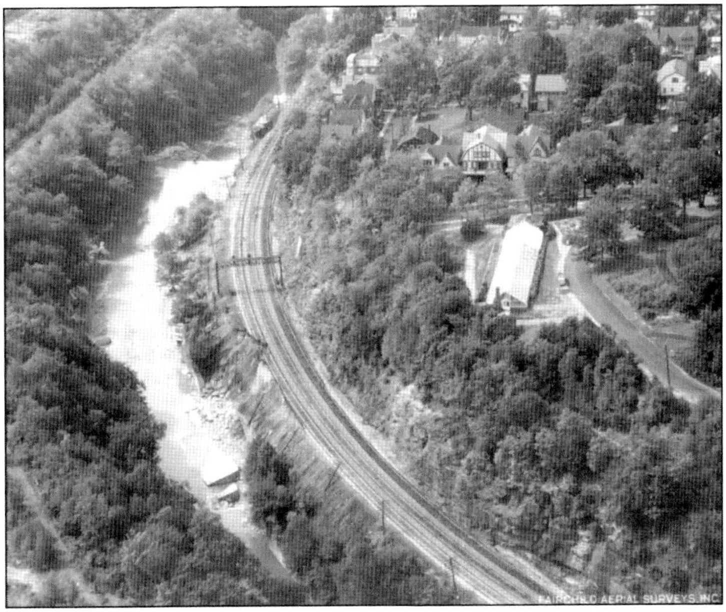

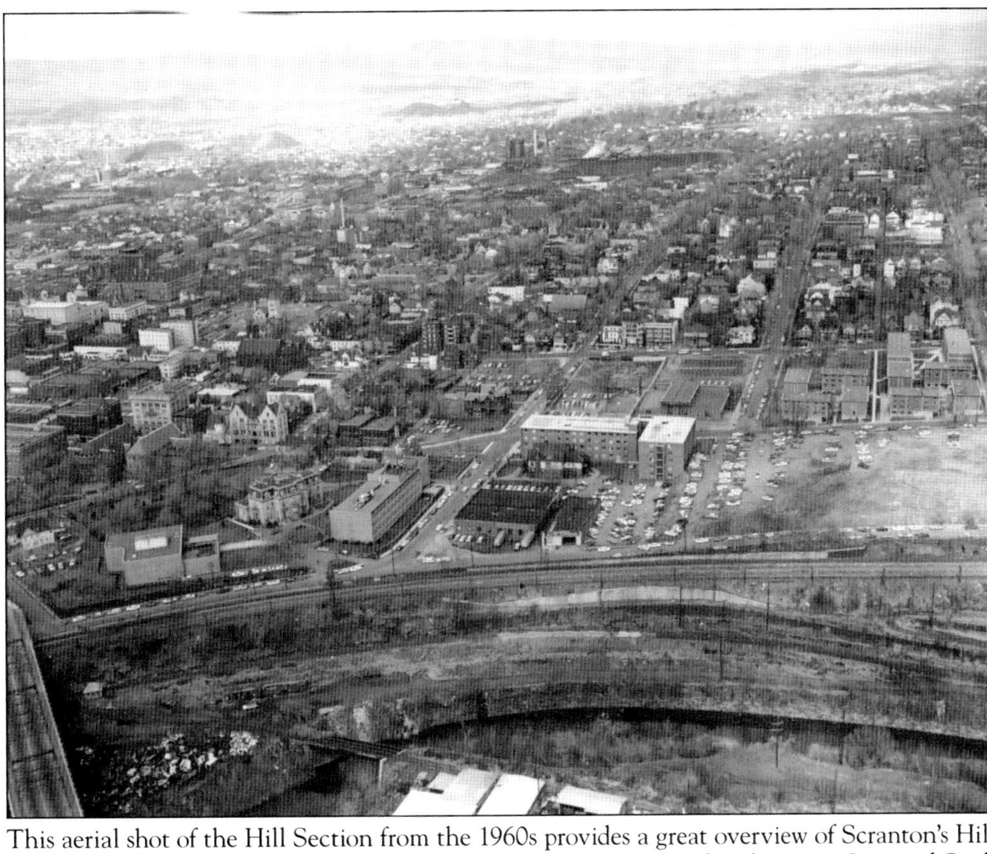

This aerial shot of the Hill Section from the 1960s provides a great overview of Scranton's Hill Section. Visible in the image are historic mansions, the former site of Lackawanna Iron and Coal, the DL&W main line, the University of Scranton's campus, and numerous other aspects of the Hill Section's heritage, as well as prospects of its future.

Consistent with our mission to preserve history on a local level, this book was printed in South Carolina on American-made paper and manufactured entirely in the United States. Products carrying the accredited Forest Stewardship Council (FSC) label are printed on 100 percent FSC-certified paper.

MADE IN THE USA